THE EUROPEANISATION OF ADMINISTRATIVE LAW

AF851291

DMU 0481590 01 8

UNIVERSITY
LIBRARY

~~341.2422 (like Craig)~~
342.26 (comparative)?

Normal loan Law Library

Please return this item at or before the date shown below.
Fines will be charged if the item is returned after this date.

Item issued subject to reservation recall

Renewals/Library information t **250 6142**

DE MONTFORT UNIVERSITY
LEICESTER • BEDFORD

© **De Montfort University Library** all rights reserved
Kimberlin library **www.library.dmu.ac.uk** PC28g
Library label series design/print **The Printing Centre**

The Europeanisation of Administrative Law

Transforming national decision-making procedures

Edited by
KARL-HEINZ LADEUR
University of Hamburg and European University Institute

Ashgate
DARTMOUTH
Aldershot • Burlington USA • Singapore • Sydney

© Karl-Heinz Ladeur 2002

All rights reserved. No part of this publication may be reproduced, stored in a retrieval system or transmitted in any form or by any means, electronic, mechanical, photocopying, recording or otherwise without the prior permission of the publisher.

Published by
Dartmouth Publishing Company
Ashgate Publishing Limited
Gower House
Croft Road
Aldershot
Hampshire GU11 3HR
England

Ashgate Publishing Company
131 Main Street
Burlington, VT 05401-5600 USA

DE MONTFORT UNIVERSITY
LIBRARY: Kimberlin
B/code Reclass 07/13
Fund: 8 Date: 25/9/02
Sequence: 342.26
Class: ~~344.026~~
Suffix: EUR

Ashgate website: http://www.ashgate.com

British Library Cataloguing in Publication Data
The Europeanisation of administrative law : transforming
national decision-making procedures
1.Administrative law - European Union countries
I.Ladeur, Karl-Heinz
342.4

Library of Congress Control Number: 2001095437

ISBN 0 7546 2223 1

Printed in Great Britain by
Antony Rowe Ltd, Chippenham, Wiltshire

Contents

List of Contributors

G. de Búrca, Professor of European Law at the European University Institute, Florence.

R. Caranta, Professor of Public Law at the University of Turin.

C. Harlow, Professor of Public Law at the London School of Economics and Political Science.

R. Hostiou, Professor of Environmental Law at the University of Nantes.

J.H. Jans, Professor of European Law at the Free University of Amsterdam.

M. de Jong, Research Assistant at the Free University of Amsterdam.

K. H. Ladeur, Professor of Public Law at the European University Institute, Florence, and the University of Hamburg.

L. Moral Soriano, Dr.jur., Researcher at the Max-Planck-Project Group on the Law of Common Goods, Cologne.

R. Prelle, Dr.jur., Research Assistant at the University of Hamburg.

Á. Ryall, Researcher at the European University Institute, Florence.

M. Shapiro, Professor of Political Science at the University of California, Berkeley.

Foreword

This book is based on a workshop held at the European University Institute, Florence, in November 1999. All the papers have since been revised and updated. Financial aid from the Institute and its Robert Schumann Centre is gratefully acknowledged.

The chapters focus on the growing impact of European law on the core elements of Member States' administrative law, and especially on their different conceptions of procedure. The book ties in with a lot of current work being conducted at the EUI in the field of the harmonisation of law, including private law. It has profited from discussions and working groups.

Martin Shapiro (Berkeley) is a regular visitor to the EUI and has injected a transatlantic perspective. Alexandra George (Sydney) has done a wonderful job editing the texts of the non-native English speakers and preparing the whole book for print. Her linguistic harmonisation has turned this book into a tricontinental endeavour!

Karl-Heinz Ladeur
Florence, March 2001

Introduction

Conflict and Co-operation between European Law and the General Administrative Law of the Member States

Karl-Heinz Ladeur

The Europeanisation of Administrative Law from a Transnational Perspective

The Europeanisation of administrative and environmental law has sparked intensive debate among legal scholars on the capacity and willingness of Member States' legal systems to respond. In addition to the transposition of EC directives regarding specific national laws, the institutions of general administrative law might also be affected. Even though the EC possesses no powers in the area of general administrative law – except for its own administration – the ECJ's "*effet utile*" case law may nonetheless undermine these competence boundaries. This could occur if the basically legitimate requirement of guaranteeing the practical efficiency of EC law in Member States tends to bring about greater homogeneity of administrative law than the division of powers would lead one to expect.

This introduction will consider the requirements to harmonise the general administrative law of Member States – especially procedural law – with the specific law of the EC. It will emerge that procedural law can be used without infringing the integrity of the various kinds of administrative law. It can be used to improve the practical effectiveness of the transposition of European law, and also to create productive transparency for the various national legal systems and for transnational practical legal comparison (or the "competition of rules") in Europe. Crossing this border can easily lead to problems of system consistency without any gain for the European integration process. This means that Member States' room for discretion in implementing specific EC law and in guaranteeing its practical effectiveness can be better shaped dogmatically, through the guarantee function of general administrative law, thus avoiding diffuse harmonisation that ignores the tradition of general administrative law in the individual Member States.

The following contributions discuss the problems of harmonising Member States' administrative procedural laws with the requirements of specific European administrative law. In addition to the problems of implementing these norms themselves, the contributions focus on the problems arising in national law and the requirements of adapting the two legal spheres to each other. These are issues that must be coped with by interpretation in conformity with the directives. They show that the national legal systems as a whole are subject to a process of Europeanisation. (The same also applies to private law, which has been similarly affected by Europeanisation, even in its general principles including the interpretation of clauses such as "good faith".) The chapters confirm – particularly with reference to environmental law – how individual Member States are faced with the difficult problems of maintaining the consistency and adaptability of their whole bodies of administrative law as a result of the special rules of European law. This is because it is difficult to create links between the doctrines and institutions of general administrative law that are necessary to the effective application of European law. European law requires a particular integration effort on the part of national legal systems, and the comparison of various Member States' strategies for coping with this demonstrates that the term "European law" is often only a mystification. Most EC law is borrowed from the systems of individual Member States and the specific logic of each example is transported into the other legal systems – which are often not adequately prepared to handle the "transplant"[1] – via Brussels. The articles in this volume are not intended to join the chorus of lamentation bewailing the threat to national "identity". Instead, they ask pragmatic questions about how productive legal integration can come about within a European multi-level system that cannot be modelled on a State pattern (not even that of a federal State), and how it would be possible to treat the self-organizing capacity and vivacity of national legal systems as a tool with which to guarantee the flexibility and adaptability of European law.

The system of administrative law in Member States constitutes a sort of memory that stores a multiplicity of experiences and possible linkages in its institutions, forms and instruments. This achievement could not – and should not – be taken over by a new unitary law. It can instead be seen that an open multi-level system with an autonomous doctrine focusing on harmonisation and co-operation can be fruitful for the process of integration as a whole. There can then be learning – even "transnationally" – through comparison of the achievements of general administrative law in Member States. It is easy to be distracted from this by concentration on problems in the hierarchical relationship between national and supranational law. "Europeanised" law should be conceived of as a heterarchical network consisting of various levels with differentiated connecting patterns, rather than as a simple layer. It can be shown that the control function of the hierarchy is ("supranationality") overestimated and the problems faced by national legal

---

1 On this see G. Teubner, "Legal Irritants: Good Faith in British Law or How Unifying Law ends up in New Divergences", in F. Snyder (ed.) *The Europeanisation of Law* (Oxford: Hart, 2000), 243 ss.

systems when adopting "legal transplants" are underestimated. This is because European law is presented as a normative production "*ex nihilo*". By contrast, it is easy to see from a transnational viewpoint that it is mostly specific legal institutions – though sometimes modified – that are drawn from national systems and Europeanised. To the extent that the (often thoroughly ambivalent) experience with these institutions in the relevant Member State(s) gets lost along the way, this is a problem. Especially in the area of environmental law, it tends to be elements that do not come from the traditional arsenal of forms that are intended to cope with new complex decision-making problems of that are Europeanised. There must instead be experiments with these forms. How, for example, will a Europeanised institution operate in conditions of uncertainty. Nor is there anything wrong with imposing common experimentation on all Member States in order to try new procedures and forms of decision; on the contrary! However, it would be more productive to openly state the advantages and drawbacks of individual legal institutions that might already have been tested by Member States, and an example of where this could occur lies in the new "reference areas" of environmental and technology law. This would let closer account be taken of the fact that the conditions for the acceptance of new legal forms in Member States will be correspondingly different on the basis of differing structures of administrative law. This is true, for instance, of the relationship between administrative decision-making freedom and the binding nature of legal (judicial) decision. Such divergences might have been used for "structured" learning through practical comparison if the exaggerated orientation towards the unity of European law had not suppressed the idea that it could be productive to experiment with various legal structures and search for functional equivalencies. Time and again the ECJ takes into account that European Community law stems from "legal interpenetrating of member states".[2] But the consequences it derived from this insight are too general: this does not necessarily allow for the presupposition of a common conception of law. The overlap and transfer of legal cultures is not a process that necessarily ends up in a deadlock,[3] but the transformation has to be regarded as a time-dependent process[4] that requires a new "transnational legal science"[5] that is adapted to the observation of a new version of a horizontal legal pluralism.[6] This means that

---

2 Case number 155/72. Rep 1982, 1610.

3 Cf. P. Legrand, "The Impossibility of Legal Transplants", *Maastricht Journal of European and Comparative Law* 4 (1997), 111; Id., "European legal systems are not converging", *International Comparative Law Quarterly* 45 (1996), 52.

4 Cf. M. Van Hoecke, "The Harmonisation of European Law – some misunderstandings", in id./F. Ost (eds), *The Harmonisation of Private Law in Europe*, Oxford (2000), 1, 5.

5 Cf. C. Schmid, "The Emergence of a New Transnational Legal Science in Europe", *Oxford Journal of Legal Studies* 19 (2000), 673. For administrative law see M. Niedobitek, "Kollisionen zwishen EG-Recht und nationalem Recht", *Verwaltungsarchiv* (2001), 58, 74 s.

6 Cf. Th. Wilhelmsson, "Jack-in-the-Box Theory of European Community Law", in L.D. Eriksson/S. Hurri (eds.), *Dialectic of Law and Reality. Readings in Finnish Legal Theory* (Helsinki: Publications of the Faculty of Law of the University of Helsinki,

member states should have more leeway in the process of implementation of European law as far as its linkages with the general doctrinal infrastructure of a certain national legal conception is concerned. The Europeanisation process should take this kind of "remodelling" of supranational norms by different doctrinal settings of member states explicitly into consideration and not just accept it in a pragmatic way. When a legal institution is transferred from one legal system into other national legal systems "via Brussels", then the following precept should apply in order to take account of the general administrative law in each case: to the extent that far-reaching changes in general administrative law are associated with the Europeanisation of new procedural components,[7] the pressure for change created through the "*effet utile*" requirement must in turn be moderated by the proportionality principle. The heavier the intervention, the higher the expectations about the "gain" for the performance capacity of the given national legal system.

The Co-ordination of General Administrative Law and Specific European Environmental Law: An Example of "Diagonal Conflicts"

For the viewpoint taken here of the linkage between specific European (environmental) law and general national administrative law,[8] it is of decisive importance to accept a distinction between general norms and specific regulations. The various procedural and decisional conceptions (openly or implicitly referred to) that constitute the conceptual infrastructure of a European norm should be distinguished from the special regulation itself. No regulation of specific administrative law can do without a conception of implementation in procedures and decisions that must be supplied by the general administrative law. There is a need for a specific European method of linking Member State and European law, and this cannot be reduced to requirements about the implementation of the specific legal rules. Since there is no unitary administrative law in Europe, we must necessarily expect conflicts of law – broadly termed "diagonal conflicts" in the

---

1999), 437, 446; Cf. also G. Teubner, "The Two Faces of Janus: Rethinking Legal Pluralism", *Cardozo Law Review* 13 (1992), 1443.

7 Cf., on the – overestimated in detail – convergence of administrative law, J. Schwarze, "The Convergence of the Administrative Laws of the EU Member States", Eur. Public Law 1998, 191ff; and from a British viewpoint, G. Anthony, "Community Law and the Development of UK Administrative Law", *Eur. Public Law* (1998), 253 ss.

8 Cf. on the method S. Kadelbach, *Allgemeines Verwaltungsrecht unter europäischem Einfluß* (Tübingen: Mohr Siebeck, 1996), 114 ss; 276 ss; C. D. Classen, *Die Europäisierung der Verwaltungsgerichtsbarkeit* (Tübingen: Mohr Siebeck, 1996), 175 ss; for criticisms Th.v. Danwitz, *Verwaltungsrechtliches System und europäische Integration* (Tübingen: Mohr Siebeck, 1996), 334 ss; R. Halfmann, *Entwicklungen des Verwaltungsrechtsschutzes in Deutschland* (Frankreich und England: VerwArch, 1999), 74 ss. D. Scheuing, "Die Europäisierung der Verwaltungsrechts. Zum mitgliedstaatlichen Verwaltungsvollzug am Beispiel der Rückforderung germeinschaftrechtswidriger Beihilfen", *Die Verwaltung* (2001), 107, 109 ss.

literature[9] – that arise alongside the problems of the conflicts to be coped with through interpretation in conformity with directives or Community law. When applied to the individual case, the European law must make use of the respective general administrative law (or also civil law!) of Member States. European law is therefore dependent on national law.[10] Even if EC law must make presumptions about the expectations of general administrative law regarding the existence and performance capacity of particular national institutions (administrative act, general legal rule, margin of assessment, discretion, review through the administrative courts, etc), it does not have competence to establish any binding framework regarding general administrative law and administrative procedural law (except for its own administration), here.

This creates a problem because the compatibility of specific European law and general administrative law will not always exist. In order to overcome this situation, the ECJ has developed a general requirement to guarantee "*effet utile*": the general administrative law of Member States must support the practical effectiveness of specific EC law, though without being bound to the utilisation of particular institutions. This seems entirely appropriate, but the concept seems so vaguely shaped that the claimed respect for the procedural autonomy of Member States can *de facto* be undermined. This is because an adjustment constraint arises from specific expectations of the European law concerning co-operation efforts by general national administrative law and, even more than the trend towards uniformisation in a federal State, it might call the balance within the EC multi-level system into question.[11] Lack of precision about the underlying goals of the "*effet utile*" case law can also bring a lack of clarity to national general administrative law that is questionable in terms of rule of law; national law incompatible with it can be reduced to an empty shell in decision-making procedures that have reference to European law.[12] The examples of environmental-impact assessment (Ladeur/Prelle) and Integrated Pollution Prevention and Control (IPPC) clearly

---

9 Cf. only C. Joerges, "The Europeanisation of Private Law as a Rationalisation Process and as a Contest of Disciplines", *European Review of Private Law* (1995), 178 ss. for civil law. For public law K. H. Ladeur, "Flexibility and "Cooperative Law": The Co-ordination of European Member States' Laws – The Example of Environmental Law", in G. De Búrca and J. Scott (eds), *Constitutional Change in the EU: From Uniformity to Flexibility?* (Oxford: Hart, 2000), 281ff.

10 For a critique see E. Schmidt-Aßmann, "Allgemeines Verwaltungsrecht in europäischer Perspektive", *Zeitschrift für öffentliches Recht* (2000), 159ss; (Berlin/New York: de Gruyter, 2000), 45.

11 Cf. only v. Danwitz, ibid, 144; in general cf. also R. Wahl, "Die zweite Phase des öffentlichen Rechts in Deutschland – Die Europäisierung des öffentlichen Rechts", *Der Staat* (1999), 495, 517.

12 Cf. again recently ECJ, ECR [1999] I 2517ss; cf. also the report by A. Epiney, "Neuere Rechtssprechung des EuGH zum allgemeinen Verwaltungs-, Umwelt- und Gleichstellungsrecht", *Neue Zeitschrift für Verwaltungsrecht* (2000), 36, 37; and J. Suerbaum, *Die Europäisierung des Verwaltungsverfahrensrechts*, Verwaltungsarchiv (2001), 169 ss; A. Scherzberg, *Die Öffentilichkeit der Verwaltung* (Baden-Baden: Nomos, 2000), 258 s.

show that even the specific EC law in each case is ultimately based on adopting particular "legal transplants" from Member States, that must accordingly involve an examination of the experience that has been gained in the "exporting" Member State. In principle, it must first be asked whether – and to what extent – the general administrative law of the Member State offers examples of institutional infrastructure that are suitable for transplant to the specific European law. It must also be asked whether these guarantee the institutions of a particular European legal tradition – which have possibly been taken as a model in formulating a directive – a functionally equivalent effectiveness. Only when in the answer is negative must one ask about the adjustment efforts that the Member State has to make in the interests of "*effet utile*". Here it must be questioned whether the functional weakness of the given system of administrative law could be compensated by a strength elsewhere. Conversely, could the advantages of a legal system that is used as a model for a European directive be balanced by functional weakness at another point? This is all the more important as systems of administrative law and their "ordering idea" are based on decades of experience. Ignoring their history might have considerable, unintended, negative consequences.

The concept of IPPC provides an example. The requirements resulting from the relevant directive regarding the integrative evaluation and control of environmental pollution in the permit-granting procedure are anything but obvious. A case-related integration concept could, for instance, fairly easily be kept compatible with French or British administrative law on the basis of the administration's broad factual discretion. This need not be superior to a model that proceeds more strictly according to general standards. In the individual case of overcoming a heterogeneous pollution situation, this tends to use an opening clause rather than dispensing entirely with the advantages of a legally-controlled and bound decision. The flexibility advantage of a situational integrated decision might be balanced by non-transparency[13] and a lack of control over the authorities' exercise of their factual discretion, and the fact that the British model can guarantee a certain regularity combined with case-relatedness only on the basis of methodological rationalisation through cost-benefit analysis. This distinguishes the situation from the German law that focuses more strongly on rule-based control of the administration when it emerges that methodical stabilisation has in practice hardly ever succeeded. If the European law calls for a comprehensive situational balance between various "pollutions",[14] the logic of a rule-bound application of the law could be called into question. But this does not seem acceptable in itself.[15] This

---

13 Cf. (Advocate-General) F. G. Jacobs, "Public Law – The Impact of Europe", *Public Law* (1999), 232, 239, who in relation to British law feels that European law requires "more explicit weighing of interests" in administrative procedures.

14 Cf. K. Lange and A. Karthaus, "Medienübergreifende Umweltverantwortung", in id. (ed.), *Gesamtverantwortung statt Verantwortungsparzellierung im Umweltrecht* (Baden-Baden: Nomos, 1997), 15, 26 ss.

15 Cf. only G. Lübbe-Wolff, "Integrierter Umweltschutz – Brauchen die behörden mehr Flexibilität?", *Natur und Recht* (1999), 241ss.; M. Schmidt-Preuß, "Integrierte

would leave decision-making authority within the discretionary competence of the environmental administration. The trade off for greater flexibility that can compensate for the contradictions among differing norm requirements in the environmental areas of law concerned, is loss of control and loss of legal – and especially judicial – review. This cannot create an efficient environmental policy. For this very reason, the decision required by the IPPC directive in accordance with the "best available techniques" is important, though it can certainly not be equated with the more strongly generalising concept of the "state-of-the-art" in the German law. The German formula ultimately refers back to the British formula, adopting the "best practicable environmental option"; it could previously be only partly operationalised through the setting up of an "integrated environmental index".[16]

These problems are connected with the complexity of a cost-benefit analysis; it all can be a thoroughly respectable method (and is much discussed in the US), but it still has to prove its performance capacity in detail. The problems of linking new European legal forms with Member States' procedural conceptions and the "ordering idea" of their administrative law can also be demonstrated with regard to environmental impact assessment. The ECJ seeks to solve these conflicts between specific European law and national general administrative law in individual cases by requiring a guarantee of "*effet utile*" for the respective European law. It considers the Member States are obliged to provide a productive infrastructure in the form of a national general administrative law that is able to guarantee the practicability of the European legal norms. These norms must first be converted into specific national laws. The requirement of a practical linkage capacity of national general administrative law that reaches into general administrative law is in turn limited by the proportionality principle, as discussed in the article by Grainne De Búrca and Áine Ryall. This may be successful from case to case, but a philosophically consistent orientation cannot be achieved this way. Such an orientation can, however, be provided by the general administrative law underlying the respective national specific administrative law. But this is problematic in a differentiated multi-level system with various "vertical" and "diagonal" conflicts (general national versus specific European law, various specific but overlapping legal areas such as broadcasting and advertising law). Over and above the individual case, a doctrinal ordering structure in the form of harmonising rules is needed. The articles in this volume should provide starting points on this issue of the legal doctrines of Europeanised administrative law. This comes about first and foremost through the presentation of the varying conceptions of administrative procedure in Member States, but also from the examples from individual legal areas such as environmental law.

Anforderungen an das Verfahren der Vorhabenzulassung – Anwendung und Umsetzung der IVU-RL", *Neue Zeitschrift für Verwaltungsrecht* (2000), 252ss.

16 Cf. Lübbe-Wolff, ibid.(Fn.10).

Towards a Conception of Practical Legal Comparison and the "Competition of Rules"

The (limited) comparison between the German and British approaches to the legal structuring regarding polluting installations confirms that Europe hosts differing regulatory models operating with differing optimisation strategies. These models are to be classified as "general administrative law" or "general environmental administrative law", on which European law can act only to a very limited extent. This limit on European law is not one that is to be merely tolerated. It is – as the very comparison between regulatory strategies in Germany and Britain shows – a potential strength of a multi-level European system that does not overestimate the advantages of a unitary legal order. The optimisation problems in the German and British laws seem to indicate a strategy of competition between legal systems,[17] which allows the various models to contend with and rely upon the possibility of mutual learning in a co-operative system. This simultaneously introduces a component of national co-operation and harmonisation of the legal systems of Member States that can exist alongside the tension between supranational and national law, in accordance with the EC "Association of States" (which is not a state itself).

The European IPPC office in Seville, where the BAT leaflets are to be produced, could make an important contribution to this development if it does not exaggerate the differences in the methodical approaches but instead makes use of them and encourages the testing of varying strategies. It might therefore be stimulating for German law to look at the performance capacity of the cost-benefit analysis method and to combine it, in part, with a method of setting prescriptive standards of conduct. Conversely, it might be stimulating for other Member States to look at the advantages of normative control through standards bought at the expense of a certain lack of flexibility. However, over-hasty recourse to a case-related "integrative approach" might prove to be a Pyrrhic victory in environmental protection if the institutional experiences regarding the "ordering idea" of general administrative law in the European States are ignored. In this way, hybrid legal formations could emerge that are more oriented towards realising good but vague intentions than to enhancing the performance capacity of the administrative legal systems.

This demonstrates a need for specific methodical rules that will form a link between the specific (environmental) law of Europe and the general administrative laws of the various member nations. This link must focus on a co-operative transnational conception of learning and mutual observation. The requirements for co-operation among the European administrations must be raised through a correspondingly polycentric model of a co-operative administrative law with a supplementary transnational "ordering idea". It is important to limit the binding

---

17 Cf. only R. Wahl, "Materiell-Integrative Anforderungen an die Vorhabenzulassung – Anwendung und Umsetzung der IVU-RL", *Neue Zeitschrift für Verwaltungsrecht* (2000), 502, 507.

effect of the directives beyond the sphere of the specific regulatory intention in each case (for example, by implementing a flexible approach that integrates formerly disparate areas of pollution regulation). It would be a mistake for all these directives to impact on conceptual questions of general administrative law without first reflecting systematically on the consequences for both the general administrative law of the member nations and the effective implementation of European law.

On the Importance of Procedural Law for the Emergence of an "Ordering Idea" of Europeanised Administrative Law

A new perspective on the results of administrative procedural law can also be developed in this way. The German debate has frequently contained descriptions of the ECJ's attempt to strengthen Europeanised procedural law (expansion of subjective rights, general enhancement of procedural law, etc) in order to turn the individual citizen into a "functionary" for the monitoring of the European law.[18] The undertones of these observations have often been critical, and might have been an important motive for the ECJ. But the stress on procedural law could be interpreted in another way. Member States act autonomously when creating and developing the general administrative law infrastructure on which specific European laws rest in each jurisdiction, so it seems entirely consistent that the procedural law is expected to be more-than-usually "rational" in relation to the effectiveness of specific European administrative laws. This helps to guarantee its implementation in a practical sense. It also has broader effects for the process of integrating European law as a whole; this is a process that requires greater transparency so that both Europe and its member nations can work towards achieving a co-operative transnational administrative law through a pattern of mutual learning.

Enhancing procedural law would seem to be a goal that is thoroughly compatible with those of the various national administrative legal systems. It meanwhile has the side effect of enabling "autonomy" for administrative procedures to be used for purposes of Europeanisation. Against the specific background of the differing decision-making models in Germany and Britain, a strengthening of the procedural idea could bring transparency for environmental-impact assessment. It could also bring transparency for implementing the IPPC directive that allows an estimate of whether, and to what degree, the various decision-making models are functionally equivalent in their legitimate claims to guarantee "integrated environment protection" despite using different instruments. Debates in Germany and other EC Member States show that higher requirements

[18] Cf. C. D. Classen, "Der Einzelne als Instrument der Durchsetzung des Gemeinschaftsrechts?", *Verwaltungsarchiv* (1997), 654 ss.; cf. also F. Schoch and G. Winter, "Individualrechtsschutz im deutschen Umweltrecht unter dem Einfluß des Gemeinschaftsrechts", *Neue Zeitschrift für Verwaltungsrecht* (1999), 457 ss and 467 ss.

on procedural rationality are also optimal for the maintenance of the specific rationality of the relevant "ordering idea" of general administrative law.[19] Indeed, they could bring a "modernising impetus" that would facilitate adjustment to the more complex decision-making situations of the European jurisdiction. For Europeanised law too, a gain in rationalisation could then be achieved that could make the concept of "subsequent improvement"[20] (used by the German Federal Constitutional Court to describe the requirements on legislation in conditions of uncertainty) a fruitful one. In this way, the search for, and testing of, decision-making models for conditions of uncertainty can replace and extend the supranational monitoring of the national implementation of European law. This is the ultimate goal as there will rarely be cases involving simple administrative procedures regarding relatively certain factual bases and problems of harmonising European (specific) and national (general) administrative law. This co-operative understanding of law accords with the precept of recognising "diagonal conflicts" because it respects the procedural autonomy of Member States. It is also an attempt by both European law and the various national general administrative legal systems to mobilise the competition between legal systems in a transnational perspective.

A strongly normative system of administrative law oriented towards the control function of legislation (as is the German one) must abandon a few myths about the function of court control being rights-based.[21] It must also devote greater attention to the rationality of administrative procedure. This makes the law more permeable to the autonomy of the procedural idea: the procedure then has more than an auxiliary function in the "proper" application of the law. To some extent, the accentuation of procedural law has different effects in the various national legal systems: in Germany it is associated with a shift towards recognising the creative administrative functions (at the expense of a one-sided conception of legal binding), whereas the room for administrative discretion in France and Britain might create the opposite effect of procedural *law* that is more binding than before. The introduction of Integrated Pollution Prevention and Control (IPPC) in Britain is claimed to have had just this effect. In her article, Carol Harlow points to the historical reasons for the high level of trust in the British administration and its expertise.

A similar difficulty arises with the IPPC directive:[22] its implementation problems cannot be attributed simply to the effects of foreign "transplants" into German administrative law. The requirement to "account" in a permit procedure

---

[19] Cf. E. Schmidt-Aßmann, "Die Ordnungsidee des allgemeinen Verwaltungsrechts" (Berlin: Springer, 1998); cf. Schoch, ibid. (Fn.5), 38 N°.156, on "procedural generation of knowledge".

[20] Bundesverfassungsgericht Reports (BverfGE), 50, 290, 374 ss.

[21] Cf. v. Danwitz, ibid. (Fn.3); it may be doubted that § 43 UGB-KomE will contribute to this; but cf. R. Breuer, Tendenzwende des Rechtsschutzes? Betrachtungen zu §§ 43 ss. UGB-KomE, Jahrbuch des Umwelt- und Technik-rechts 1998, 161 ss.; cf. also Schmidt-Preuß, op. cit. (Fn.10).

[22] Cf. K. H. Ladeur, "Integrierter Umweltschutz im Genehmigungsverfahren", *ZUR* (1998), 245 ss.

for differing impacts on the environment must ultimately lead to abandonment of the fiction of strict binding by law (of the one right decision) in the procedure. This does not mean that the doors are now wide open to administrative arbitrariness. The margins for decision can and must be better shaped according to type and level of decision, and this would be the alternative to a case-by-case system of recognition of "exceptional cases". Then the administration's freedom can be easily limited to a very narrow corridor (in permit proceedings, for example); but this is also necessary in order to better adapt the philosophy of administrative law to the requirements of complex administrative decisions that can no longer be "subsumed" under a legal norm.

The Challenge to Member States' Administrative Procedural Law from "Diagonal Conflicts" with European Law: A Survey of the Papers in this Volume

The introductory chapter by Martin Shapiro confirms the American experience that the autonomy of procedural rationality is not easy to picture. The attempt to enhance the "procedural reasonableness" of the administrative decision-maker by redirecting attention to the decision-making *process* and not at illusory concepts of the substantive "rightness" of the decision creates extremely strict requirements. It is easy for this to irritate the administrative courts and the administration itself by enhancing the trend towards an unstructured collection of as many detailed elements oriented to individual cases as possible. In light of the American experience, Shapiro is sceptical about the possibility of developing a conception of procedural rationality that avoids these dangers.

Carol Harlow sets out the implicit assumptions underlying British administrative law and its procedural conceptions. It trusts the reliability of knowledge, and the practical decision-making rules and patterns accumulated as administrative experience. Associated with this is scepticism about the importance of legislation controlling the administration. The associated conception of procedure and its administrative rationality leads to a weakening of the binding effect of procedural *law*. The chapter highlights the tendency of European law to bypass the stores of experience and practical orientation patterns contained in individual national legal systems without replacing them with anything of equal value. It thereby shows how important the historical backgrounds to the administrative legal system are for a more precise classification of the relationship between the powers involved in law-making (the legislature, executive and judiciary). This perception is of great importance for developing the law of the multi-level European system.

René Hostiou investigates how the French legal system, is developing a conception of cost-benefit analysis (*bilan coûts-avantages*) that seeks to respect traditions while structuring administrative freedom of action through procedural balancing rules. Hostiou uses the example of French planning law and discusses the issue in the light of the challenge from complex new decisions going beyond the existing model of far-reaching administrative self-management and limited judicial control. The cost-benefit analysis expresses an insight into the limited utility of accumulated administrative knowledge when it comes to complex planning decisions that have to balance a multiplicity of factors against each other. It portrays a new legal infrastructure for the administration from which other countries facing similar problems can benefit by observation. But this evolution of the French law must first be formally recognised if there is to be serious consideration about legal transplants and fitting them into various legal systems.

Jan Jans and Marianne De Jong use Dutch law to investigate the problems arising in using the "*effet utile*" formula to link European and national law. They show that uncertainty about the European Court's case law is transferred to national law, and that there are limits to the benefits of a case-oriented case law.

Roberto Caranta studies the Italian law and its specific adjustment problems in the Europeanisation process. He suggests that European law can contribute to a productive "irritation" of the administration and of administrative law by providing a modernising impetus that might meanwhile help to enhance the structuring effects of national administrative law.

The chapter by Karl-Heinz Ladeur and Rebecca Prelle analyses the specificities of German administrative law and its emphasis on binding through law at the expense of the administration's creative freedom., Due to its stress on guaranteeing substantive correctness through binding by law, the German law neglects the autonomy of procedure; procedure is reduced to a merely auxiliary function. The paper shows that the strengthening of procedural law – particularly in environmental law – should not only be viewed from the viewpoint of effective implementation of European law (particularly through judicial protection of rights), but might also lead to a modernisation of procedure in the national law. It also increases the transparency of the administration, and this might contribute to mutual observation and co-operation among European administrations.

Grainne De Búrca and Áine Ryall follow the development of the administrative procedural case law of the European courts. They find that, while the courts certainly leave room for developmental discretion by Member States, their case law is generally oriented too strongly to individual cases to be able to contribute to shaping the adjustment effects one should be able to expect from European law.

The chapter by Leonor Moral Soriano adds a theoretical appendix to Martin Shapiro's discussion of proceduralisation. While Shapiro casts a theoretical glance at the concept of proceduralisation, Moral Soriano takes a theoretical view of one important technical area – British environmental case law – and its problems in coping with constraints to decide under conditions of uncertainty. The methodological problems for general administrative law when dealing with complexity are shown clearly through the example of the British law. That closes the circle. The papers published in this volume provide approaches towards legal comparison with practical intentions, oriented to the objective of developing a specific legal dogma and method to fit the specific features of the multi-level European system. They do this on the basis of two theoretical considerations on proceduralisation and one central technical area (environmental law). And they show that procedural law, in particular, can contribute to an open, process-based conception of the Europeanisation of administrative law that cannot be tied down to the national pattern of a unitary, hierarchically structured legal system.

Chapter 1

Two Transformations in Administrative Law: American and European?

Martin Shapiro

What is referred to as rule-making in American administrative law is the exercise of law-making power delegated by the legislature to administrative agencies to create supplementary norms that fill in the details of the generally worded provisions of statutes. The English often use the expression *delegated legislation*, the French *regulement*, the Germans *rechsverordungen*. The American administrative law governing agency rule-making underwent a major transformation from the mid-1960s to the late 1980s.[1] This transformation was accomplished largely by case law seconded by Congressional legislation but without amendment of the relevant provisions of the Administrative Procedures Act. (In US federal practice, individual statutes creating new agencies or new government programs typically contain their own particular administrative procedure provisions. The APA is a residual statute. Its provisions come into play only where a particular statute itself fails to contain specific procedural norms. Typically in the period under discussion new doctrines first announced in court decisions would later be echoed by Congress in the procedural provisions of new statutes. Thus the meaning of the APA was fundamentally altered by judicial "interpretation", but Congress gave indirect approval to these judicial alterations by itself adopting most of them in one or another subsequent statute such as the Clean Air Act.) These changes in administrative law were particularly important because in this period the U S passed a large number of new, sweeping regulatory statutes that delegated an enormous amount of rule-making authority to administrative agencies.

To some degree this transformation was triggered by the internal dynamics of administrative law itself. Lawyers and judges acted to bring the huge new body of agency discretion to make law under some sort of procedural and even substantive norms. The history of administrative law everywhere is a story of continuously

1 R. Stewart, "The Reformation of American Administrative Law" (1975) 88 *Harvard Law Rev*, 1667-1813; Martin Shapiro, *Who Guards the Guardians: Judicial Control of Administration* (Athens: University of Georgia Press, 1988).

seeking to bring new discretions under rules. To some degree the transformation was the result of exterior, American, intellectual forces. At the very time when a wave of new, highly technical environmental, health, safety and consumer protection legislation necessarily depended upon implementation by government technocratics, the US was going through a wave of anti-technocratic, pro-democratic sentiment. At that time democracy was conceived largely in pluralist terms. A democratic government decision was one in which all relevant groups had participated so that the outcome aggregated group preferences. Thus a proper administrative decision-making process was one characterised by maximum transparency and access for all interests resulting in a democratic check on the discretion granted to government technocrats. In American administrative law, the intrusiveness of judicial review into the administrative process was greatly increased in part so that judges, who were not themselves technically trained, could provide a lay or common sense check on the technically trained bureaucracy and in part so that judges could insure that sufficient transparency and participation had been introduced into technical decision-making processes so that non-governmental groups could themselves act as a check on technocratic administration.

The transformation was embodied in a number of now well-known doctrines. The courts declared themselves the "partners" of administrative agencies in rule-making. And since judges have the final say on the lawfulness of agency made rules, courts really became the senior partners. The courts liberalised standing both to participate in agency proceedings and to seek judicial review until a "scintilla" of injury in fact including non-economic injury was sufficient to establish standing. Congress sometimes went even further. Some statutes specifically granted "any person" judicial standing although their constitutionality is in doubt. The courts also expanded the "notice" requirements of the APA, in effect requiring agencies contemplating rule-making to allow outsiders to participate from the very earliest moment that the agency began to think about a new rule and to know all the data and analysis the agency was generating as soon as it generated it. Then comes the famous judicially created "dialogue" requirement. The agency must receive and *adequately respond to* every point raised by outside groups. The extremes of the dialogue requirement are slightly constrained by judicial warnings against purely strategic behaviour by outside groups, that is inadequately explained or supported points raised simply to delay proceedings. In short, there should be perfect, pluralist, democratic, transparency and participation in rule-making. The technocrats of government must conclusively show the reviewing judge that they have provided all the information and access possible to all outside groups, that they have meticulously considered every legitimate point raised by those groups, and that the final rule promulgated can be fully justified in terms of all the points raised. The agency must compile a "rule-making record" sufficient to allow effective judicial inquiry into all these matters.

The relationship between substantive and procedural review is a tricky one in all systems of administrative law. Whatever the formal legal doctrine, it is obvious that the more of the facts and analysis on which a rule-making agency relied is spread upon the reviewable record the more opportunity for substantive judicial review presents itself. Moreover where a government agency is required to give reasons for what it has done, a reviewing court is pressed from the purely procedural requirement that the agency produce a statement of reasons to the substantive requirement that the agency give good reasons. For surely an agency that procedurally correctly offers a reasons statement but one that reads "We made this rule because on the date of its issuance Mars was in the seventh house of Jupiter and in conjunction with the moon" can hardly be said to really have met a giving reasons requirement. It is one very short, and often almost unnoticed, step from a judicial requirement that an agency respond to all points raised to a requirement that it respond to all points that could have or should have been raised. Finally, it is easy and avoids a direct judicial-administrative confrontation for a court which is really in substantive disagreement with an agency to quash the agency rule on the grounds that it has not paid adequate attention to all the points that were or could have been raised. Such a judicial decision may contain the strongest substantive condemnation between the lines while still being cast in the form "Perhaps ultimately you may have even this extremely stupid rule if you go back and go through the proper procedural motions". Such judicial review is a kind of suspensive rather than absolute veto.

The American courts certainly moved right up to the line between a perfect pluralism and synopticism (I use the term "synopticism" in this paper to refer to a requirement that an agency have considered all relevant facts and analysis before enacting a rule) and may well have crossed it. In preparing for judicial review, American agencies today certainly try to demonstrate not only that they took everybody seriously but that they made not simply an acceptable or plausible rule but the substantively best rule it is possible to make given the state of the world and the state of human knowledge and capacity. American agencies expect that if they cannot make a persuasive substantive case for their rule in court they stand a good chance of being reversed for what the judges will say is procedural error.

In parallel to this intimate connection between procedural and substantive judicial review lies the substantive dimension of "lawfulness" review. Does the rule violate the substantive terms of the statute that delegated rule-making authority to the agency? Statutory interpretation may be about the ambiguity of words but it is also sometimes a vehicle for judicial rejection of agency policy choices. In its much commented upon *Chevron* decision,[2] the Supreme Court announced that courts should defer to agency interpretations of ambiguous statutory language. Such a doctrine, however, no matter how clearly and loudly announced itself always remains ambiguous. If a court is charged with the duty of judicial review, ultimately it must strike down the unlawful acts of agencies and so ultimately it must have the final authority as to what the statute means. Courts cannot accept agency interpretations of statutes that are "clearly" or "manifestly" in error "on their face". Thus the *Chevron* doctrine in practice can only mean that where an agency has chosen one from among a number of alternative statutory

2 *Chevron U.S.A. v. National Resources Defense Council*, 467 U.S. 837 (1984).

interpretations that a court finds plausible then the court will defer, but that courts will strike down agency interpretations that they deem to be clearly incorrect. The US Supreme Court's decisions since *Chevron* have fallen precisely into this pattern. The statutory intent of Congress could hardly be that agencies make bad policy, so whenever an agency makes a policy that the court views as substantively very wrong, the court necessarily is tempted to find an error in agency statutory interpretation. *Chevron* did not end statutory interpretation based judicial reversals of agency decisions.

The result of the extremely aggressive judicial review in the US has been a learning process in which agencies have come to lean over backwards to avoid the risk of judicial reversals. Agencies have maximised transparency and outside participation in their decision-making processes and devote enormous care to preparing fully supported rebuttals to points raised in opposition. They offer very fully elaborated defences of the outcomes they have chosen as the best possible rules. Indeed they have learned to cover themselves in huge screens of technological camouflage. The result is that the American rule-making process has become extremely open to anyone and everyone who has the interest, knowledge and resources to play and that the substance of agency rules is much more carefully thought out and critically tested than it once was. The result is also that the agencies lose fewer cases as they construct huge records of data analysis that reviewing courts cannot really understand. The attempt to exert lay control over technocratic government through judicial review leads to the technocrats playing the specialised knowledge card even harder. And finally the result has been not only more open and better substantive rule-making, but enormous time and resource costs for rule-making. It is often easier and quicker now to get Congress to amend its statute than for an agency to exercise the discretion to make rules delegated to it by the statute.

Today the growth industry or leading edge of administrative law in the US is figuring out ways that an agency can make new policies *without* making new rules. One avenue has been to move to the ultimate level of pluralism, so-called "negotiated rule-making" in which no rule is promulgated until all interested parties have reached consensus. The agency is reduced from the legislator to one of the negotiating parties. In return for veto power, all of the negotiating groups agree not to subsequently challenge the consensual rule in court. An alternative is "soft law", agency policy statements which do not have the force of law but contain the implied threat of various government imposed difficulties for those who choose to ignore them. The APA provides that "interpretive rules", that is those that are designed solely for the internal guidance of agency personnel and which do not have the force of law, are non-reviewable. Agencies may seek to achieve more easily through such internal rules policy changes that might have been sought through the legislative rule-making process. For many years some Washington agencies made all policy through "case law", that is doctrines announced in the course of administrative adjudications. Such an approach does not avoid judicial review but does tend to reduce the number of parties and the range of issues and evidence considered compared to rule-making. These agencies used to be much criticised for this "piece meal" approach and urged to employ rule-making procedures. Today case-by-case policy-making looks more attractive. Finally, some agencies are in a position to announce soft law with quite hard enforcement mechanisms. Where the private party cannot proceed without a government license, permit, planning permission, grant, tax exemption or collaborative effort, that party may simply be told that, absent its compliance with agency policy, the favourable government action it needs will not be forthcoming. And if it goes to court to challenge one government refusal to act favourably on one of its needs, by the time the case is decided adversely to the government, the agency will have found something else not to give it that it cannot go forward without.

Critics of the pluralist transformation of American administrative law sum up their case as follows. Rule-making now takes far too long and costs too much in agency resources so that regulatory agencies, which usually operate on very constrained budgets, simply don't make enough of the rules needed. The law now encourages strategic behaviour rather than good faith participation by outside parties. Transparency and lay control is actually reduced as agencies learn to throw up huge technological smoke screens to protect their policy guesses from judicial second-guessing. Both transparency and participation are reduced as agencies move to sub rosa policy-making to avoid the costs of rule-making.

Because the proponents of the new pluralism have won, they are less vocal, but generally their argument is a simple one. Fifty years ago judges presumed that the agencies had the facts to justify their rules and deferred to "expert" agency policy discretion. Although the agencies had to receive outside comments, they didn't have to make it clear what needed to be commented on nor did they have to really listen to the comments. Today agencies may not make new law without encouraging the expression of and taking seriously the full range of interests that will be affected by their new law. Such a process may be time consuming, but the time is worth it in terms of both greater democracy and greater substantive rationality. In the realm of regulation, the regulated and those outsiders seeking regulation often know more and care more than does the government bureaucrat. In regulation the public interest is better achieved through a pluralist process than technocratic wisdom.

Whichever side one takes, there is a fair level of agreement among leading American scholars of US administrative law that pluralism has triumphed, that government now does a much better job of rule-making than it used to but that there is increasing concern for the costs and delays of rule-making and judicial "partnership" (intrusion) in agency rule-making.

This set of pragmatic concerns about the transformation of US administrative law has been accompanied by ideological changes as well. Pluralist democratic theory, which had been the orthodoxy of the 1950s came under attack in the late 1960s and 1970s as did nearly every establishment aspect of American life. If pluralism was orthodox then it was a defence of the status quo and the status quo must be wrong because it gave us Viet Nam and racism. Moreover, pluralism as a political theory was linked to utilitarianism as a moral philosophy, and utilitarianism was under general attack by a movement sometimes called post consequentialist ethics. It was argued both that the resources for participation enjoyed by various groups inevitably were highly unequal in a capitalist system so that the equality of participation that would be a pre-requisite to truly democratic pluralism was unattainable and that the aggregation of group interests did not necessarily constitute morally best public policies.

For the last decade in the US there has been less talk of transparency and participation in conjunction with administrative law and more talk of "deliberation". No one has figured out just what deliberation is or how you know when you have it. What is clear is that the word "deliberation" registers an aspiration to move beyond the mere aggregation of group preferences to a process that yields morally superior results. Deliberation appears to entail both technocratic themes in the form of requiring the best possible data collection and analysis and pluralist themes in the form of requiring the broadest possible public participation. It then, however, adds a magic and intangible element. This full range of technical and lay participants is to arrive not at an aggregation of preferences but at a truly better policy. How do we know when a pluralist process of negotiating outcomes that at least minimally satisfy all participants has turned into a true deliberation? I don't know. The observable procedural elements of both would appear to be the same. Both require broad participation, good data and adequately explained conclusions. The same people meet in the same rooms and say the same things in both. It seems to me that you would only know that pluralist procedures had turned into deliberative procedures by knowing that you had achieved a substantively better outcome than aggregation alone would have achieved or at least a very good substantive outcome. I don't know how you are going to know that you got an outcome better than some other outcome that you didn't get.

All the talk of deliberation in administrative law seems to me indeterminate as to the scope and level of intrusiveness of judicial review. Given that deliberation seems to require all the procedural transparency and participation that pluralism did plus the complete information and analysis that synopticism does, deliberation does not seem to imply less procedural judicial review than now exists. And it would seem to lean toward even more aggressive substantive judicial review because that's the only way a reviewing court can tell whether a very good outcome occurred.

Indeed the one thing that is clear about deliberation is that it demands more than ever of the rule-making administrative agency. The agency cannot content itself with being only a referee or arena provider for groups engaged in a struggle to achieve a rule that at least minimally satisfies most or all participants. The agency somehow must also assure that the participants rise above their initial self-interested positions to achieve a genuinely best or better outcome.

Some years ago in a paper written before but published soon after certain crucial ECJ and CFI decisions,[3] I predicted that the European courts would move from their previous position and begin using the then Article 190 (giving reasons

---

3 ECJ, Case C-269/90, *Hauptzollamt Munchen-Mitte v. Telchnische Universitat Munchen* [1991] ECR 1-5469; *CFI*, Case T 44/90, *La Cinq v. Commission* [1992] ECR II-1.

requirements) of the Treaties to exercise more active judicial review of administrative rule-making.[4] At the time I also suggested that even while moving in the American direction, European courts would consciously seek to avoid going to the American extreme of requiring that EU administrators respond to every point raised and ultimately even to every point not raised but relevant. There is now some evidence that my predictions were correct, although there is a debate about just how far the EU courts have gone and some indication that the CFI wants to move faster than the ECJ.[5]

My predictions were not based on some hypothesised general tendency toward the globalisation of American law but rather on more concrete comparative considerations. The American transformation had occurred when there was a big new outburst of regulation at a time of strong anti-technocratic sentiment and great concern for democratic legitimacy expressed as demands for pluralist transparency and participation. I argued that following a "constitutional" phase in which European law was creating a common market by sweeping away national laws, it was entering a new phase of heightened regulatory activity by the Union to replace or "harmonise" the national regulations swept away. This new European regulatory wave was occurring in a climate of hostility to technocracy, concern for democratic legitimacy and constant calls for more transparency and participation. Moreover, regulated industries which had very much been insiders to national regulatory processes, which were highly syndicalist in character, had become somewhat more outsiders in regulatory processes conducted in Brussels and, like all outsiders, would be more interested in transparency and participation. Thus it would follow, or so I argued, that facing the same situation in the 1990s and after that the US had faced in the 1960s and after, Europe would proceed in the same direction. However, given the knowledge obtained from the American experiment, Europe would try not to go quite so far.

Certain other concrete European factors may be added to this line of argument. The peculiar structure of EU governance leaves Parliament largely an "outsider" attempting to penetrate the decision-making processes through which the Commission proposes and the Council enacts public policies. Thus in the EU outsider demands for more transparency and participation are pushed not only by NGOs and economic enterprises but by an organ of the government itself. For instance it has been the EP that has led the way in trying to penetrate the comitology process. Moreover EU regulation becomes more and more pervasive but is administered largely by national bureaucracies. The result inevitably will be national regulatory variation. Multinationals will litigate more and more against regulatory actions not so much because they oppose regulation as such but because they want uniformity of regulation across national boundaries. Once a multinational's lawyers are set loose against any regulatory action they will try to

---

4 Martin Shapiro, "The Giving Reasons Requirement" (1992) *University of Chicago Legal Forum*, 179-220.

5 H. P. Nehl, *Principles of Administrative Procedure in EC Law* (Oxford: Hart, 1999), 145, 160-165.

win any and every way they can. So they will challenge not only the lack of uniformity but the procedural and substantive regularity of the underlying EU rule. Thus a broad and rapid stream of litigation will give the EU courts the opportunity to create a new and elaborate administrative law of rule-making if they want to. Finally as EU regulation grows, the Council almost inevitably resorts to more delegation of rule-making discretion to the comitology process and to the independent agencies. The creation of administrative discretion creates heavy internal pressures within administrative law for more norms to govern that rule-making discretion.[6] Given that the Commission is unlikely to vigorously champion an administrative code, at least in the short run, and both Parliamentary pressures and stream of litigation is likely to exist, case law is likely to develop rapidly.

Will the case law be pluralist, technocratic or deliberative? At the academic level the battle is already underway.[7] Our distinguished colleague Majone calls for technocracy. Democratic politics should be excluded from regulatory rule-making which should be based solely on objective "efficiency" criteria and thus should be conducted exclusively by experts. Any social justice problem that may arise from this apolitical, expert administration should be handled by a pluralist redistributive politics that directly pays off those adversely affected rather than protecting them through inefficient regulation.[8] On the other hand our distinguished colleague Dehousse suggests that a pluralist rationale for policy-making by the "independent" agencies may be in order.[9] And our distinguished colleague Harlow tells us that a European administrative law of rule-making may be forthcoming but cautions us against going too far in American pluralist directions.[10] In a recent book on EU administrative law, the author discovers the Union courts to be inventing, or deriving from European legal traditions, a duty of good administration or due diligence incumbent on the Commission. This duty, particularly when combined with the duty to give reasons, certainly requires pluralist transparency and participation but may require synopticism and/or deliberation as well.[11] If you run your eye randomly over writing on European administrative law you will find the word deliberation popping up more and more frequently, albeit with the usual vagueness about what it is and how you would know whether you had it.

Thus I believe that Europe today stands in the following position vis-à-vis earlier American experience. First forces previously present in the US and now present in Europe, plus some forces peculiar to Europe, push the EU courts toward an American style transformation of administrative law emphasising maximum transparency and participation. That transformation will be resisted and will be less

---

6 C. Harlow and R. Rawlings, *Pressure through Law* (London: Routledge, 1992).

7 C. Joerges and J. Neyer, "Transforming Strategic Interaction into Deliberative Problem Solving" (1997) 4 J.E.P.P., 609-625.

8 G. Majone, ed., *Regulating Europe* (London/New York: Routledge, 1996).

9 R. De Housse, "Regulation by Networks in the European Community, the Role of European Agencies" (1997) 4 J.E.P.P., 246-261.

10 C. Harlow, "Codification of EC Administrative Procedure? Fitting the Foot to the Shoe or the hoe to the Foot" (1996) 2 E.L.J., 3-25.

11 H. P. Nehl, above Fn.5., p. 1.

radical in Europe than in the United States. Pluralism is now weaker and technocratic themes again stronger than they were in the immediate past. The now-known high costs of the American transformation and knowledge of current American efforts to avoid those costs will reduce European enthusiasm for absolutely maximising pluralism. Nevertheless, greater EU court emphasis on procedural judicial review in the form of judicial demands for more complete administrative "rule-making records", that is administrative reason giving and proof of due diligence, will lead to greater substantive judicial review as well. And the resort of administrative law scholars to a discourse of "deliberation" is more likely than not also to push courts further into substantive review.

Chapter 2

Procedural Errors and Substantive Legality in Italian Administrative Law

Roberto Caranta

Sources of Italian Administrative Procedural Law

Judge-Made General Principles

It has been said that "[u]ntil 1990 [...] the administrative procedure was regulated only with reference to some special aspects, while the general principles were derived by the jurisprudence of the *Consiglio di Stato* and the Regional Administrative Courts (T.A.R.)".[1] Administrative law has traditionally been characterised as judge-made law and the *plenum* of the judicial sections of the Italian *Consiglio di Stato* once remarked that administrative law is not only made of statutory rules, but it consists also of principles systematically developed in scholarly works and judicial decisions.[2]

Italian courts developed general principles of administrative law from a basis of specific statutory provisions ruling given administrative procedures, such as those leading to expropriation.[3] It could be debated whether courts really created anything new in this way, or whether they just applied existing rules by analogy.[4] However, one recent opinion suggests that the rules applied by analogy soon started to give way to general principles that were far more detached from specific statutory provisions.[5]

---

1 M. Chiti, "Italian Report" in J. Schwarze (ed.), *Administrative Law under European Influence* (Baden Baden: Nomos, 1996), 248.

2 Cons. St., Ad. plen., 28 gennaio 1961, n. 3, *Foro amm.* 1961, I, 561; the Court speaks of "principi che dottrina e giurisprudenza hanno elevato a dignità di sistema".

3 See generally G. Sala, *Potere amministrativo e principi dell'ordinamento* (Milano: Giuffrè, 1993), 149 ff. and 282 f.

4 Even the latter activity can to some extent be regarded as creative: M.S. Giannini, "Genesi e sostanza dei princìpi generali del diritto" in *Scritti in onore di A. Predieri*, vol. II (Milano: Giuffrè, 1996), 900 ff.

5 G. Sala, *Potere amministrativo e principi dell'ordinamento*, cit. supra n. 3, at 29 ff.

This was particularly the case with the development of procedural rules and principles through the case law on *eccesso di potere* [translating roughly to "excess of power"]. *Eccesso di potere* derives from the French *excès de pouvoir*, but the Italian idea has diverged from the original model.[6] It is one of three forms of invalidity, the other two being *incompetenza* (incompetence, *incompétence*) and *violazione di legge* (infringement of the law, *violation de la loi*). *Eccesso di potere* initially performed the role played in France by *détournement de pouvoir*,[7] but soon come to cover the breach of a rather vague general principle of reasonableness. Little by little, this has since crystallised around a number of recurring hypotheses in the case law. As is often the case with judge-made law (procedural) principles are here moulded in a negative way: a decision affected by *eccesso di potere* and is ruled invalid and, in this negative response, the path that should have been followed by the administration is laid out, and the principle that has been infringed is thereby elucidated.[8]

It is not necessary here to go further into the general theory and practice of *eccesso di potere*; moreover, any pretence at being exhaustive would ultimately be frustrated since the possible applications of *eccesso di potere* are endless and new examples could be added by the courts at any time.[9] It is more important, once the creative role played by courts is understood, to point out that some of the principles distilled through *eccesso di potere* concern administrative procedure.

For instance, courts have consistently held that, once the administration has decided to follow a given procedure, a decision adopting a different procedure is affected by *eccesso di potere* unless a reason is given to explain the different course.[10] Any decision whose outcome is at odds with the facts ascertained during the procedure is also deemed to be affected by *eccesso di potere*, and therefore

---

6 See M. D'Alberti, *Diritto amministrativo comparato* (Bologna: Il Mulino, 1992), 133 ff.; M. D'Alberti, "Mutamenti e destini del «recours pour excès de pouvoir»" in *Scritti in onore di M.S. Giannini*, vol. III (Milano: Giuffrè, 1988), 300 ff.

7 For a comparison of the Community and Italian notions of *détournement de pouvoir* see L. Musselli, "Evoluzione del détournement de pouvoir in ambito comunitario ed ipotesi di raffronto con l'ordinamento amministrativo interno", *Riv. dir. pub. comunitario*, 1996, 119.

8 See, albeit critically, G. Sala, *Potere amministrativo e principi dell'ordinamento*, cit. supra n. 3, at 166 f. and 206 ff.

9 See S. Piraino, *La funzione amministrativa tra discrezionalità e arbitrio* (Milano: Giuffrè, 1990); M. S. Giannini, *Diritto amministrativo*, 2nd ed. (Milano: Giuffrè, 1988), 775 f., however, points how that, given the extent now reached by *eccesso di potere*, new developments today are more apparent than real.

10 For instance Cons. St., Sez. V, 24 maggio 1996, n. 585, *Cons. Stato* 1996, I, 863; Cons. St., Sez. VI, 14 dicembre 1991, n. 1081, *Foro amm.* 1991, 2973; a rule contrary to the English one against fettering of discretion applies in Italy.

invalid.[11] Indeed, the procedure must allow the interested parties to make their points clear to the administration.[12]

The role played by Italian courts in procedural matters must not be overestimated. Indeed, administrative courts have tended to share the traditional wisdom that places all the emphasis on the administrative decision; they have consequently downplayed the importance of the administrative procedure.[13] For example, before the Administrative Procedure Act 1990 entered into force, the administrative courts consistently refused to recognise due process as a general principle of administrative law.[14] Today, both administrative courts and the Constitutional court usually deny any constitutional underpinning to the due process principle.[15]

Case law can turn a specific rule into a general principle; it can build a general principle from nothing but reason. However, when it has turned down a proposed principle, it can even curtail the application of a subsequent statute adopting that principle. This has sometimes been the case with due process clauses embodied in the Administrative Procedure Act 1990. A 1995 decision almost made scrap paper of that statute. In a case concerning an alleged breach of due process with reference to a procedure to withdraw a decision which the administration thought to have been illegally adopted, the court ruled that due process could not help a person who opposed the withdrawal of an invalid decision.[16, 17]

---

11 For instance Cons. St., Sez. IV, 13 maggio 1991, n. 357, *Riv. amm. R.I.* 1991, 1277; T.A.R. Calabria, Sez. Catanzaro, 29 giugno 1994, n. 771, *Foro amm.* 1994, 2549.

12 Con. St., Sez.VI, 13 aprile 1992, n. 256, *Cons. Stato* 1992, I, 606.

13 See V. Cerulli Irelli, *Corso di diritto amministrativo* (Torino: Giappichelli, 1997), 416 f.; A. Zito, *Le pretese partecipative del privato nel procedimento amministrativo* (Milano: Giuffrè, 1996), 4 ff.

14 This was still the position one year before the statute was passed: Cons. St., Sez. V, 18 marzo 1989, n. 170, *Foro amm.* 1989, 596.

15 Corte cost., 19 marzo 1993, n. 103, *Regioni* 1993, 1671, note S. Staiano, "Lo scioglimento dei consigli comunali e provinciali nella lotta alla criminalità organizzata tra Corte costituzionale e giudice amministrati"; Cons. St., Sez. VI, 24 agosto 1996, n. 1072, *Giur. it.* 1997, III, 1, 72; on due process see E. Palici Di Suni, "Inerzia della p.a. e giusto procedimento", *Giur. it.* 1992, I, 1, 13; A. Franco, "Leggi provvedimento, principi generali dell'ordinamento, principio del giusto procedimento", *Giur. cost.* 1989, II, 1041; G. Roehrssen, "Il giusto procedimento nel quadro dei principi costituzionali", *Dir. proc. amm.* 1987, 47; G. Sala, "Regole costituzionali dell'azione amministrativa e principio del giusto procedimento nella giurisprudenza dei TA.R.", *Dir. proc. amm.* 1985, 637. A shift of attitude can be detected in Cons. St., Ad. Plen., 15 settembre 1999, n. 14, *Urbanistica e appalti* 1999, 1014, con nota di R. Caranta, "Comunicazione di avvio del procedimento e annullamento ministeriale di autorizzazione paesaggistica".

16 Cons. St., Sez. VI, 16 ottobre 1995, n. 1141, *Foro amm.* 1995, 2279.

17 Due process will be dealt with later in this chapter.

Scholarly Opinions

For most of the last century, scholarly works have offered very limited help to courts trying to supplement incomplete legislative provisions. These works were minded to draw the *Allgemeiner Teil* (the general principles) of administrative law, which had to include administrative procedure.[18] But they were strongly influenced by and drew heavily on the most abstract of German theories of the time. If they quoted a piece of domestic legislation, it was only to ease the way to an understanding of the systematic structure they envisaged.[19] While the courts derived general principles from existing pieces of legislation, the professors used them to exemplify general principles which were deduced from "more general", general principles.

However, two decades of refined scholarly works[20] paved the way to L. 7 agosto 1990, n. 241, *Procedimento amministrativo e diritto di accesso ai documenti amministrativi* ("Administrative Procedure Act 1990", hereafter "APA").[21] A whole philosophy, a *Weltanschauung*,had come under growing criticism for its emphasis on the strength of the administration *vis à vis* the citizen, the latter having been reduced to a passive subject of the exercise of State powers. Italian academia began to give proper weight to the fundamental rights vested in individuals by the 1948 Constitution.[22] The forbidding, hierarchical character traditionally assigned to the relationship between the administration and the citizen by was challenged by influential writings that advocated *un diritto amministrativo paritario* (translating roughly to "parity of administrative law"). That is, they called for a more balanced adjudication between the powers and rights of the two poles of the dialectic relationship between the citizen and the State.[23]

---

18 Foremost among them A.M. Sandulli, *Il procedimento amministrativo* (Milano: Giuffrè, 1940, repr. 1964).

19 Ibid., at 166 s.

20 For a general overview see G. Corso, "El procedimiento administrativo en Italia" in J. Barnez Vasquez (ed.), *El procedimiento administrativo en el derecho comparado* (Madrid, Civitas, 1993), 473 ff.

21 There are many commentaries; the most authoritative are: V. Italia and M. Bassani (eds.), *Procedimento amministrativo e diritto di accesso ai documenti*, 2nd ed. (Milano, Giuffrè, 1995); G. Corso and F. Teresi, *Procedimento amministrativo e accesso ai documenti. Commento alla legge 7 agosto 1990,* n. 241 (Rimini: Maggioli, 1991); A. Travi (cur.), "Commentario della legge 7 agosto 1990, n. 241" *Nuove leggi civ. commentate* 1995, 1; P. Alberti et al., *Lezioni sul procedimento amministrativo* (Torino: Giappichelli, 1992).

22 A most important work was V. Bachelet, *La giustizia amministrativa nella Costituzione* (Milano: Giuffrè, 1966).

23 The seminal work was F. Benvenuti, "Per un diritto amministrativo paritario", in *Studi in memoria di E. Guicciardi* (Padova: CEDAM, 1975); see also G. Berti, "Procedimento, procedura, partecipazione", *ivi*; recent assessments in the works collected by G. Berti and G.C. De Martin (eds.), *Gli istituti della democrazia amministrativa* (Milano: Giuffrè, 1996).

Denying the omnipotence of the State meant a shift of focus towards administrative law. The administration's decision was no longer be the exclusive subject matter of interest. Administrative procedure – where the State and the citizen meet, and possibly conflict – acquired a new relevance. A search began for institutions more in line with the new constitutional framework, and some scholars turned their attention abroad. Foreign models were viewed with interest and their details scrutinised.[24] In particular, the German *Verwaltungsverfahrensgesetz* of 1976 was translated into Italian, as were some relevant preparatory works and commentaries by leading German scholars.[25]

In 1983 the Government set up a Commission chaired by a leading scholar, the late Prof. Mario Nigro,[26] to draft a statute on administrative procedure.[27] The outcome engendered lively debate among experts.[28]

The Administrative Procedure Act 1990

Though its most innovative aspects were considerably diluted in the Governmental bill and by the following Parliamentary readings, Commisione Nigro's draft eventually took the form of the APA. Administrative proceedings lost their reputations as points at which authoritative decisions were taken to bind citizens, and they instead became stages for participation. They became points at which conflicting interests could be balanced one against the other to find outcomes that are plausible, and even agreeable, to all concerned.[29]

Without labouring the details, it should be noted that the subject matter of the statute is twofold: on the one hand it deals with administrative procedure; on the other hand it provides a comprehensive framework for access to administrative documents that is not dependent on whether or not an administrative procedure is in question.[30] In the area of administrative procedure, it should be noted that the

---

24 See G. Pastori, *La procedura amministrativa* (Padova: CEDAM, 1964).

25 A. Masucci (ed.), *La codificazione del procedimento amministrativo in Germania* (Napoli: ESI, 1979); the book included C.H. Ule and H.W. Laubinger, "Diritto del procedimento amministrativo", and P. Badura, "Il procedimento amministrativo".

26 See his contribution to the discussion titled "Procedimento amministrativo e tutela giurisdizionale contro la pubblica amministrazione (il problema di una legge generale sul procedimento amministrativo)", published in *Riv. dir. proc.* 1980, 267.

27 See M. Nigro, "Commissione per la revisione della disciplina dei procedimenti amministrativi. Appunto amministrativo (dic. 1983)", *Riv. trim. sc. amm.* 1984; see also G. Pastori, "Commento all'Article 1", A. Travi (ed.), "Commentario della legge 7 agosto 1990, n. 241", cit. supra n. 21, at 5 ff.

28 For a wide overview see *La disciplina del procedimento amministrativo. Contributi alle iniziative legislative in corso, Atti del XXXII° Convegno di scienza della amministrazione*, Milano, 1989.

29 G. Corso, *El procedimiento administrativo en Italia*, cit. supra n. 20, 502.

30 Generally I. F. Caramazza, "Dal principio di segretezza al principio di trasparenza. Profili generali di una riforma", in *Scritti in memoria di A. Piras* (Milano: Giuffrè, 1996), 77.

subject matter of the Italian act is somewhat narrower than, for instance, the Spanish *Lei de régimen jurídico de las administraciones públicas y procedimiento administrativo común* of 1992 or the German *Verwaltungsverfahrensgesetz* of 1976. Indeed, the Italian statute does not deal with the general discipline of administrative decisions; in particular, nothing is said about what is a valid decision and what is not. Moreover, proceedings leading to the adoption of general rules and planning decisions are excluded from the application of the APA.[31]

The APA, and the philosophy behind it, has met considerable resistance from the bureaucracy and even, though to a more limited extent, from administrative courts.[32] Its goals were far too ambitious given the state of most Italian administrative authorities.[33] It is thus no surprise that the APA has failed to rejuvenate the Italian administration.[34] To give new impetus to administrative reform, many institutions were refined by two 1997 statutes, *Bassanini I* and *Bassanini II* (named after the Minister for the Public administration who proposed them).[35] It is too early to say whether these will have a deeper affect on Italy's administration.

Finally, it should be remembered that the APA is not a self-sufficient framework for administrative proceedings (other than rule making and planning),

---

31 For references to the case law see R. Caranta and L. Ferraris, *La partecipazione al procedimento amministrativo* (Milano: Giuffrè, 2000), at 27 ff.

32 A. Travi, "Note introduttive", in A. Travi (ed.), "Commentario della legge 7 agosto 1990, n. 241", cit., *supra* n. 20, 1 ff.; A. Corpaci, "Spunti critici sulla giurisprudenza applicativa della legge sul procedimento amministrativo", *Dir. pub.* 1995, 185; G. Vesperini, "L'attuazione della legge sul procedimento amministrativo", *Giorn. dir. amm.* 1995, 251 ff.; P. Duret, *Partecipazione procedimentale e legittimazione processuale* (Torino: Giappichelli, 1996), 47 f.

33 G. Della Cananea, "The Reform of Finance and Administration in Italy: Contrasting Achievements", *Frank Cass Journals* 1997, 203, exactly points out that "there was no systematic reform of the public apparatus – in particular the administrative sector [...]. Instead, there was a series of initiatives (such as the law no. 241/1990 on administrative procedure) put together with varying degrees of effectiveness. However, these were still isolated cases, in so far as they were not coordinated with other structural reforms, and were not followed up by a period of committed implementation, either at the regulatory or administrative level". See also G. Azzariti, "Trasformazioni dell'amministrazione e procedimento amministrativo", in P. Alberti et al., *Lezioni sul procedimento amministrativo*, cit. supra n. 21, at 20 ff.; P.G. Lignani, "La disciplina del procedimento amministrativo e le sue contraddizioni", in *Studi in memoria di F. Piga*, vol. I (Milano: Giuffrè, 1992), 489.

34 See generally S. Cassese, "La riforma amministrativa all'inizio della quinta Costituzione dell'Italia unita", *Foro it.* 1994, V, 9 ff.; S. Cassese, "Hypotheses on the Italian Administrative System", 16/2 *West European Politics* (April 1993), 316 ff.

35 See generally A. Sandulli, "La semplificazione", *Riv. trim. dir. pubbl.* 1999, 757; V. Parisio (ed.), *Semplificazione dell'azione amministrativa e procedimento amministrativo alla luce della legge 15 maggio 1997, n. 127* (Milano: Giuffrè, 1998); F. Mele, "La semplificazione del procedimento amministrativo nelle leggi 15 marzo 1997, n. 59 e 15 maggio 1997, n. 127 (c.d. «riforma Bassanini»)", *Dir. proc. amm.* 1997, 781.

but must be read with the statutes applicable to the various proceedings. Some diverge from the principles laid down by the APA.[36] Others, such as that dealing with local government, lay down rules applicable to a vast array of proceedings[37] and their consistency with the provisions of the APA can sometimes be questioned.[38] Attention will nevertheless be drawn mainly by the APA as its general nature allows it to influence the reading of other statutes.[39]

Does EC Law Influence Italian Procedural Law?

The influence of EC law on Italian procedural law has been aptly summarised by Mario Chinti, who notes that "[t]he Italian situation does not seem to be particularly influenced by European law, as the general principles of the national administrative procedure were already, on the whole, similar or identical to those of the Community".[40] Even the APA, he notes, seems "to reflect more the development of events in Italy than to be the result of European law".[41]

Though generally adequate, these statements do require some qualification. The Italian legislation was greatly influenced by pre-existing national legislation in other (mainly European) legal systems, such as the German *Verwaltungsverfahrengesetz*. Thus Italian law has been exposed to the same forces that have modelled EC law – it is the same body of law that influenced the case law of the Court of justice of the European Communities – and this further explains the similarities existing between the two.

Moreover, scholars trying to systematically appraise and construe the provisions of the APA have turned their eyes to EC law. Their research shows that many important aids to interpretation can be drawn from the case law of the Court of Justice.[42]

---

36 See for instance T.A.R. Basilicata, 9 maggio 1994, n. 63, *Foro amm.* 1994, 2224 (s.m.)

37 L. 8 giugno 1990, n. 142 (Local Government Act 1990), is analysed by V. Italia and M. Bassani (eds.), *Le autonomie locali* (Milano: Giuffrè, 1990). L. 3 agosto 1999, n. 265, has now brought the Local Government Act 1990 into full line with the Administrative Procedure Act 1990.

38 See the analysis by G. Sciullo, "Sintonie e dissonanze tra le L. 8 giugno 1990, n. 142 e 7 agosto 1990, n. 241: riflessioni sull'autonomia normativa locale", *Foro amm.* 1990, 2199.

39 E.g. T.A.R. Lazio, Sez. II, 6 marzo 1991, n. 456, *Foro amm.* 1991, *fasc.* 9 (s.m.); moreover, according to Article 29, the Administrative Procedure Act 1990 is to a large extent applicable to the proceedings which fall under Regional competence.

40 M. Chiti, *Italian Report*, cit. supra n. 1, 248; but see G. Greco, "Incidenza del diritto comunitario sugli atti amministrativi italiani", in M.P. Chiti and G. Greco (eds.), *Trattato di diritto amministrativo europeo. Parte generale* (Milano: Giuffrè, 1997), 592.

41 M.P. Chiti, ibid.

42 The most developed work is M. Cartabia, *La tutela dei diritti nel procedimento amministrativo. La legge n. 241 del 1990 alla luce dei principi comunitari* (Milano: Giuffrè, 1991).

The same Court has often been asked to assess the consistency of national administrative proceedings with national obligations under Treaties and secondary legislation. The proportionality requirement under Article 36 of the EC Treaty provides an example. The Court of Justice has frequently made it clear that, in lieu of harmonisation, the Member States may to limit the use of foodstuff additives, however:

> by virtue of the principle of proportionality, traders must also be able to apply, under a procedure which is easily accessible to them and can be concluded within a reasonable time, for the use of specific additives to be authorised by a measure of general application.[43]

Indeed, many principles of administrative procedure law are scattered through the Reports of the decisions by the Court of Justice. That their influence seems to have been limited thus far, is mainly because they are not well known to those working with and within the administration.[44]

Finally, some specific administrative procedures, such as those in the field of public procurements, are now governed by statutes drawn along the lines of EC directives.[45] In this way, procedures which are sometimes alien to the Italian tradition have nevertheless found a place in Italian law.[46] In due course, the principles underlying these rules are likely to affect national procedures.[47]

---

43 E.g. Case 178/84 [1987] ECR 1227, point 45.

44 The principle of proportionality has recently been the object of two attentive scholarly works: D.U. Galletta, *Principio di proporzionalità e sindacato giurisdizionale nel diritto amministrativo* (Milano: Giuffrè, 1998), and A. Sandulli, *La proporzionalità dell'azione amministrativa* (Padova: CEDAM, 1998).

45 See E. Picozza, "Il regime giuridico del procedimento amministrativo comunitario", *Riv. dir. pub. comunitario* 1994, 330 f.

46 E. Picozza, "Alcune riflessioni circa la rilevanza del diritto comunitario sui principi del diritto amministrativo italiano", in *Studi in memoria di F. Piga*, vol. I (Milan: Giuffrè, 1992), 745 ff.; the different conceptions underlying Community and Italian procedural rules in this field are pointed out by G. Greco, "L'adeguamento dell'ordinamenti italiano alle direttive comunitarie in tema di appalti di lavori pubblici", in G. Greco (ed.), *Gli appalti dei lavori pubblici nel diritto amministrativo comunitario e italiano* (Milano: Giuffrè, 1990), 12 f.

47 On spill over generally M. L. Fernandez Esteban, "National Judges and Community Law: The Paradox of the Two Paradigms of Law", 4 (1997) *Maastricht Jour. Eur. and Comp. L.* 143; with specific reference to the directives on remedies in public procurement see M. Protto, *L'effettività della tutela giurisdizionale nelle procedure di aggiudicazione di pubblici appalti* (Milano: Giuffrè, 1997).

Functions of Administrative Procedural Law in Italy

Administrative procedural law is instrumental to the organisation of administrative management and it protects those to whom authoritative decisions are addressed, particularly by allowing their participation in the proceedings.

The reciprocal importance of these functions and the way in which they have been interpreted, has changed throughout the years. Most administrative procedural law was traditionally about organisation; procedural rules were established to protect the integrity of the public decision-making process.[48] Since the beginning of the twentieth century, Italian law has been under the spell of French administrative law. One of the germinal ideas of procedural law is the opinion, attributed to Napoléon, according to which *administrer est le fait d'un seul, conseiller est le fait de plusiers*; this approach implies two central stages of administrative proceedings, an examination leading to an advice, and a final decision. Accordingly, procedural law was mainly concerned with questions such as who could start the procedure, which body would be entrusted with the procedure, whose advice must be taken, and who would make the final decision. The citizen could enter into the administrative decision-making procedure only in so far as his or her cooperation was deemed necessary by the administration.[49]

Procedural law slowly began to be read as a tool designed also to protect the citizen against *Eingriffsverwaltung* (public interference with private action).[50] Since administrative decisions could not, as a rule, be challenged on their merits, the respect of procedural rules became paramount to assess the validity of the final decision; if a procedural error was found, the administrative decision was set aside and the citizen was able to recover his freedom or his goods. The respect of procedural law was both a by-product of the same idea of *Rechtsstaat*,[51] and the application of an older idea (probably originating in the Germanic roots of the Middle Ages), according which a free man could be deprived of his life or goods only after a ritualised procedure had been followed.[52] Italian scholars and courts did not share the common law *penchant* for procedure; rather, the review of procedural errors matched their formalistic approach to judicial review and, more generally, to administrative law.

---

48 See e.g. A. M. Sandulli, *Il procedimento amministrativo*, cit. supra n. 18, at 12 ff.

49 See M. Terrasi, *Procedimenti amministrativi e garanzie del cittadino* (Napoli: Jovene, 1991), at 5 ff.; P. Duret, *Partecipazione procedimentale e legittimazione processuale*, cit. supra n. 32, at 8 ff.

50 This function too surfaces in A. M. Sandulli, *Il procedimento amministrativo*, cit. supra n. 18, at 14 ff.

51 *Ex multis* F. Benvenuti, *Prefazione*, to G. Pastori, *La procedura amministrativa*, cit. supra n. 24, at xiv; A. Masucci (ed.), *La codificazione del procedimento amministrativo in Germania*, cit. supra n. 25, xv, at f.

52 For a hint see A. Weber, "El procedimiento administrativo en el derecho comunitario", in J. Barnez Vasquez, *El procedimiento administrativo en el derecho comparado*, cit. supra n. 20, 75.

The shift from *Eingriffsverwaltung* to *Leistungsverwaltung,* from the administration of a liberal state to that of a welfare state, can lead to a less formalistic approach. Citizens want their demands to be met. They are more interested in getting positive replies than having administrative decisions set aside on technicalities. However, it is debatable whether Italian law has understood the full consequences of this momentous change. Democratisation of administrative activities meanwhile results in more emphasis being laid on openness and transparency of procedures.[53]

A clear example of this is the importance of transparency and participation under the APA. Procedural rules are no more a mere shield against administrative decisions; they empower all concerned people and public interest organisations to engage with the administrative authorities in order to find the best compromise possible for all with an interest in the outcome.

The recognition of the right of both individuals and public interest groups to take part in proceedings could point to different aims: on the one hand, protecting individual interests, and, on the other hand, allowing representation of every public and private interest concerned by the administrative decision.[54]

Following the enactment of the APA, some decisions have gone so far as to claim that procedural rules exist to allow interested parties to look into the choices left to the public administration.[55] Individual rights are therefore not just sheltering behind procedural rules, but play a more pro-active role in shaping the administrative decision-making process.

However, to date most decisions and many scholars have been happy with just the two traditional functions of procedural rules, that is protecting both the integrity of the public decision-making process and the individual rights of the people affected by administrative decisions.[56]

---

53 See M. Shapiro, *Two Transformations in Administrative Law: American and European?*, supra: "A democratic government decision was one in which all the relevant groups had partecipated so that the outcome aggregated group preferences".

54 Some hints can be found in A. Valorzi, "*Dalla procedura amministrativa al processo giurisdizionale*" (Padova: CEDAM, 1999), at 60 f.

55 See specially Cons. St., Sez. VI, 16 aprile 1998, n. 515, *Urbanistica e appalti* 1999, 415, note G. Rizzo, "Ancora sulla partecipazione del privato al procedimento di imposizione del vincolo".

56 See the analysis by F. Fracchia, "Manifestazioni di interesse del privato e procedimento amministrativo", *Dir. amm.* 1996, 11, and F. Ledda, "Problema amministrativo e partecipazione procedimentale", *Dir. amm.* 1993, 133, specially at 147 f., and 152 ff.

Procedural Rules Allowing Participation in the Administrative Procedure Act 1990

The openness principle enshrined in the APA has an obvious and conspicuous bearing on participation.[57] Administrative decisions do not suddenly appear out of nowhere, but are instead made with the participation, if not the assent, of their addressees.[58] Under Article 7 of the APA:

> If there is no special urgency, both those who can be directly affected by the final decision and those who are called to take part in the procedure by the law are informed of the opening of the file following the rules laid down in Article 8. In the same way, when the final decision can adversely affect people, other than the addressee of the final decision, whose identity either is known or can easily be known, the authority is under a duty to inform those people in, the same ways, of the opening of the file.[59]

---

[57] See generally R. Caranta and L. Ferraris, *La partecipazione al procedimento amministrativo*, cit. supra n. 31; G. Virga, *La partecipazione al procedimento amministrativo* (Milano: Giuffrè, 1998); A. Zito, *Le pretese partecipative*, cit. supra n. 13; P. Duret, *Partecipazione procedimentale e legittimazione processuale*, cit. supra n. 32; see also the review by A. Travi, "Interessi procedimentali e 'pretese partecipative': un dibattito aperto (A proposito di due contributi di Duret e Zito)", *Dir. pub.* 1997, 531; see further C. E. Gallo, "La partecipazione al procedimento", in P. Alberti et al., *Lezioni sul procedimento amministrativo*, cit. supra n. 21, 55 ff.; S. Fuochi, "Commento all'Article 7", in A. Travi (ed.), "Commentario della legge 7 agosto 1990, n. 241", cit. supra n. 21, 41 ff.; M. Occhiena, "Prime riflessioni sugli interessi procedimentali dopo la legge sul procedimento amministrativo", *Dir. proc. amm.* 1997, 728.

[58] See F. Patroni Griffi, "Un contributo alla trasparenza dell'azione amministrativa: partecipazione procedimentale e accesso agli atti", *Dir. proc. amm.* 1992, 56 ff.; see also Cons. St., Sez. VI, 20 settembre 1996, n. 1244, *Foro amm.* 1996, 2665; Cons. St., Sez. VI, 16 gennaio 1996, n. 98, *Giur. it.* 1996, III, 1, 274.

[59] See generally R. Caranta and L. Ferraris, *La partecipazione al procedimento amministrativo*, cit. supra n. 31, at 37 ff.; F. Mariuzzo, "Commento all'Article 7", in V. Italia and M. Bassani (eds), *Procedimento amministrativo e diritto di accesso ai documenti*, cit. supra n. 21, 127 ff.; T. Tessaro, "Atti vincolati, provvedimento di decadenza della concessione edilizia e comunicazione di avvio del procedimento amministrativo", *Riv. amm. R.I.* 1996, 530; L. Centofanti, "Comunicazione di avvio del procedimento (Article 7 legge n. 241 del 1990). Ambito di applicazione oggettivo", *Riv. amm. R.I.* 1994, 906; L. Mercati, "La comunicazione dell'avvio del procedimento: primi passi verso la partecipazione procedimentale in tema di contratti della p.a.", *Rass. giur. umbra* 1994, fasc. 3, 234; G. Terraciano, "Sull'obbligo di comunicazione dell'avvio del procedimento", *Foro amm.* 1994, 2177; the case law is analysed by A. Corpaci, "La comunicazione dell'avvio del procedimento alla luce dei primi riscontri giurisdizionali", *Regioni* 1994, 303, and A. Martin, "Comunicazione di avvio del procedimento e giudice amministrativo: primi orientamenti giurisprudenziali sull'Article 7 della l. 7 agosto 1990 n. 241", *Dir. regione* 1994, II, 1099.

No doubt that this provision is essential to allow a real participation of the persons concerned.[60] Under Article 8:

(1) The administrative authority gives notice of the opening of the file by way of an individual communication.
(2) The communication must list:
  a) the competent authority;
  b) the subject matter of the proceeding;
  c) the office and the person responsible for the proceeding (*responsabile del procedimento*); and
  d) the office where is possible to see the documents of the file.
(3) When so many people are concerned by the decision that individual communication to each is either impossible or extremely burdensome, the information listed in Subsection (2) is to be made known in a way appropriate to the situation. This method is chosen by the authority itself.
(4) Compliance with the duty to give notice of the opening of the file can be enforced only at request of a person who should have been informed.[61]

Under Article 9 of the APA:

> Everyone representing an interest, be it public or private, and the associations and bodies representing diffuse interests that could suffer harm as a result of a final decision, are allowed to take part in the procedure.[62]

This provision has allowed widespread participation that extends well beyond those people directly concerned. Of great importance is the admission of diffuse interest to participation in administrative proceedings.[63] Before the APA, a similar provision could be found only in a statute concerning environmental matters.[64]

Special rules concerning complex decision-making procedures generally predate the APA and they tend to be less structured regarding participation. The l.

---

60 C. E. Gallo, "La partecipazione al procedimento", cit. supra n. 57, at 70.

61 See generally R. Caranta and L. Ferraris, *La partecipazione al procedimento amministrativo*, cit. supra n. 31, at 102 ff.; F. Mariuzzo, "Commento all'Article 8", in V. Italia and M. Bassani (eds), *Procedimento amministrativo e diritto di accesso ai documenti*, cit. supra n. 21, 159 ff.

62 See generally R. Caranta and L. Ferraris, *La partecipazione al procedimento amministrativo*, cit. supra n. 31, at 120 ff.; A. Zucchetti, "Commento all'Article 9", in V. Italia and M. Bassani (eds), *Procedimento amministrativo e diritto di accesso ai documenti*, cit. supra n. 21, 180 ff.

63 See generally M. Cresti, *Contributo allo studio della tutela degli interessi diffusi* (Milano: Giuffrè, 1992).

64 See generally C. Dell'Acqua, "Lo Stato, gli enti territoriali e le associazioni nella legge 8 luglio 1986, n. 349", in *Scritti in onore di M.S. Giannini*, vol. II (Milano: Giuffrè, 1988), 149 ff.; some decision has traced the right to partecipation back to Article 2 of the Italian Constitution: e.g. T.A.R. Lazio, Sez. III, 22 aprile 1992, n. 433, *T.A.R.* 1992, I, 1838; this however happened only after the 1990 Act was passed.

17 agosto 1942, n. 1150 (the Town Planning Act 1942) simply provides that planning projects must be publicised. Public interest groups, and the owners of land parcels affected by the project, are empowered to submit written observations.[65] The same applies to projects which are to undergo an Environmental Impact Assessment under Article 6 of the l. 8 luglio 1986, n. 349.[66]

Consequences of Breach of the Duty to Give Prior Notice of the Opening of the File

Breaches of the duty to give prior notice of the opening of the file under Articles 7 and 8 of the APA has quickly become the most conspicuous testing ground regarding of procedural errors in Italian administrative law.

Sharply conflicting trends can be detected in the case law.[67] Many decisions downplay the importance of the duty to give notice to be given under Article 7 and 8.[68] Administrative courts often allow administrative authorities to forgo the notice when the latter do not enjoy discretionary power; such decisions are based on the reasoning that there is no room for discussion with the addressee of a decision when the authority is bound to follow precise rules.[69] Some decisions go so far as to refuse to quash a decision which seems sound on its meritsbut that is prima facie invalid because the required notice was not served.[70]

---

65 The case law allows the administration to give almost cursory attention to those observations: Cons. St., Sez. IV, 15 luglio 1992, n. 682, *Riv. giur. edilizia* 1993, I, 112; T.A.R. Marche 14 novembre 1985 n. 360, *Foro amm.* 1986, 1463 (s.m.).

66 See C. Dell'Acqua, "Lo Stato, gli enti territoriali e le associazioni nella legge 8 luglio 1986, n. 349", cit. supra n. 64.

67 There are other questions as well, such as the applicability of Article 7 and 8 to proceedings in the competence of municipal authorities: see the different stances taken on the one hand by Cons. St., Sez. V, 26 maggio 1997, n. 560, *Giur. it.* 1997, III, 1, 570, and Cons. St., Sez. V, 2 febbraio 1996, n. 133, *Giur. it.* 1996, III, 1, 193, and, on the other hand, by T.A.R. Friuli Venezia Giulia, 13 gennaio 1997, n. 17, *Giur. it.* 1997, III, 1, 488, note S. Verzaro.

68 See A. Zito, *Le pretese partecipative*, cit. supra n. 13, at 142 ff.; in the case law Cons. St., Sez. IV, 11 febbraio 1999, n. 150, *Foro amm.* 1999, 324 (s.m.); Cons. St., Sez. V, 16 novembre 1998, n. 1615, *Foro amm.* 1998, 3109; Cons. St., Sez. V, 11 ottobre 1996, n. 1223, *Foro amm.* 1996, 2882; *Cons. Stato* 1996, I, 1501; T.A.R. Toscana, Sez. I, 17 febbraio 1995, n. 92, *Foro amm.* 1995, 1679; T.A.R. Sicilia, Sez. Catania, 1° settembre 1994, n. 1941, *T.A.R.* 1994, I, 4214; T.A.R. Sicilia, Sez. Catania, 31 gennaio 1994, n. 67, *T.A.R.* 1994, I, 1274; T.A.R. Lombardia, Sez. III, 14 febbraio 1994, n. 61, *T.A.R.* 1994, I, 1406; T.A.R. Veneto, Sez. II, 13 maggio 1992, n. 442, *Giust. civ.* 1993, I, 828.

69 Cons. St., Sez. V, 11 ottobre 1996, n. 1223, *Foro amm.* 1996, 2882; T.A.R. Calabria, Sez. Catanzaro, 17 dicembre 1996, n. 900, *T.A.R.* 1997, I, 753; T.A.R. Lazio, Sez. Latina, 1 aprile 1996, n. 300, *T.A.R.* 1996, I, 1779 (s.m.); T.A.R. Lombardia, Sez. Milano, 27 gennaio 1996, n. 113, *Foro amm.* 1996, 1984 (s.m.).

70 T.A.R. Valle Aosta, 24 settembre 1996, n. 157, *Foro amm.* 1997, 842 (s.m.).

Other decisions view the notice as a cornerstone of participation that must be served at the very beginning of the procedure,[71] and they are reluctant to condone its absence.[72] From this perspective, a duty to give notice of the opening of the file results in the illegality of the final decision.[73] The absence of discretion is no reason to withhold the notice and participation is considered to be necessary because every administrative proceeding rests on material facts that are best ascertained and evaluated with the widest participation possible.[74]

Sometimes these two conflicting approaches find a compromise in cases where the futility of participation in a given case is ascertained *in concreto* by the courts. According to this position, the applicability of Article 7 is presumed unless its futility is proven.[75] For example, a 1993 decision was held valid notwithstanding that an interested authority had not been duly invited to take part in the proceedings, as the authority had participated regardless.[76] The same stance has been taken in cases concerning the participation of private parties.[77] Other judgments have held final decisions to be valid notwithstanding the failure to serve the required notices, as the addressee had become aware of the existence of the proceedings in other some.[78] Another decision held that invalidity would not follow

---

71 E.g. T.A.R. Lombardia, Sez. Brescia, 23 ottobre 1995, n. 1009, *T.A.R.* 1995, I, 4831.

72 E.g. Cons. St., Sez. V, 5 giugno 1997, n. 606, *Giur. it.* 1997, III, 1, 636; Cons. St., Sez. V, 26 maggio 1997, n. 560, *Giur. it.* 1997, III, 1, 570; Cons. St., Sez. VI, 16 gennaio 1997, n. 57, *Foro amm.* 1997, 183; T.A.R. Trentino Alto Adige, Sez. Trento, 18 dicembre 1995, n. 331, *Foro amm.* 1996, 1626.

73 E.g. T.A.R. Sicilia, Sez. III, Catania, 24 maggio 1996, n. 857, *Riv. giur. polizia* 1997, 115 (s.m.); T.A.R. Lazio, Sez. I, 3 aprile 1996, n. 567, *T.A.R.* 1996, I, 1694 (s.m.); T.A.R. Toscana, Sez. I, 9 marzo 1995, n. 220, *Foro amm.* 1995, 1974; T.A.R. Sicilia, Sez. Catania, 22 luglio 1995, n. 1870, *T.A.R.* 1995, I, 4395.

74 See Cons. St., Sez. V, 13 novembre 1995, n. 1562, *Foro it.* 1996, III, 260; *Foro amm.* 1995, 2604; *Dir. regione* 1996, 893; Trib. Sup.re Acque, 2 maggio 1995, n. 38, *Cons. Stato* 1995, II, 1086 (s.m.). This line of cases is followed among others by Cons. St., Sez. IV, 17 febbraio 1999, n. 167, *Foro amm.* 1999, 326 (s.m.), and T.A.R. Campania, Sez. IV, 28 maggio 1996, n. 346, *Foro amm.* 1997, 277 (s.m.).

75 E.g. Cons. St., Sez. V, 19 marzo 1996, n. 283, *Giust. civ.* 1997, I, 844; T.A.R. Campania, Sez. IV, 28 maggio 1996, n. 346, *Foro amm.* 1997, 277 (s.m.); T.A.R. Lazio, Sez. II, 14 novembre 1996, n. 2051, *T.A.R.* 1996, I, 4405; T.A.R. Calabria, Sez. Catanzaro, 11 settembre 1996, n. 711, *T.A.R.* 1996, I, 4320. See also Cons. St., Sez. V, 1° aprile 1997, n. 306, *Foro amm.* 1997, 1076 (s.m.); in this case the concerned person had written to the administrative authority speaking his mind about the subject matter of the proceeding.

76 T.A.R. Lazio, Sez. II, 8 giugno 1993, n. 657, *T.A.R.* 1993, I, 2310.

77 Cons. St., Sez. V, 1 aprile 1997, n. 306, *Foro amm.* 1997, 1076 (s.m.).

78 Cons. St., Sez. VI, 9 agosto 1996, n. 1000, *Giur. it.* 1997, III, 1, 224, note S. Verzaro, "In tema di comunicazione dell'avvio del procedimento amministrativo: l'Article 7 e la normativa previgente"; Cons. St., Sez. VI, 12 agosto 1996, n. 1028, *Giur. it.* 1997, III, 1, 78; Cons. St., Sez. IV, 2 gennaio 1996, n. 3, *Foro amm.* 1996, 53; T.A.R. Friuli Venezia Giulia, 13 gennaio 1997, n. 17, *Giur. it.* 1997, III, 1, 488, note S. Verzaro; T.A.R. Veneto, Sez. I, 9 febbraio 1994, n. 82, note T. Tessaro, "Comunicazione

necessarily from a breach of the duty to give notice of the opening of the file. On the contrary, it was held that invalidity could be established unless the administration could establish that participation was useless or that the examination had been thorough.[79]

Uncertainty about the consequences of a breach of the duty to give prior notice flows from a clash of form verses substance that has yet to be resolved.

A case-by-case *a posteriori* judgment is, however, somewhat unpredictable. Given the triviality of sending a notice every time a new file is open, it would seem sensible to adhere to the more rigorous position. Article 8 already limits the possibility of invalidity flowing from a breach of the duty to serve the notice; and, contrary to the general rule about the consequences of a breach of procedural provisions,[80] only the beneficiary of the duty to inform is allowed to raise the issue in courts.[81]

Procedural Errors and Mere Irregularities

Beyond Articles 7 and 8 of the APA, the infringement of formal and procedural requirements is generally held to be a breach of the law causing the illegality of the final administrative decision. In so far as it is not a mere irregularity,[82] a procedural error that has not been rectified during the decision-making process invalidates the final decision.[83] For instance, a decision was invalid because it was made after receiving an advice from a consultative body whose panel was not formed according to the applicable legal provisions.[84]

The line dividing procedural errors from mere irregularities depends on the purpose of the infringed provision. In theory, a procedural error should not make the final decision invalid if the purpose of the legislation was nevertheless fulfilled. In the case law, the division between errors and mere irregularities is sometimes expressed in terms of the "character" of the breach: if the breach is essential, and

individuale, normativa sul procedimento e procedimenti già 'normati': appunti per una riflessione", *Foro amm.* 1995, 1649.

79 T.A.R. Toscana, Sez. I, 17 febbraio 1995, n. 92, *Foro amm.* 1995, 1679.

80 A. Zito, *Le pretese partecipative*, cit. supra n. 13, 134.

81 The final decision is invalid when the notice has not been served (e.g. Cons. St., Sez. VI, 16 gennaio 1997, n. 57, *Foro amm.* 1997, 183; T.A.R. Lazio, Sez. I, 3 aprile 1996, n. 567, *T.A.R.* 1996, I, 1694; V. Cerulli Irelli, *Corso di diritto amministrativo*, cit. supra n. 13, 433), but standing to challenge the same decision under this ground is severely restricted.

82 E.g. Cons. St., Sez.V, 12 dicembre 1984, n. 918, *Quaderni regionali* 1985, 489.

83 See Cons. St., Sez.VI, 13 aprile 1992, n. 256, *Cons. Stato* 1992, I, 606.

84 Cons. St., Sez. V, 9 aprile 1994, n. 291, *Foro amm.* 1994, 796 (s.m.).

the aim of the legislation therefore cannot be attained, the final decision is invalid. Otherwise, it is only irregular.[85]

Given the formalistic approach characterising Italian administrative law, irregularity is the exception rather than the rule.[86] A recent decision states the standard doctrine that, since public law rules are generally binding, a mere irregularity can be found only in case of formal infringement relating to marginal aspects of the administrative decision.[87] This rule has been upheld, for example, in many cases in which the *audi alteram partem* principle (according to which the administrator listens to both sides of a dispute) had been broken in relation to the imposition of fines.[88]

Beside the contentious decisions relating to the duty to give prior notice of the opening of a case, mere irregularities are found in four main areas.

First, under Article 3 (4) of the APA, every decision must state the authority with jurisdiction to hear objections to the decision, and the term for the commencement of the action. An advice by the *Consiglio di Stato* has held that a breach of Article 3 (4) does not make the decision invalid.[89] On this view, the only consequence of the breach is that an addressee who has challenged the decision before an authority that is not competent to decide the claim is permitted to reargue its case before the correct authority, notwithstanding the exhaustion of the period in which challenges may be brought. Following this advice, the competent administrative authority is estopped from pleading the timebar.[90]

Second, a decision is not invalid simply because the required notice of the opening of the file is silent about some of the items listed in Article 8 of the APA (for example, the identity of the person responsible for the proceeding). According to the prevailing case law, the recipient of the notice can obtain this information

---

85 Cons. St., Sez.V, 12 dicembre 1984, n. 918, *Quaderni regionali* 1985, 489. T.A.R. Lazio, Sez. Latina, 6 marzo 1995, n. 225, *Foro amm.* 1995,2374 (s.m.); the Court held not to be invalid but merely irregular a notice given by way of phonogram instead of telegram as required by the law.

86 For a detailed analysis see A. Romano Tassone, *Contributo sul tema dell'irregolarità degli atti amministrativi* (Torino: Giappichelli, 1993).

87 Cons. St., Sez. IV, 17 febbraio 1997, n. 123, *Foro amm.* 1997, 446 (s.m.).

88 Cass. civ., Sez. I, 7 ottobre 1996, n. 8758, *Giust. civ. Mass.* 1996, 1383; Cass. civ., Sez. I, 19 maggio 1995, n. 5554, *Giust. civ. Mass.* 1995, 1039; Cass. civ., Sez. I, 17 settembre 1992, n. 10658, *Arch. giur. circol. e sinistri* 1993, 535; Cass. civ., Sez. I, 16 febbraio 1993, n. 1880, *Giust. civ. Mass.* 1993, 310 (s.m.); Cass. civ., Sez. I, 17 settembre 1992, n. 10658, *Giust. civ. Mass.* 1992, *fasc.* 8-9.

89 Cons. St., Sez. II, 11 gennaio 1996, n. 1958, *Cons. St.* 1997, I, 611; see also the judgments by Cons. St., Sez. V, 15 aprile 1996, n. 434, *Giur. it.* 1996, III, 1, 387, and T.A.R. Lombardia, Sez. Brescia, 6 maggio 1996, n. 503, *Foro amm.* 1996, 3425 (s.m.).

90 See also T.A.R. Sicilia, Sez. Catania, 3 maggio 1995, n. 1267, *T.A.R.* 1995, I, 3369; T.A.R. Campania, Sez. III, 26 aprile 1995, n. 194, *T.A.R.* 1995, I, 3195. Both T.A.R. Lazio, Sez. II, 14 ottobre 1988 n. 1247, *T.A.R.* 1988, I, 3254, and T.A.R. Toscana, 18 marzo 1983 n. 60, *Foro amm.* 1983, I, 1676 (s.m.), held the same with reference to the similar rule laid down in Article 1 d.P.R. 24 novembre 1971, n. 1199.

elsewhere.[91] However, withholding the name of the *responsabile del procedimento* (acting person) results in the invalidity of the final decision.[92]

Third, most of the cases outside the scope of the APA that condone breaches of law as "mere irregularities", relate to the working rules of collegial administrative bodies. The failure to give a prior notice of a meeting is held to be a mere irregularity with no effect on the validity of a collegial decision if the person concerned nevertheless attends the meeting and does not complain of not having been served the notice.[93] Imperfect recording of the minutes does not lead to the invalidity of a collegial decision if it is plain what the decision was.[94] Errors in vote counting are mere irregularities if the final outcome is not affected.[95] Finally, even if Article 53 of the Local Government Act provides that every decision taken by local elective bodies must be preceded by a technical advice on the legality of the proposed decision, administrative courts have held that both the absence or the illegality of the prior advice cause only the "mere irregularity" of a final decision that is not otherwise invalid.[96]

If the real identity of the underwriter and the exact date can be otherwise inferred, the absence of: the protocol number on a copy of a decision, the clear signature of the person having made the decision, or the date at which the decision was taken, are considered to be miscellaneous irregularities.[97]

---

91 Cons. St., Sez. VI, 14 aprile 1999, n. 433, in *Foro amm.* 1999, 787 (s.m.); T.A.R. Basilicata, 23 marzo 1998, n. 86, in *Foro amm.* 1998, 3293; T.A.R. Sicilia, Sez. Palermo, 30 novembre 1996, n. 1730, in *T.A.R.* 1997, I, 368; T.A.R. Friuli V.G. 3 febbraio 1996, n. 64, in *Giust. civ.* 1996, I, 2451; T.A.R. Friuli V.G. 17 ottobre 1994, n. 357, in *Giust. civ.* 1995, I, 1114; in *Foro amm.*, 1994, 2905 (s.m.); in *Foro it.* 1995, III, 266; in *Giur. it.* 1995, III, 1, 320, e T.A.R. Friuli Venezia Giulia, 9 dicembre 1996, n. 1241, in *Foro amm.*, 1997, 1469.

92 E.g. Cons. St., Sez. II, 8 marzo 1995, n. 2532, *Cons. St.* 1996, I, 116 (s.m.).

93 Cons. St., Sez. V, 30 marzo 1994, n. 194, *Foro amm.* 1994, 468; *Cons. Stato* 1994, I, 385; Cons. giust. amm. Sicilia, 11 febbraio 1986, n. 3, *Foro amm.* 1986, 1088 (s.m.); T.A.R. Lazio, Sez. II, 8 giugno 1993, n. 657, *T.A.R.* 1993, I, 2310.

94 Generally Cons. St., Sez. VI, 3 maggio 1994, n. 680, *Foro amm.* 1994, 1145 (s.m.); *Cons. Stato* 1994, I, 832 (s.m.); T.A.R Campania, Sez. I, 21 luglio 1993, n. 274, *Foro amm.* 1994, 655 (s.m.); T.A.R. Calabria, Sez. Catanzaro, 22 novembre 1986, 367; *Foro amm.* 1987, 1586; T.A.R. Lombardia, Sez. III, 12 dicembre 1994, n. 844, *T.A.R.* 1995, I, 547 (a decision is held to have been taken unanimously if not otherwise recorded).

95 T.A.R. Molise 22 marzo 1994, n. 59, *T.A.R.* 1994, I, 2120; *Foro amm.* 1994, 1919; the same rule is followed with reference to electoral procedures in general by T.A.R. Molise 12 novembre 1985, n. 199, *Foro amm.* 1986, 1511 (s.m.).

96 Ad es. Cons. St., Sez. V, 27 febbraio 1998, n. 219, *Foro amm.* 1998, 445 (s.m.); *Cons. Stato* 1998, I, 258 (s.m.); T.A.R. Emilia Romagna, Sez. Parma, 23 aprile 1998, n. 209, *T.A.R.* 1998, I, 2533.

97 T.A.R. Molise 18 maggio 1988, n. 87, *Foro amm.* 1989, 324 (s.m.); Cass. 14 giugno 1979, n. 3342, *Giust. civ. Mass.* 1979, *fasc.* 6, and T.A.R. Lazio, Sez. II, 14 ottobre 1988, n. 1247, *T.A.R.* 1988, I, 3254.

Form and Substance in Judicial Review of Administrative Action: The Story so Far

Apart from the decisions concerning the breach of the duty to give prior notice of the opening of a file under Articles 7 and 8 of the APA, Italian administrative courts have generally been rather wary of condoning breaches of formal and procedural rules. Even judicial trends towards reducing the emphasis on formal requirements do not go unresisted. Quite to the contrary and with a view to strengthening the rights of participants in the decision-making process, some scholars think that the greatest range of remedies possible (including the ability to bring an action for damages),[98] should be allowed in cases of procedural violations.[99]

The general approach is consistent with the traditional character of Italian judicial review of administrative action. As a rule, Italian administrative courts perform only a limited review of administrative decisions. In theory at least, administrative courts never inquire into the merits of administrative decisions. In English terminology, they do not have appellate jurisdiction;[100] in French (and Italian) terms, they act, *vis à vis* the administrative decision, as *cours de cassation.*

Various aspects contribute to this character. First, Italian administrative courts can quash an administrative decision but they are forbidden replace it with one of their own. Second, due to a deferential attitude towards administrative discretion, discretionary decisions are quashed by Italian administrative courts only if they are manifestly wrong and give rise to an *eccesso di potere* due to *ingiustizia manifesta* (which can be translated literally as "manifest injustice"). Last, because the Italian administrative courts cannot independently ascertain the facts alleged by the administrative decision,[101] all material facts ascertained during the administrative procedure must be taken at face value unless they are plainly wrong. If they are clearly wrong, the decision is found to be in *eccesso di potere* due to *travisamento dei fatti* (an error in fact), and it is reversed.[102] Under the current procedural rules of

---

98 See A. Romano Tassone, "I problemi di un problema. Spunti in tema di risarcibilità degli interessi legittimi", *Dir. amm.* 1997, 76 ff.

99 P. Duret, *Partecipazione procedimentale e legittimazione processuale*, cit. supra n. 32, 269 ff.

100 E.g. *Brind and others* v. *Secretary of State for the Home Department* [1991] 1 All ER 720, at 739 *per* Lord Lowry. For more details see C. Harlow, "Proceduralism in English Administrative Law", *infra.*

101 See C. E. Gallo, "Istruzione nel processo amministrativo", in *Digesto IV, Disc. pubbl.*, IX (Torino: UTET, 1994), 9. In the case law see for example T.A.R. Lombardia, Sez. Brescia, 16 maggio 1984 n. 459, in *Foro amm.* 1984, *fasc.* 11, concerning the question whether a building has such a historical importance to be considered part of the national heritage. For a case concerning a planning decision see T.A.R. Lombardia, Sez. I, 4 settembre 1997, n. 1471, *Foro amm.* 1998, 1153 (s.m.).

102 Cons. St., Sez. IV, 8 settembre 1997, n. 955, *Cons. Stato* 1997, I, 1184 (s.m.); T.A.R. Piemonte, Sez. II, 18 novembre 1995, n. 612, *Riv. trim. app.* 1995, 386, note R. Roffi,

general application, an administrative court can do no more than ask the administration for a new assessment of the relevant facts (the "*verificazioni*"); Article 26 R.D. 17 agosto 1907 n. 642, is still in force and its application was extended to the procedures in front of the *Tribunali amministrativi regionali* by Article 19 L. 6 dicembre 1971, n. 1034.[103]

This approach ties judicial review strictly to both the final decision adopted and the procedure followed by the administration. Substantive judicial review creeps into the system mainly by way of the duty to give reasons for the decision. In Italy, as elsewhere, if a government agency is required to give reasons for what it has done, a reviewing court is required to demand that the agency produce a statement of reasons to meet this substantive requirement.[104] *Eccesso di potere* due to *insufficienza*, *contraddittorietà* and *perplessità della motivazione* provide good examples of this.

The self-restraint characterising the approach to administrative decisions by Italian court usually is not confined to adjudication relating to discretionary powers. Even fact-finding reports and factual evaluations are traditionally reviewed only if they are manifestly wrong.[105] The judicial attitude is epitomised by a decision concerning the building of a new road. According to the *Consiglio di Stato*, courts must limit themselves to an external review of existence and reasonableness of the reasons given, and the adequacy of the fact-finding procedure employed by the administration. They may not substitute the administration's evaluations concerning the alternative decisions available or the respective costs and benefits of these various alternatives.[106]

As a rule, an administrative authority is not required to show that the final decision was the best outcome available from the alternatives considered. For

---

"Nel giudizio di legittimità di cui all'Article 13, comma 2, della l. 19 febbraio 1992 n. 142, che può fare il giudice?". See also, with reference to a similarly limited power of review allowed to the Government, Cons. St., Sez. VI, 12 maggio 1994, n. 772, *Giust. civ.* 1994, I, 2374.

103 See e.g. Cons. St., Sez. IV, 24 marzo 1998, n. 495, *Cons. Stato* 1998, I, 367; Cons. St., Sez. VI 27 maggio 1991, n. 321, *Foro it.* 1992, III, 114; Cons. St., Sez.VI, 13 luglio 1985, n. 422, *Riv. giur. edilizia* 1985, I, 779; the differences between the *verificazioni* and the expertise, to which generally administrative courts can have no recourse, is underlined e.g. by Cons. St., Sez. VI, 13 luglio 1985, n. 422, *Foro amm.* 1985, 1379.

104 M. Shapiro, "Two Transformation in Administrative Law: American and European?", supra.

105 See for example T.A.R. Lombardia, Sez. Brescia, 16 maggio 1984 n. 459, in *Foro amm.* 1984, *fasc.* 11, concerning the question whehther a building has such a historical importance to be considered part of the national heritage.

106 Cons. St., Sez. IV, 28 dicembre 1994, n. 1093, *Cons. Stato* 1994, I, 1723 (s.m.): the summary reads: "il giudice amministrativo deve limitarsi ad una verifica estrinseca in ordine all'esistenza, sufficienza e congruità della motivazione addotta ai fini della scelta, nonché in ordine all'adeguatezza dell'istruttoria espletata in via amministrativa, senza che possa sostituirsi all'amministrazione attiva in valutazione di merito ad essa istituzionalmente spettanti".

instance, a decision relating to the location of high tension power lines held that the competent authority had to consider only the alternative solutions that had been put before it by the private parties concerned.[107] The same applies to planning decisions;[108] alternative solutions are to be taken into account and discounted only if limitations on the use of privately owned land are reiterated after a first decision has elapsed without any future taking procedure having been commenced.[109]

As substantive review has a very limited and somewhat disguised reach, it is not surprising that the traditional judicial review system relies very heavily on formal and procedural legality. An authority whose decision is challenged in court cannot show that a decision infringing procedural or other formal requirements is nonetheless sound on its merits. For instance, inadequate reasons given at the time the decision was taken cannot be supplemented in court.[110] Conversely, the administration is entitled to adopt a decision identical to that overturned due to formal or procedural inadequacies, provided that its new decision confirms with the appropriate formal and procedural constraints.[111]

In a context in which formal and procedural requirements are usually taken very seriously, scholarly opinion has supported judgements condoning a breach of the requirement to serve a notice under Articles 7 and 8 of the APA by referring to the rules on formal infringements and procedural mistakes laid down in the 1976 German *Verwaltungsverfahrengestez*.[112] However, the German rules are grafted into a judicial review system that allows a full reappraisal of the administrative decision by the courts. Administrative discretion is accepted in marginal hypothesis

---

107 Cons. St., Sez. VI, 24 agosto 1996, n. 1072, *Cons. Stato* 1996, I, 1244; T.A.R. Lombardia, Sez. II, 3 novembre 1994, n. 618, *Rass. giur. Enel* 1995, 954; T.A.R. Lombardia, Sez. II, 14 maggio 1994, n. 302, *Rass. giur. Enel* 1994, 243; T.A.R. Veneto, Sez. I, 18 maggio 1994, n. 550, *Rass. giur. Enel* 1994, 240; T.A.R. Campania, Sez. V, 21 dicembre 1994, n. 485, *Rass. giur. Enel* 1995, 508; T.A.R. Marche 9 ottobre 1992, n. 588, *T.A.R.* 1992, I, 4903.

108 See for instance T.A.R. Sardegna 11 agosto 1989 n. 675, *Foro amm.* 1990, 2154 (s.m.).

109 See for instance Cons. St., Sez. IV, 20 febbraio 1998, n. 312, *Appalti urbanistica Edilizia* 1999, 243; T.A.R. Lazio, Sez. I, 17 settembre 1994, n. 1354, *T.A.R.* 1994, I, 3528.

110 *Ex multis* Cons. St., Sez. IV, 20 maggio 1992, n. 546, *Cons. Stato* 1992, I, 716; the rule is distinguished rather than departed from in Cons. giust. amm. Sicilia, 20 aprile 1993, 507, and *ivi* 1994, 577, with note by A. Zito, "L'integrazione in giudizio del provvedimento amministrativo: una questione ancora aperta"; the case concerned an appeal against a refusal to allow access to a file, a matter where peculiar powers are give to administrative courts. More difficult to reconcile with the traditional case lawseems Cons. St., Sez. IV, 7 maggio 1998, n. 773, *Foro amm.* 1998, 1364 (s.m.).

111 *Ex multis* Cons. St., Sez. VI, 31 maggio 1994, n. 899, *Giur. it.* 1994, III, 1, 593; T.A.R. Lazio, Sez. III, 1° febbraio 1985, n. 142, *Foro amm.* 1985, 1193.

112 E.g. F. Mariuzzo, *Commento all'Article 8*, cit. supra n. 59, at 168 ff.; G. Virga, *La partecipazione al procedimento amministrativo*, cit. supra n. 57, at 107 ff.

only to a very limited extent.[113] The German system is much more like an appeal system than a judicial review system. German courts are quite well placed to ascertain whether the administration has arrived at a substantially sound decision as it is part of their function to determine the soundness of a decision. The disregard for merely formal or procedural rules is a by-product of this role. On a smaller scale, this relationship is confirmed by recent developments in Dutch law: the courts can disregard formal and procedural requirements if they have the power to assess the merits of a case and replace a decision of the administration with one of their own.[114]

The situation is different in Italy.

Form and Substance in Judicial Review of Administrative Action: A Different Future?

Or, maybe more correctly, the situation used to be different in Italy.

Two new factors must be now taken into account. First, a very important decision by the *Sezioni Unite* of the *Corte di cassazione* in 1999 greatly widened the sphere within which the administration can be liable to pay damages as a result of making an illegal decision. To avoid paying damages for decisions that are sound on their merits but that constitute a breach of either formal or procedural requirements, courts are expected (and, indeed, are asked by the *Sezioni unite*) to go beyond illegality and to assess the merits of the case.[115] Substantive illegality is to be treated differently from formal illegality and it is doubtful whether the distinction will be limited to actions for damages.

A spillover effect on annulment actions is more probable when a second factor is considered. Articles 33-35 of d.lgs. 31 marzo 1998, n. 80,[116] which entered into force few weeks before the above-mentioned decision was delivered by the *Corte di cassazione*, allow administrative courts full access to the facts of a case and empower the courts to substitute decisions taken by the administration.[117] However,

---

113 See the chapter by K. H. Ladeur and R. Prelle, "Judicial Control of Administrative Procedure and Court Control of Procedural Mistakes. The Example of Environmental Impact Assessments – a European-law and comparative-law view", supra.

114 See the chapter by J. H. Hans and D. De Jong, "Between Direct Effect and Rewe/Comet: Remarks on Dutch Administrative Law, Procedural Defects and the EIA Directive".

115 Cass., Sez. un., 1999, n. 500, in *Foro it.* 1999, I, 3201, note R. Caranta, "La pubblica amministrazione nell'età della responsabilità".

116 *Gazz. Uff.* 8 aprile 1998, n. 82, s.o. 65/I.

117 See F. Caringella and R. Garofoli, "Il rito degli appalti e la tutela risarcitoria degli interessi legittimi dopo il D.Lgs. 80/1998", *Urbanistica e appalti* 1999, 299; A. Travi (ed.), "La nuova giurisdizione esclusiva del giudice amministrativo", *Nuove leggi civ. commentate* 1998, 207; E.A. Apicella, "Il d.lgs. n. 80 del 1998 (c.d. Bassanini-*ter*)", *Giust. civ.* 1998, II, 245; M. Lipari, "La nuova giurisdizione amministrativa in materia edilizia, urbanistica e dei pubblici servizi", *Urbanistica e appalti* 1998, 592. More

the new law applies only to some subject matters, such as the provision of services to the general public, urban planning and building permissions, and (possibly) environmental matters.[118]

This partial reform could help spearhead a different judicial attitude to the administration. For instance, a 1999 decision by the *Consiglio di Stato* overruled long-standing case law to allow administrative courts to assess the administration's fact finding and factual evaluation.[119]

The present tendency of strengthening substantive judicial control on administrative decisions and allowing the courts to substitute administrative decisions with their judgements could, in the long run, lead Italian administrative law in the direction of the German precedent. The present situation – where form prevails over substance – could ultimately be reversed.

Conclusion, or Where (Formal and) Procedural Requirements are Proved to be Different

In the *form* verses *substance* clash, substance has an evident appeal. "Formalism" (an evident derivation from "form"), has a plain pejorative flair.[120]

However, it is submitted that not all formalities are the same and not all can be discarded just because a decision has been reached that is sound on its merits. Some procedural rules play a more significant role than just helping the administration arrive at the best decision possible. They contribute to the openness and democratic character of the decision-making process. They cannot be disregarded just because the outcome of the procedure meets the applicable substantive requirements.

Procedural rules allowing for the participation of concerned parties and public interest groups have aims that are not necessarily met just because the final

---

recently I. Franco, *Strumenti di tutela del privato nei confronti della pubblica amministrazione (dall'annullamento dell'atto lesivo al risarcimento)* (Padova: CEDAM, 1999), at 399 ff.

118 The exact sphere of application of the new rules are not so easy to fathom: see M. Lipari, "La nuova giurisdizione amministrativa in materia edilizia, urbanistica e dei pubblici servizi", cit. supra n. 117.

119 Cons. St., Sez. IV, 9 aprile 1999, n. 601, *Cons. St.* 1999, I, 584; *Giorn. dir. amm.* 1999, 1183, note D. De Pretis, "Discrezionalità tecnica e incisività del controllo giurisdizionale"; a forerunner was T.A.R. Lombardia, Sez. III, 12 maggio 1997, n. 586, *Giorn. dir. amm.* 1997, 1262, note A. Travi, "Valutazioni tecniche e istruttoria del giudice amministrativo". The first decision recalled was however doubted by Cons. St., Sez. IV, 10 febbraio 2000, n. 715, not yet reported. It is therefore too early a stage to say that the old case law is gone for good.

120 See C. Harlow, "Proceduralism in English Administrative Law", infra, where the author notes that "procedural requirements face courts with the dilemma that, if they enforce them too rigidly, everything may have to be redone, causing delay and expense".

decision is sound.[121] They encourage a more pro-active role of citizens and public interest groups in the administrative decision-making process.[122]

This realisation seems to be at the roots of the recent decision by the Court of Justice of the European Communities in the Bozen airport case.[123] The applicable legislation was Council Directive 85/337/EEC on the assessment of the environmental effects of certain public and private projects. The directive provides that projects that are likely to have significant effects on the environment by virtue, *inter alia*, of their nature, size or location, are to be subject to an Environmental Impact Assessment ("EIA"). The EIA procedure designed by the directive requires the developer to inform the public about the project. The municipal law applied by the local authority provided for a sort of simplified EIA procedure without any public participation. Asked by the referring *Verwaltungsgericht* whether the participation of the public within the meaning of Article 6 of the Directive is an essential requirement of an environmental assessment, the Court held that an EIA procedure must necessarily include public participation.[124]

---

121 Participation is essential in an even stronger meaning under American pluralist theories claiming that the only correct decisions are those aggregating all interested group preferences: see the report by M. Shapiro, "Two Transformation in Administrative Law: American and European?", supra; the approach is criticised by K. H. Ladeur and R. Prelle, "Judicial Control of Administrative Procedural Mistakes in Germany: A Comparative European View of Environmental Impact Assessments", infra, who claim that correct procedure in by no means a guarantee for the substantive correctness of a decision.

122 See specially Cons. St., Sez. VI, 16 aprile 1998, n. 515, *Urbanistica e appalti* 1999, 415, con nota di G. Rizzo, "Ancora sulla partecipazione del privato al procedimento di imposizione del vincolo".

123 Case C-435/97, *WWF* v. *Autonome Provinz Bozen*, judgement of September 16, 1999, *nyr*.

124 Point 54 of the judgment. Some precedents could be found in French law: see the references by K. H. Ladeur and R. Prelle, "Judicial Control of Administrative Procedural Mistakes in Germany: A Comparative European View of Environmental Impact Assessments", infra, at nt. 53.

Chapter 3

Proceduralism in English Administrative Law

Carol Harlow

General Characteristics of Administrative Adjudication[1]

Administrative Justice

Common law procedure Some characteristics of legal process in England should be briefly stated so that they can be borne in mind in considering what follows. First, the English proverbially like their "day in court". Judicial proceedings have, until very recently, tended to be oral rather than written, so that a procedure which does not involve orality would tend to be seen as non-judicial, hence possibly contrary to the rules of natural justice (explained below).[2]

Second, there is a general feeling – one can put it no higher, as it has never been formalised – that every decision, administrative or judicial, should admit of some appeal.[3] As society gets more litigious, citizens look increasingly for a way to challenge even trivial decisions, such as a state school's requirement that pupils wear uniform or officers' routine commands in the armed forces. As we shall see, this tendency is likely to increase as a result of the Human Rights Act 1998, which incorporates the main provisions of the European Convention into the domestic

---

1 The main texts to be consulted for a fuller account of what follows are: C. Harlow and R. W. Rawlings, *Law and Administration* (London: Butterworths, 1997), hereafter 'HR'; P. P. Craig, *Administrative Law* (London: Sweet and Maxwell, 1999), hereafter 'Craig'; H. W. R. Wade and C. Forsyth, *Administrative Law* (Oxford: Oxford University Press, 1994), hereafter 'Wade'; de Smith, Woolf and Jowell, *Judicial Review of Administrative Action* (London: Sweet and Maxwell, 1995), hereafter 'WJS'. Reference will also be made to S.A. de Smith, *Judicial Review of Administrative Action* (London: Stevens, 1980, 4th edn by J. M. Evans), hereafter 'de Smith'; to the useful outline by P. Cane, *An Introduction to Administrative Law* (Oxford: Clarendon, 1996), hereafter 'Cane'.

2 H. Street, *Justice in the Welfare State* (London: Stevens, 1975).

3 See W. A. Robson, *Justice and Administrative Law* (London: Stevens, 1951). The first edition appeared in 1929. See also the Report of the Franks Committee on Tribunals and Inquiries (Cmnd 218) 1957.

legal system. There may also be an increase in formal methods of adjudication under the influence of ECHR Article 6(1).

Third, common law proceedings are typically adversarial rather than inquisitorial. This is the pattern in the system of administrative tribunals which has emerged during the second half of this century as the characteristic English contribution to administrative adjudication. Welfare tribunals are, for example (at least nominally) adversarial. A case is made by the claimant, either in person or through a representative, though not generally a lawyer, since no legal aid is available. A specialised 'Presenting Officer' from the Department of Social Security attends to respond. As the claimant typically does not appear, this has proved problematic and is one reason for experiments with written procedures.

Fourth, there is a long tradition of lay justice in common law countries, reflecting the jury system which has historically been of such importance. This tradition has found its way into administrative justice, where the typical tribunal consists of a legally qualified chair with two lay members. In cases which turn on specialised knowledge, such as appeals against the decision to detain persons diagnosed as mentally ill in hospital handled by Mental Health Review Tribunals, professional assessors may be substituted. An experiment has also begun in welfare law to eliminate the lay element from tribunals in the name of expense and greater efficiency.[4]

The present system of administrative tribunals generally admits two appeals: the first on questions of fact and law, the second only on questions of law. A further characteristic, and one of constitutional importance endorsed by the two most important official inquiries into administrative justice of this century,[5] is that, at the end of the day, there should be appeal to, or review by, the "ordinary courts" of the land.[6] The existing system is neither orderly nor regular – a further general characteristic of the pragmatic English system of administration and adjudication. A typical appeals structure would be that used in welfare adjudication:[7]

(i) decision by an administrative official;
(ii) full appeal to the Social Security Appeals Tribunal, normally presided over by a legal practitioner with two lay members (but see above);
(iii) appeal on a point of law to a specialised and legally qualified tribunal (in this case, the Social Security Commissioner);
(iv) appeal on a point of law to the Court of Appeal (elsewhere the High Court might be substituted).

Final appeal to the House of Lords lies only with permission and on a point of law of particular public interest. The courts will encourage the use of this appeal

---

4 M. Adler, "Lay tribunal members and administrative justice" [1999] *Public Law* 616.

5 The Donoughmore Committee on Ministers' Powers, Cmnd 4050 (1932); The Franks Committee on Tribunals and Inquiries, Cmnd 218 (1957).

6 This forms part of Dicey's rule of law principle: see A. V. Dicey, *Introduction to the Study of the Law of the Constitution* (London: MacMillan, 1959), ECS Wade, 187-196; HR 37-47.

7 HR at 472-486. The system has recently been modified by the Social Security Act 1998, on the provisions of which see M. Adler, "Lay tribunal members and administrative justice" [1999] *Public Law* 616.

system, disallowing parallel applications to the High Court for judicial review other than in exceptional circumstances.[8]

The expense of this type of appeal procedure in a system of mass welfare administration has led to experiments with documentary procedures – an interesting parallel here to recent reforms of procedure in the civil courts.[9] In welfare adjudication, not all appeals now go to the well-established and administered independent tribunal system. In the case of the "social fund" (a system of discretionary loans made to welfare claimants in cases of exceptional need) an inspectorate has been established under the control of the Social Fund Commissioner, a semi-independent official.[10] Social Fund inspectors handle reviews of cases primarily on the papers, though they could hold an informal interview with the claimant if they wished. This is essentially an administrative procedure, which moves away from the classic English oral model towards inquisitorial procedure. The question must arise, however whether it would satisfy the requirements of ECHR Article 6, unless a further appeal structure is built in.

Basic Procedural Requirements Classic English administrative law distinguished sharply between "administrative" and "judicial";[11] the rules of natural justice, requiring a measure of independence and trial-type procedure applied to the latter but not the former. More recently, however, this distinction has become blurred. There is a general feeling that any decision involving an element of individuated adjudication imposes "a duty to act fairly".[12] This duty is procedural in character, the parameters being set by the judicial standards of natural justice. Natural justice has expanded from its original starting point as a principle of adjudication until today it covers a variety of functions better described as administrative.

Natural justice in classic English law contained two main rights:

(i) the right to present a case or make representations (the *audi alteram partem* principle);

(ii) the right to an independent or unbiased judge or decision-maker, a right in practice limited to cases which are strongly adjudicative in character.[13]

Clear and simple as this may sound, in practice the requirements of natural justice have always been unpredictable and have today become extremely variable.[14] At

8 See *Chief Adjudication v Foster* [1993] AC 754. And see below.

9 As recommended by Lord Woolf, *Access to Justice*, Report to the Lord Chancellor on the civil justice system in England and Wales (London: Lord Chancellor's Department, 1996).

10 HR 486-491. See also G. Dalley and R. Berthoud, *Challenging Discretion, The Social Fund Review Procedure* (London: Policy Studies Institute) 1992.

11 HR at 31-5; de Smith at 58-9. "Quasi-judicial" procedures blended both; they were seen as primarily adjudicative but allowed for the introduction of a strong policy element.

12 *Re HK* [1967] 2 QB 617; *Schmidt v Home Secretary* [1969] 2 WLR 337.

13 Craig at 451-9.

14 The relevant case law with theoretical explanations are discussed in HR, Chapter 15, "A flexible friend: procedural fairness". See also D. Galligan, *Due Process and Fair Procedures: A Study of Administrative Procedures* (Oxford: University Press, 1996).

one end of the spectrum,[15] where a mass administrative system is in operation or the interests involved are very small,[16] little may be expected of the decision-maker: in selecting students for university, for example, it is doubtful whether any formal fact-finding process, reasoned decision or appeal system would be required. Any feedback to an unsuccessful applicant pointing to reasons for failure would be purely voluntary and would be likely to be considered gratuitous (unless it pointed to a clear breach of the law, such as racial discrimination). At the other end of a scale, procedural requirements are becoming more stringent and it may be that natural justice is gaining additional requirements. It may, for example, be strictly true to state that the common law has never insisted (as does the EC Treaty) on reasoned administrative decisions. But recent case law is insisting on reasoned decisions over such a wide range of circumstances that, whatever the courts say,[17] the statement is rapidly becoming fictitious.

This point can be illustrated by reference to prison practice and procedure. It is fair to say that prisoners' rights have not been a high priority either for English courts[18] or for politicians, alert to powerful negative sentiments on the part of large sections of the electorate. Much power is accorded in the British system to the Home Secretary, who has important discretions both in policy making and in individual cases. Courts have been slow to move in to control these discretionary powers, though, at a lower level of prison governance, they have moved a little more swiftly. They have, for example, insisted that prisoners subjected to disciplinary hearings which can result in serious penalty – accusations of drug-dealing or riot in prison, for example – should be brought before an impartial tribunal and may sometimes need legal representation.[19] But where prisoners claim the privilege of parole or are detained for life and are thereafter subject to the discretionary power of the Home Secretary,[20] it must be admitted that, without the more liberal jurisprudence of the European Court of Human Rights,[21] there would probably have been little movement.

---

15 For the 'spectrum' theory of adjudicative decision-taking, see HR, loc cit and D. Mullan, "Fairness: the New Natural Justice?" (1975) 25 *University of Toronto LJ* 281. See also, P. Craig, "Procedures and Administrative Decision Making: A Common Law Perspective" (1993) *European Review of Public Law* (Special Issue) 55.

16 HR at 502.

17 HR at 522-529; G. Richardson, "The Duty to Give Reasons: Potential and Practice" [1986] *Public Law* 437.

18 G. Richardson, *Law, Process and Custody: Prisoners and Patients* (London: Weidenfeld and Nicolson) 1993.

19 *R v Home Secretary ex p. St. Germain* [1978] QB 678; *R v. Home Secretary ex p. Tarrant and Anderson* [1985] QB 85.

20 HR at 184-199; M. Loughlin and P. Quinn, "Prisons, Rules and Courts: A Study in Administrative Law" (1993) 56 *Modern Law Review* 497.

21 HR, loc. cit; G. Douglas and S. Jones, "Prisoners and the European Convention on Human Rights" in M. Furmston, R. Kerridge, and B. Sufrin (eds), *The Effect on English Domestic Law of Membership of the European Communities and Ratification of the European Convention on Human Rights* (The Hague: Martinus Nijhoff, 1983).

In the important case of *R v. Home Secretary ex p. Doody*,[22] prisoners challenged the rather arbitrary procedures connected with life sentences. The Home Secretary, who takes the final decision as to the actual period of years served by a prisoner sentenced to life, in practice consults the judiciary (usually, the Lord Chief Justice). Prisoners were simply informed of the result. When this practice was challenged, the House of Lords ruled that prisoners were entitled to know the reasons for the Home Secretary's decision and Lord Mustill spoke of a general trend to reasoned decision making:

> I find in the more recent cases on judicial review a perceptible trend towards an insistence on greater openness, or if one prefers the contemporary jargon "transparency", in the making of administrative decisions... I accept without hesitation... that the law does not at present recognise a general duty to give reasons for an administrative decision. Nevertheless, it is equally beyond question that such a duty may be implied.

Referring to the particular case in issue, he continued:

> The giving of reasons may be inconvenient, but I can see no ground at all why it should be against the public interest: indeed, rather the reverse. This being so, I would ask simply: is the refusal to give reasons fair? I would answer without hesitation that it is not... It is not... questioned that the decision... is subject to judicial review. To mount an effective attack on the decision, given no more material than the facts of the offence and the length of the penal element, the prisoner has virtually no means of ascertaining whether this is an instance where the decision-making process has gone astray. I think it important that there should be an effective means of detecting the kind of error which would entitle the court to intervene, and in practice I regard it as necessary for this purpose that the reasoning of the Home Secretary should be disclosed.

While it may just be true to say that there is no general duty to give reasons in English administrative law an administrator would, except in the most trivial of cases, today be very unwise to issue a decision without giving reasons. In addition, there should probably be at least an informal opportunity for representations to be made by the person affected. One could describe this development of the law either as an illustration of the flexible character of the natural justice principle (rule (i) above); or in terms of the emergence of a new principle of natural justice: (iii) a duty to give reasons.

Judicial Review of Administrative Action

Review and Appeal The classic distinction in English law is between "review" and "appeal". The main remedy for abuse of power is judicial *review* of administrative action. This allows the procedures by which a decision is taken to be attacked, a formula which allows the court to assure itself that some evidence justifying the

---

22 [1993] 3 WLR 154.

decision did exist and was considered. But the court cannot require further evidence to be brought nor can it substitute its own view of the evidence for that of the decision maker, unless the decision is so far from correct that it can be labelled wholly unreasonable. Amongst many explanations of the role of courts in judicial review, a passage from a recent President of the Court of Appeal (Master of the Rolls) is particularly authoritative. The courts had been asked to review the findings of the Boundary Commission, an independent statutory body set up by and answerable to the Home Secretary, which exists to settle the boundaries of electoral constituencies in England and Wales. It was generally admitted that changes to the constituencies recommended by the Boundary Commission, though dictated by population change, would disadvantage Labour at the next election. Arguing that the Commission had failed to give proper weight to the principle of equal representation, the applicant, who was then Leader of the Opposition, asked for an order restraining the Commission from submitting its report to the Home Secretary. Sir John Donaldson, MR explained:[23]

> Since a very large number of people are interested in this appeal and since it is most unlikely that our decision, whether for or against the applicants, will meet with universal approval, it is important that it should at least be understood. In particular it is important that everyone should understand what is the function and duty of the courts. Parliament entrusted the duty of recommending changes in English constituency boundaries to the commission. It could, if it had wished, have further provided that anyone who was dissatisfied with those recommendations could appeal to the courts. Had it done so, the duty of the court would, to a considerable extent, have been to repeat the operations of the commission and see whether it arrived at the same answer. If it did, the appeal would have been dismissed. If it did not, it would have substituted its own recommendations. Parliament, for reasons which we can well understand, did no such thing. It made no mention of the courts and gave no right of appeal to the courts... There are some who will think that in that situation the courts have no part to play, but they would be wrong. There are many Acts of Parliament which give ministers and local authorities extensive powers to take action which affects the citizenry of this country, but give no right of appeal to the courts. In such cases, the courts are not concerned or involved as long as ministers and local authorities do not exceed the powers given to them by Parliament. Those powers may give them a wide range of choice on what action to take or to refrain from taking and so long as they confine themselves to making choices within that range, the courts will have no wish or power to intervene. But if ministers or local authorities exceed their powers – if they choose to do something or to refrain from doing something in circumstances in which this is not one of the options given to them by Parliament – the courts can and will intervene in defence of the ordinary citizen.

It has to be said that this situation has not generally recommended itself to the Court of Human Rights, which has on several occasions indicated that judicial review procedure may not measure up to the standard required by ECHR Article 6(1).[24]

---

23 *R v. Boundary Commission ex p Foot* [1983 QB 600.

24 *Weeks v. United Kingdom* [1987] 10 EHRR 293. In *Chahal v. United Kingdom*, where

Establishing Facts The centrepiece of judicial control of administration is in England "the application for judicial review",[25] a term which refers to the special High Court procedure used to attack the legality of administrative proceedings. For historical reasons, judicial review procedure has always been documentary in character. Facts are established through a series of written questions (interrogatories) posed by the applicant to the respondent and oral evidence is very rarely given. This practice runs counter to the main thread of common law procedure, which requires oral evidence given by witnesses before the court to be tested through cross-examination. It has been defended by a senior judge on the ground that the facts are seldom in dispute in proceedings against the administration.[26]

Immigrants and asylum-seekers would certainly not agree; disputes over simple factual issues of age or relationship or financial matters lie behind many such cases. They would no doubt give a great deal to be able to cross-examine immigration officials about the factual basis for decisions. This point is all the stronger when we realise that, in many immigration proceedings, the applicant is outside the country and has to pursue his claim from overseas. The fact-finding process will then take place overseas, typically in an embassy, and outside the real control of the immigration tribunal hearing any appeal.[27] A similar position arises where an immigrant seeking to enter is turned back at the frontier; his appeal too will have to be pursued from overseas.

Where the immigrant applies directly for judicial review, his case is not much better. *Zamir v. Home Secretary*[28] illustrates the difficulties which may arise. Z, aged 15 and unable to read or speak English, applied from Pakistan to enter the UK as a dependent child. Three years on, when his application was finally processed, he arrived at Heathrow. He was by then married but did not inform the immigration officer, not realising it to be relevant, though it would in fact have ended his right of dependency. When, two years later, Z applied to bring in his wife and children, he was detained as an illegal immigrant. In the House of Lords, discussing the factual basis for judicial review, Lord Wilberforce said:

> The [court] on judicial review of a decision to remove and detain... considers the case on affidavit evidence, as to which cross-examination, though allowable, does not take place

---

deportation on grounds of national security was in issue, ECHR Articles 5(4) and 13 were held to have been breached.

25 See generally R. Gordon, *Judicial Review: Practice and Procedure* (London: Sweet and Maxwell, 1999); M. Fordham, *Judicial Review Handbook* (Chichester: Wiley, 1994).

26 H. Woolf, *Protection of the Public – A New Challenge* (London: Stevens, 1990).

27 A process described in greater detail in C. Harlow and R. Rawlings, *Law and Administration* (London: Weidenfeld and Nicolson, 1984), Chapters 16 and 17. (It should not be assumed that the law and procedures are identical today.)

28 [1980] 2 All ER 768 (HL). The House of Lords held that immigrants were bound by a "positive duty of candor" to tell immigration officers all material facts. This harsh and unfair ruling had to be reversed soon after by *Khawaja and Khera v. Home Secretary* [1983] 1 All ER 765 (HL).

> in practice. It is... not in a position to find out the truth between conflicting statements: did the applicant receive notes, did he read them, was he capable of understanding them, what exactly took place at the point of entry... It cannot possibly act as, in effect, a court of appeal as to the facts on which the immigration officer decided. What it is able to do, and this is the limit of its powers, is to see whether there was evidence on which the immigration officer, acting reasonably, could decide as he did.

To sum up, there are usually two stages to a contested immigration appeal:

(i) Tribunal hearings, which are unsatisfactory in that appellants are not always present and legally represented, a defect made worse by recent legislation.[29] These find the facts.

(ii) Judicial review, by no means always available.[30] This provides more satisfactory remedies for abuse of power by immigration officials but the fact-finding opportunities are less. If a judge on review is dissatisfied, he is likely to return the case to the immigration tribunal to find the facts and come to a new decision.

Although taken from a decision rightly discredited on other grounds, the citation does give an excellent impression of the limited role played by fact in judicial review proceedings. This gap in the protection of the individual against the administration has led to adverse criticism from the Court of Human Rights, which has commented adversely on the limited opportunity to contest either the facts or the merits of a decision in judicial review proceedings, suggesting that this is not a sufficient remedy for purposes of ECHR Articles 13 and 6(1).[31]

Reviewing Discretionary Power The traditional grounds for judicial review were said to be: error of law, *ultra vires* or excess of power, and breach of the rules of natural justice. Currently, a reformulation of the grounds by Lord Diplock[32] is preferred. Lord Diplock stated that the present grounds for review were: illegality, irrationality, and procedural impropriety. By irrationality was meant what can by now be succinctly referred to as "*Wednesbury* unreasonableness". It applies to a decision which is so outrageous in its defiance of logic or of accepted moral standards that no sensible person who had applied his mind to the question to be decided could have arrived at it.

Lord Diplock here refers back to a classic case in which unreasonableness was defined by the Court of Appeal, when considering the powers of a local authority to include in a cinema licence a provision forbidding entrance of children on Sundays.[33] Lord Greene MR said:

> When an executive discretion is entrusted by Parliament to a body such as the local authority in this case, what appears to be an exercise of that discretion can only be

29 See Asylum and Immigration Appeals Acts 1993, 1996; Wade, p. 232.

30 See below.

31 See *Weeks v UK* (1987) 10 EHRR 293.

32 *Council of Civil Service Unions v. Minister for the Civil Service* [1985] AC 374.

33 *Associated Provincial Picture Houses v. Wednesbury Corporation* [1948] 1 KB 223.

> challenged in the courts in a strictly limited class of case... it must always be remembered that the court is not a court of appeal. When discretion of this kind is granted the law recognizes certain principles upon which that discretion must be exercised, but within the four corners of those principles the discretion, in my opinion, is an absolute one and cannot be questioned in any court of law. What then are those principles? They are well understood... The exercise of such a discretion must be a real exercise of the discretion. If, in the statute conferring the discretion, there are to be found expressly or by implication matters which the authority exercising the discretion ought to have regard to, then in exercising the discretion it must have regard to those matters. Conversely, if the nature of the subject-matter and the general interpretation of the Act make it clear that certain matters would not be germane to the matter in question, the authority must disregard those irrelevant collateral matters...

Whether this is one test or two has been much disputed. Clearly, however, the first formulation entitles the court to look closely at the evidence on which the decision maker has based his decision. As Lord Greene went on to say:

> a person entrusted with a discretion must, so to speak, direct himself properly in law. He must call his own attention to the matters which he is bound to consider. He must exclude from his consideration matters which are irrelevant to what he has to consider. If he does not obey those rules, he may truly be said, and often is said, to be acting "unreasonably".

Modern cases have built on this to monitor both the reasoning process of decision makers and the weight given to policy factors. In one famous case,[34] for example, Lord Diplock used the formula to reason that, in setting fares for public transport, the interests of passengers and environmental factors should be weighed against the financial interests of local taxpayers. He felt able to conclude that preference should be given to the latter. This case was said by administrators to give rise to a change in practice whereby *all* the facts and evidence thought to be potentially relevant to decision making was placed before the decision maker, causing paper mountains to accumulate throughout the administration!

The second part of Lord Greene's test allows courts to intervene where decisions are "so absurd that no sensible person could ever dream that it lay within the powers of the authority".

It will be immediately obvious that this test, although extremely flexible, adopts a different starting point from that used in many continental versions of the proportionality principle. These start from the assumption that the citizen possesses a right or interest which ought not to be invaded without good reason and then only to the extent that is necessary to achieve a stated administrative goal. Reasonableness adopts an opposite approach. The assumption is that anything authorised by the supreme Parliament is lawful and the question therefore is always whether administrative action falls within the powers granted. Originally established as a way to protect the administration from undue judicial interference in policy matters, the test has in later years been used to require the administration

[34] *Bromley LBC v. Greater London Council* [1983] AC 768.

to justify its actions by reference to reasons and evidence which it must bring forward.[35] This is marked by the shift in the terminology used by Lord Diplock (above): rationality replaces reasonableness.

Despite this development, the Court of Human Rights is clearly uncomfortable with the traditional reasonableness test and has used it to cast doubt on the adequacy of judicial review as machinery for control of the administration. In *Smith*,[36] service personnel dismissed from the armed forces for being of "homosexual tendency", applied for judicial review of the decision on the ground that the policy was unreasonable. The settled policy of the Ministry of Defence expressed in regulations had recently been approved by Parliament. Reluctantly, the Court of Appeal held that there were no grounds for intervention, applying the following test:

> The court may not interfere with the exercise of an administrative discretion on substantive grounds save where the court is satisfied that the decision is unreasonable in the sense that it is beyond the range of responses open to a reasonable decision-maker. But in judging whether the decision-maker has exceeded this margin of appreciation the human rights context is important. The more substantial the interference with human rights, the more the court will require by way of justification before it is satisfied that the decision is reasonable in the sense outlined above.

This variant of the *Wednesbury* test is generally known as the test of "anxious scrutiny" and is today adopted in all cases where serious breach of a human right is alleged.

The victims in *Smith* went on, however, to contest the decision in the Court of Human Rights, on the ground that judicial review procedure did not afford a sufficient remedy for breach of a human right (ECHR Articles 6(1), 13) because the merits of the decision could not be tested. The Court found for them on all counts,[37] requiring the proportionality test of human rights law to be applied by the UK courts. This decision highlights a serious difference of opinion between the ECtHR and the British courts. Applying separation of powers theory rather strictly, English law, as we have seen, distinguishes sharply between appeal and review. As Lord Bingham explained in the *Smith* case (above):

> It is not the constitutional role of the court to regulate the conditions of service in the armed forces of the Crown, nor has it the expertise to do so. But it has the constitutional role and duty of ensuring that the rights of citizens are not abused by the unlawful exercise of executive power. While the court must properly defer to the expertise of responsible decision-makers, it must not shrink from its fundamental duty "to do right to all manner of people".

---

35 See *Padfield v. Minister of Agriculture* [1968] AC 997.

36 *R v. Ministry of Defence ex p. Smith* [1996] 1 All ER 257.

37 *Lustig-Prean and Beckett, Smith and Grady v. United Kingdom* (Judgement of ECtHR 27 September 1999).

He deduced from this that the irrationality or unreasonableness test traditionally applied by the courts was legitimate, subject to the "anxious scrutiny" development and the tendency of modern courts to require increasing detail of the facts on which decisions are based and the reasoning by which it was arrived at. As we have indicated, the ECtHR has not only required our courts go further and to apply the European proportionality test but is also unhappy about the reach of judicial review into questions of fact and control of the merits of an administrative decision. Both would require a fundamental shift in the balance of judicial and governmental power – a basic issue of law and democracy.[38] Only the recent authorisation of such a shift by Parliament in the Human Rights Act 1998 could justify such fundamental constitutional change.

Impact

Direct Impact

It is important to stress that every common law system of judicial review relies heavily on the mandatory orders which the courts have at their disposal: injunctions and interim injunctions (suspensory orders) plus the two public law orders of mandamus and prohibition.[39] An order of mandamus tells a public official to carry out a public duty and lies to all public bodies. This enables potential breaches of procedure to be challenged at an early stage and prospectively prevented through injunctions. In *Padfield's* case,[40] for example, a minister publicly announced that he would not be referring the question of price rises for milk producers to an advisory committee, as he had power to do. Holding the procedures to be mandatory in the teeth of the wording of the statute (below), the House of Lords issued an order of mandamus to the minister, ordering him to make the reference. This he did; though famously he declined to accept the committee's recommendation.

Prohibition prevents a tribunal or administrative body from taking a decision which it is not empowered to make; its use is uncommon, though there is one interesting example of the use of prohibition to enforce administrative procedures. A local authority had undertaken not to embark on a scheme to reorganise taxi licenses until it had consulted with the taxi drivers' association. When it took steps to move forward without consultation, an order of prohibition was awarded to prevent further action.[41]

---

[38] On which see the views of the present Lord Chancellor, A. Irvine, "Judges and Decision-makers: The Theory and Practice of *Wednesbury* Review" [1996] *Public Law* 59. See also HR, chapter 17; K. Ewing, "The Human Rights Act and Parliamentary Democracy" (1999) 62 *Modern Law Review* 79.

[39] Craig 721-752.

[40] *Padfield v. Minister of Agriculture* [1968] AC 997. HR 98-100.

[41] *R v. Liverpool Corporation ex p. Liverpool Taxi Fleet Operators' Association* [1972] 2

The order of *certiorari* quashes the decision of a tribunal or administrative body once made. Normally the case is then returned to the decision maker to make a new decision, this time following proper procedures, though there are limited powers for the court in a clear case to substitute its own decision.

Until recently, it was thought that neither injunctions nor mandamus were available against the Crown, a serious gap in protection, as this term can cover ministers, at least when they do not have statutory backing for their decisions. Today, injunctive relief in all its forms lies to the Crown. This is the consequence of the celebrated *Factortame* case,[42] where the Court of Justice advised that the statutory prohibition on injunctions against the Crown should be set aside if it was the only barrier to remedy. The House of Lords duly disapplied the statute and awarded an interim injunction. Shortly afterwards, in a case where the Home Secretary had failed to comply with an order to return an expelled immigrant to the UK so that the legality of his asylum status could be determined, the House of Lords ruled that the Crown's immunity from injunctive relief did not apply to any public law proceedings.[43]

Remedies are at the discretion of the court,[44] which may prefer to substitute for injunctive relief a declaratory statement that a procedural breach has occurred.[45] This is often done where the court is aware that a change is being made in the law. A declaratory judgment may also be made against government in the knowledge that it will be complied with. Courts also possess limited power to issue "advisory declarations" where uncertainty exists as to the legality of administrative action. This power is not used frequently but it would in theory be possible, if a local authority was unclear (for example) as to the meaning of procedural regulations governing planning inquiries, to seek a declaration as to the proper course of action.[46]

In the leading *Datafin* case,[47] the court moved to establish its jurisdiction over the statutory system of self-regulation which controls financial markets and the City, ruling that the private, contract-based system was "public" in character because the body which operated it carried out a public function and was therefore subject to judicial review. Significantly, no injunction to stop the questioned transactions was awarded and the Court of Appeal made an important statement as

---

WLR 1262.

42 *R. v. Secretary of State for Transport ex p. Factortame (No. 1)* [1990] 2 AC 8, Case C213/89 *R v. Secretary of State for Transport ex p Factortame (No 2)* [1990] ECR I-2433, *R. v. Secretary of State for Transport ex p. Factortame (No. 2)* [1990] 3 WLR 818. The statutory provision in question was s. 21 of the Crown Proceedings Act, 1947.

43 *M v. Home Office* [1993] 3 WLR 433 (HL). For an explanation of the reasoning see my note, "Accidental Death of an Asylum Seeker" (1994) 57 *Modern Law Review* 620.

44 T. Bingham, "Should Public Law Remedies be Discretionary?" [1991] *Public Law* 64.

45 *R v. Aston University ex p Roffey* [1969] 2 QB 538.

46 See, J. Laws, "Judicial Remedies and the Constitution" (1994) 57 *Modern Law Review* 213.

47 *R v. Panel on Take-Overs and Mergers ex p Datafin* [1987] QB 815.

to the future use by the courts of their "new" powers. Sir John Donaldson MR explained this choice:

> I wish to make it clear beyond a peradventure that in the light of the special nature of the Panel, its functions, the market in which it is operating, the timescales which are inherent in that market and the need to safeguard the position of third parties.... all of whom are entitled to continue trade on an assumption of the validity of the Panel's rules and decisions, unless and until they are quashed by the court, I should expect the relationship between the Panel and the court to be historic rather than contemporaneous. I should expect the court to allow contemporary decisions to take their course, considering the complaint and intervening, if at all, later and in retrospect by declaratory orders which would enable the Panel not to repeat any errors and would relieve individuals of the disciplinary consequences of any erroneous finding of breach of the rules.

This reasoning leaves scope for the court to overlook trivial breaches of procedure, especially if they feel that the outcome of the case would have been the same had the procedure been followed to the letter.

In rule-making, as opposed to judicial or quasi-judicial proceedings, there are no general duties to consult interested parties or to make reasoned decisions nor is there any equivalent of the American Administrative Procedures Act.[48] (It should be pointed out that central governments normally consult widely before law or regulations are made.) The position has been the subject of criticism in an unofficial report from the respected Hansard Society.[49] No action has been taken – indeed, there is probably no agreement as to what should be done – but the present government has introduced, on an experimental basis, a consultative stage before Bills are debated by Parliament.

It is generally conceded that the courts have been more vigilant in the protection of individuated due process than in supervising consultative procedures in rule-making. Where these are imposed by statute, the courts could have a powerful role in developing participatory rule-making procedures but they have not to date seized their opportunity. Whether they will hold consultation procedures to be "mandatory", hence enforceable, or purely "directory" is in any specific case hard to predict; the law has, indeed, recently been described as "an inextricable tangle of loose ends".[50]

Mandatory or Directory?

"Mandatory" procedures are those imposed by law, typically through use of the word "must" or other mandatory formula in the governing statute. The term

---

48 HR, Chapter 6; Craig 376-383.

49 *Making the Law: Report of the Hansard Society Commission on the Legislative Process* (London: Hansard Society, 1992).

50 WJS para 5-058. paras 5-057-5-077 nonetheless contain the best account of the underlying principles of review in this area.

"directory" signifies discretion or choice, often indicated by the word "may" in the statutory formula. A remarkable feature of the *Padfield* decision (above) was that the House of Lords construed a discretionary formula ("if the Minister in any case so directs") as a mandatory requirement. It is more usual for this process to be reversed.

The flexible attitude of courts to procedural breaches can be illustrated by a series of old cases involving disputes over selection in the state education sector after 1944. In 1967, when selection became a matter of hot political controversy, the parents and governors of selective schools turned to the courts to frustrate the policy of comprehensive education. In one such case, an education authority, acting on legal advice, did not follow the statutory consultation procedures in some of their schools, believing it to be inapplicable. Challenged by the parents, their decision was quashed by the court for procedural impropriety. This left them with insufficient time properly to consult and get the new, non-selective system in place for the next school year. With the help of the minister, they resorted to a notice which allowed only a four-day period over a weekend for consultation. The court ruled this invalid, awarding a declaration and injunction.[51] By way of contrast, in a case where the education authority had publicised their comprehensive scheme and consulted widely but had overlooked the requirement to post a notice at or near the main entrance of two of their schools, the judge overlooked the breach, saying:[52]

> What the regulations require is that notices should be published in a manner designed to show a representative number of people what their rights are, and leave to them the organisation of others. In fact that is what happened in this case. Some people, I think a great number, saw the notice. They organised the parents' association... If there had been more notices, even if the number of objectors had been doubled, it does not seem to me that that would be sufficient to make any real difference to the problem which troubled the Minister who sat down with the proposals on the one hand and the objections on the other.

The casual style of this passage may seem strange to continental lawyers but it typifies the highly pragmatic attitude of English judges and their tendency to base decisions on the facts of the particular case. This judge does not lay out principles or criteria by which the reality of consultation may be measured; he is broadly satisfied that enough parents will have seen the notices to provide the minister with enough information on which to base his decision. One explanation may be that the judge saw the objectors as simply trying to delay an inevitable change. In the earlier *Enfield* cases, the outcome was perhaps less clear; moreover, the minister had acted in an underhand manner likely to meet with the court's disapproval. It could perhaps be said that the improper motive rendered this breach of procedure

---

51 *Bradbury v Enfield LBC* [1967] 1 WLR 1311, *Lee v Department of Education and Science* (1967) 66 LGR 211.

52 *Coney v Choice* [1975] 1 WLR 422. To bring this story up-to-date, decisions to abolish selection are today taken by parents' ballot, a move from consultation to popular decision-making.

qualitatively different from the second, more trivial, failure to comply with the letter of the law. It is nonetheless hard to identify a principle which would explain both cases and serve as a guide in future cases.

Procedural requirements face courts with the dilemma that, if they enforce them too rigidly, everything may have to be redone, causing delay and expense. Given modern trends in the law of liability, this may expose the administration to liability in damages or at least to statutory compensation payments. There is the additional danger that administrators will become obsessive in following every procedural step to the letter, causing further delay and expense.

Planning Procedures [53]

Minor procedural errors cause particular problems in the land use planning process, where feelings run very high and the parties are prepared to push every legal argument to its limit; for environmental protestors, every delay is a victory. Over the years since the passage of the Town and Country Planning Acts 1971, which established and codified the broad outlines of modern planning procedure,[54] the procedures have become increasingly complex. One reason is undoubtedly the influence of lawyers. Property is an important and well-protected right at common law, and courts incline to provide strong protection for land and property owners. Equally, government faces strong pressure to make planning a more participatory process and steps towards this goal have occasionally been taken.[55] The consequence is a set of cumbersome procedures which crawl along at a snail's pace. There is then a temptation – for politicians as well as administrators – to replace the procedures by informal procedures which are less transparent, less participatory and less strictly controlled. When the Conservative Government of Mrs Thatcher came into power in 1979, one of the first things they did was to introduce legislation to simplify and streamline planning law. Today, in smallscale developments, written procedure has been largely substituted for the type of enquiry described below.

Planning inquiries are conducted by an inspector who is appointed by the minister, usually from the planning inspectorate attached to the ministry, though in important cases a senior lawyer may be chosen instead. The inspector makes a

---

53 See generally, M. Grant, *Urban Planning* (London: Sweet and Maxwell, 1982).

54 The legislation has since been amended and consolidated by the Planning Acts 1990, Planning and Compensation Act 1991 and the consolidated General Development Order 1995. For details, consult D. Heap, *An Outline of Planning Law* (London: Sweet and Maxwell, 1996); R. Duxbury, *Telling and Duxbury's Planning Law and Procedure* (London: Butterworths, 1996).

55 For an interesting theoretical explanation, see P. McAuslan, *The Ideologies of Planning Law* (Oxford: Pergamon) 1980. For the way in which the process was shaped until 1980, see C. Harlow and R. Rawlings, *Law and Administration* (London: Weidenfeld and Nicolson) 1984, Chapters 14 and 15. On the attitude of the judiciary, see the early article by M. Grant, 'Planning, Politics and the Judges' [1978] *Journal of Planning Law* 512.

report, including recommendations, to the Minister. It is the Minister for the Environment who takes the final decision.

Bushell's case[56] illustrates the tensions of the planning process very well. The case concerned a public enquiry into the building of a motorway. It was hotly contested by local amenity groups. Much turned on the volume of traffic which would use the new road. Objectors at the enquiry wished to question departmental witnesses on the accuracy of their traffic flow predictions and on the standard method used for calculating traffic flow. After the enquiry but before the Minister's decisions, a revised method was introduced which cast doubt on the original figures. The objectors asked for the enquiry to be re-opened but the minister refused. The applicants applied for certiorari to quash this decision on the grounds that the failure to allow cross-examination and the use of new evidence post-enquiry were breaches of procedure and of natural justice. The Law Lords differed hotly over whether the contested material was "fact" or "policy". In his dissenting speech, Lord Edmund-Davies cogently reasoned:

> The inspector could – and should – disallow questions relating to the merits of government policy. But matters of policy are matters which involve the exercise of political judgement and matters of fact and expertise do not become 'policy' merely because a department of government relies on them. And, as the Franks Committee had put it in 1957: We see no reason why the factual basis for a departmental view should not be explained and its validity tested in cross-examination ... [T]here is a massive body of accepted decisions establishing that natural justice requires that a party be given an opportunity of challenging by cross-examination witnesses called by another party on relevant issues.

The majority ruled, however that the "priorities between one stretch of motorway and another" were matters of policy for the minister and Lord Diplock described the material as "government policy in the relevant sense of being a topic unsuitable for investigation by individual inspectors upon whatever material happens to be presented to them at local inquiries held throughout the country". The enquiry did not have to be re-opened.

It has to be said that this highly controversial decision, though still good law, has an old-fashioned look. In many ways it harks back to an era of administrative law when a sharp distinction between "administrative" and "judicial" functions was in use. Lord Diplock concentrates on the ministerial decision, which he views as a matter of policy, hence essentially administrative in character. Lord Edmund-Davies focuses on the enquiry, which he classifies as quasi-judicial in character, hence requiring the protections of natural justice. If this view was correct (and arguably, it was) this could have important consequences today. At least where the compulsory purchase of land is in issue,[57] planning enquires might not measure up to the standards of ECHR Article 6(1): on the one hand, the inspectorate is not

---

56 *Bushell v Environment Secretary* [1980] 3 WLR 22.

57 *Zander v Sweden* A 279-B (1993), *Sporrong and Lonroth v Sweden* A 52 (1982).

independent of the respondent department; on the other, the minister, a politician, is entrusted with a decision which is primarily judicial in character.[58]

The tactics used by objectors in controversial planning cases range from direct political action and obstruction to use of the law and litigation. They have been replicated in every recent enquiry, with the additional twist that EC law, with its added procedural requirement of an Environmental Impact Assessment[59] can now be prayed in aid. The first instance of its use was the hotly contested affair of the Twyford Down motorway, where protestors attempted to stop government from pushing the M3 motorway through an ancient Iron Age encampment on hills near the historic town of Winchester. Objectors contested the outrageous decision through planning inquiries, ending with an action for judicial review[60] in which they argued that no EIA had been prepared and that consequently the public information and consultation stages had been omitted. The judge considered the linked questions of whether the directive was directly effective (ruling that it was) and, if so, whether the applicants must and were able to show that they had suffered by the failure to implement (ruling that they must and could not). The action was not pursued on appeal, probably because, by that time, the UK Government was arguing that the decision fell into a transitional category, being made before the EIA directive had come into force. After some negotiation between the Commission and UK government, it was reported in the press that the Commission had backed away from infringement proceedings under EC Article 169.

EC law was used in two further transitional cases. In the first, which never came to court, the government resiled from the contested scheme. In the Newbury Bypass affair, the unpopular scheme to build a motorway through virgin country was pushed through. This time the Commission refusal to bring EC Article 169 proceedings was challenged by a group of dissatisfied protestors in a complaint to the European Ombudsman.[61] The only result was that the EO examined the file to satisfy himself that the decision to close it had been taken in conformity with general principles of good administrative behaviour.

Although these two cases were unsuccessful, the EIA Directive is now an enforceable part of land use planning procedures. As our courts are on balance very compliant to precedents from the Court of Justice, it is likely that the recent decision in *Commune de Bolsana* will be honoured. This casts doubt on the *Twyford Down* case and should provide better protection for consultation rights in planning cases.

---

58 *McGonnell v UK* (8 February 2000) suggests that this might be the outcome.

59 Environmental Impact Directive 85/337.

60 *Twyford Parish Council and others v Environment Secretary* (1992) CMLR 276 (QBD).

61 *132/21.9.95/AH/EN v Commission re Newbury Bypass*, Annual Report of the European Ombudsman for 1996, 66-7. The wider impact of the complaint was an EO request to the Commission to examine its procedures under EC Article 169, resulting in a more user-friendly and transparent procedure.

Void or Voidable?

A further technique which can be used to blunt the impact of procedural requirements on the administrative process is via a distinction between "void" and "voidable" decisions.[62] A void decision is wholly without effect, requiring the situation to be returned to what it was before the invalid decision was taken. Voidable decisions are valid until successfully ruled invalid by a court; they can thus have legal consequences.

For a certain period, the void/voidable distinction was very important in the context of time limits and the planning process.[63] As Craig puts it, "where an expensive planning and building project is undertaken then the traditional response of retrospective nullity will be difficult to apply".[64] It may be impossible or very hard to return to the *status quo ante*. By holding the decision voidable, its validity until such time as it is set aside by a court can be preserved, obviating the difficulty of reinstatement.

The question may also arise as to whether compensation should be paid. Here the situation has been eased by the introduction of statutory compensation.[65] Where money has been paid to the administration under a void[able] decision, an order for restitution can now be made.[66] The position as to damages is less clear. In the leading case of *Dunlop v Woollahra Municipal Council*,[67] a planning decision to limit the height of an apartment block was quashed because of a minor procedural irregularity. The owner sued for loss of profit caused by the invalid decision but failed because it was held that no action lay for mere invalidity; proof of negligence or bad faith was necessary for liability to accrue. In defence, it has to be said that the possibility of major financial compensation creates a presumption against implementing planning decisions before appeal is exhausted or even embarking on development projects; this runs counter to the short, six-week limitation period and can add to planning delays.[68]

---

62 WJS paras. 5-044-056; Craig, Chap 20.

63 *R v Secretary of State ex p. Ostler* [1977] QB 122.

64 Craig 819.

65 By the Land Compensation Act 1973. See HR 617-9.

66 *Woolwich Building Society v Inland Revenue Commissioners* [1992] 3 WLR 366; HR 628-630.

67 [1982] AC 158. This case was decided by the Privy Council, at that time final appellate court for Australia, and is thus authoritative in the United Kingdom.

68 For some of the difficulties, see the Special Report of the ombudsman (Parliamentary Commissioner for Administration) in the Channel Tunnel affair, where "planning blight" was caused over many years to property on the projected fast rail link from London to the coast but owners were refused compensation: *The Channel Tunnel Rail Link and Blight: Investigation of complaints against the Department of Transport*, HC 193 (1994/5); HR 439-40.

Procedural Irregularity as a Defence

How does the court distinguish a void from a voidable decision? Some of the case law suggests a distinction between "procedural" irregularity and "substantive" error. We are told that a substantive error exists where "the decision is unreasonable or is *ultra vires* in the narrow sense".[69] One would not wish to examine this unhelpful definition too closely; it amounts to saying that minor irregularities may sometimes be labelled "procedural" and overlooked, leading to a finding of voidability.

The distinction has recently been examined in a set of cases which involve the "collateral review" of public law decisions in the course of alternative proceedings. The problem arises because, according to the so-called "exclusivity rule", issues of public law can normally be raised only by way of an application for judicial review and not in other proceedings.[70] This may in practice make it impossible or difficult to challenge a procedural irregularity once the time limit for judicial review has expired.

We have noted too that applicants are generally required to exhaust all lesser remedies before applying for judicial review.[71] This rule may operate to preserve the integrity of a code of procedure with its specialised remedies. Both these points are illustrated in *R v Wicks*,[72] where a builder had been in dispute with the local planning authority over planning restrictions. Finally, when planning procedures had been exhausted, a planning enforcement notice, enforceable by criminal prosecution, was served by the authority. At this last stage, the builder sought to raise the invalidity of the notices with which he had been served, opening the possibility of an enquiry into the facts as well as the law.

On appeal, the House of Lords took the line that planning law amounted to a self-contained code affording ample opportunity to dispute the validity of planning conditions. It was not open to the subject to stand on his rights and ultimately raise public law points before a magistrates' court, which might lack the expertise to deal with them. There was some suggestion, too, that only serious or substantive errors could be challenged in collateral (criminal) proceedings. The *Wicks* decision is, however, highly contestable. It deprives the defendant in a criminal case of his defence. Doubt is cast on it by the later case of *Boddington*,[73] where a defendant prosecuted for smoking in a train was allowed to raise the defence that the by-laws were invalid. Here the House of Lords stood strongly on the over-arching principle

---

69 WJS at paragraph 3-075.

70 Wade, 680-695; WJS, paras. 3.067-3.073. And see C. Emery, "Collateral Attack – Attacking *Ultra Vires* Action Indirectly in Courts and Tribunals" (1993) 56 *Modern Law Review* 643 and "Public Law or Private Law? The Limits of Procedural Reform" [1995] *Public Law* 450; C. Harlow, "Why Public Law is Private Law: An Invitation to Lord Woolf", in R. Cranston and A. Zuckerman (eds), *The Woolf Report Reviewed* (Oxford: Clarendon, 1995).

71 *R v Hillingdon LBC ex p Puhlhofer* [1986] 2 WLR 259; HR at 535.

72 *R v Wicks* [1997] 2 WLR 876.

73 *Boddington v British Transport Police* [1998] 2 WLR 639.

of the rule of law and doubted the validity of the unworkable substance/procedure distinction.

Conclusion: Proceduralism, Process Review or Juridification?

In contemporary England, administrative law and public administration are undergoing parallel shifts of style, though whether they are moving in the same direction is a moot point.

The classic model of English judicial review is procedural in character. Its objective was always the protection of individual interests. Traditionally, a wide discretion is permitted to government and administration, the expectation being that they will use their powers properly or "reasonably" and the justification being the constitutional one that accountability is to be ensured through the parliamentary and political process.[74] A vestige of separation of powers theory is to be found in the belief, often expressed by the judiciary, that judges should not engage in policymaking; this is the sphere of government and administration. These underlying constitutional principles are reflected in the essential distinction between "review" and "appeal". They are also reflected in the celebrated *Wednesbury* formula. The traditional boundaries of judicial review can be summarised by saying that judicial control is limited to the procedures or process by which a decision is taken and does not extend to its merits. Common law courts are comfortable with this traditional, procedural model of review which sits well with their "Westminster" systems of parliamentary government.[75] To allow wide powers of policy-making to an unelected judiciary raises the spectre in common law jurisdictions of "government by judges".

For Richardson and others of liberal persuasion,[76] English proceduralism should be pushed towards the American theory of "process review" often linked to

74 J. A. G. Griffith, "The Political Constitution" (1979) 42 *Modern Law Review* 1.

75 For a defence, see J. A. G. Griffith, "Judges and the Constitution", in R. Rawlings (ed.), *Law, Society and Economy* (Oxford: Oxford University Press, 1997); Lord Irvine of Lairg, "Judges and Decision-makers: The Theory and Practice of *Wednesbury* Review" [1996] *Public Law* 59; K. Ewing, "The Human Rights Act and Parliamentary Democracy" (1999) 62 *Modern Law Review* 79. See also A. Mason, "Courts, Constitutions and Fundamental Rights" in R. Rawlings (ed.) *Law, Society and Economy* (Oxford: Oxford University Press, 1997). (Sir Anthony Mason was previously Chief Justice of Australia.) For the United States, see J. Hart Ely, *Democracy and Distrust: A Theory of Judicial Review* (Cambridge, Mass: Harvard University Press, 1980).

76 G. Richardson, "The Legal Regulation of Process", in G. Richardson and H. Genn, *Administrative Law and Government Action* (Oxford: Clarendon, 1994). See also P. Craig, *Public Law and Democracy in the United Kingdom and the United States of America* (Oxford: Clarendon, 1990); D. Galligan, *Discretionary Powers, A Legal Study of Official Discretion* (Oxford: Clarendon, 1990) and *Due Process and Fair Procedures: A study of administrative procedures* (Oxford: University Press, 1996).

civic republicanism.[77] This envisages a humane society, in which citizens participate in deliberative democracy. In such a framework, claims to due process are best justified in terms of a "dignitary theory of legal process":[78] in short, a relaxed and benign theory of legal process. In modern Britain, this would link to the coming into force of the Human Rights Act later in the year which might be expected to produce, with the aid of ECHR Article 6(1), a new generation of universal procedural rights.[79] Transparency and respect for human dignity coupled with a light framework of regulation would suffice to protect individual interests. This would certainly represent a logical variance in traditional English patterns of governance.

It has, however, already been suggested that the traditional constitutional understanding of the proper ambit of judicial review could be at risk from the jurisprudence of the Court of Human Rights, with its vision of a rule of law founded in strong judicial independence and of an expanding right to contest each and every civil or administrative right and obligation through an independent adjudicative process.[80] It will be equally hard to accommodate the proportionality test, familiar in several European jurisdictions, into English law. It has been suggested that reasonableness and proportionality start from diametrically opposed assumptions. The first is permissive to reasonable executive action; the second limits any administrative action which interferes with human rights to what is deemed by a judge to be necessary and proportionate.[81] Both developments can be explained in terms of a European predilection for a strong system of public law in the framework of a written constitution.

What is developing in the actual context of a heavily regulated and punitive society is an arid form of proceduralism. Inside the administration, there has been a rapid shift from the relaxed and informal traditional style of administration to a regulatory and bureaucratic model, heavily dependent on the promulgation of rules.[82] This is usually theorised in terms of a move from a "group" or "trust" society, in which elite groups are both trusted and trust each other, to a "grid" society, in which obligations are imposed on individuals by external authorities.[83] The courts may have some responsibility – and certainly like to take credit for – promoting adjudicatory procedure in administration, at least in the case of

---

77 See C. Sunstein, *The Partial Constitution* (Cambridge: Harvard University Press, 1993).

78 J. Mashaw, "Dignitary Process: A Political Psychology of Liberal Democratic Citizenship" (1987) 39 *University of Florida Law Review* 155. See also J. Mashaw, *Due Process in the Administrative State* (New Haven: Yale University Press, 1985).

79 A. Bradley, "Administrative Justice: A Developing Human Right?" (1995) 1 *European Public Law* 347.

80 See especially *Osman v. United Kingdom* (1998) 5 BHRC 293.

81 Though see J. Jowell and A. Lester, "Proportionality: neither novel nor dangerous" in J. Jowell and D. Oliver (eds), *New Directions in Judicial Review* (London: University College, 1988).

82 HR, chaps 6 and 7.

83 D. Chalmers, "Judicial Preferences and the Community Legal Order" (1997) 60 *Modern Law Review* 164, 167.

individuated decision-making.[84] The real motor is the modern administrative style encapsulated in the phrase "New Public Management" or NPM.[85] The goals of NPM are expressed in terms of the "Three Es" of Economy, Effectiveness and Efficiency. Transparency and accountability are stated to be key values, but enforced through bureaucratic structures. Public lawyers tend to be hostile to the NPM model because it "transforms traditional mechanisms of public sector accountability to Parliament and the courts into an ever more fragmented and unsatisfactory form".[86] The model of regulation combines wide discretion on the part of the regulator with detailed rules to enable constant monitoring and audit of the lower administrative echelons. This is one side of the development of a pattern of "juridification", a term coined to describe the tendency of modern and post-modern societies to formalise and encapsulate all social relations in terms of law.[87]

The second side of the process of juridification and the negative side of the new model of rights is the development of an Americanised society, where individuals increasingly see their desires as rights and are quick to test and see them enforced through lawyers and litigation.[88] The "complaints culture" which features high on the agenda of NPM both as an internal management tool and as machinery for the external enforcement of standards and performance indicators has fuelled this process. This is really the message of the acclaimed "Citizens' Charter". There has recently been a shift in English judicial review to a model more friendly towards group litigation.[89] This too follows earlier American precedents and is also reflected both at the European and international levels,[90] where a rapid survey of litigation patterns shows that cases in the main transnational courts, if not brought by multinational corporations, are typically supported by NGOs. The lobbying and representational functions of pressure groups are being replaced by a public advocacy function and they are gradually tempted to turn away from the frustrations of the political process towards the illusory finality of courts. These developments are not an outcome of a growing respect for humanity and for its democratic rights reflected in liberal dignitary theory. They reflect popular disillusion with a style of governance which, while preaching accountability and participation, is actually increasingly centralised, bureaucratic and distant from the citizenry. Unfortunately, salvation through juridification is highly unlikely.

---

84 Little is actually known about the impact on administration of judicial decisions: see G. Richardson and M. Sunkin, "Judicial Review: Questions of Impact" [1996] *Public Law* 79.

85 C. Hood, "A Public Management for All Seasons" (1991) 69 *Public Administration* 3. See generally, HR, Chap 5.

86 C. Scott, "Regulation inside government: re-badging the Citizen's Charter" [2000] *Public Law* 595, 595-6.

87 C. Scott, "The Juridification of Regulatory Relations in the UK Utilities Sectors", in J. Black, P. Muchlinski and P. Walker (eds), *Commercial Regulation and Judicial Review* (Oxford: Hart, 1998).

88 M. Galanter, "Law Abounding: Legalisation around the North Atlantic" (1996) 55 *Modern Law Review* 1.

89 HR at 539-552.

90 C. Harlow and R. Rawlings, *Pressure Through Law* (London: Routledge, 1992).

Chapter 4

Between Direct Effect and Rewe/Comet: Remarks on Dutch Administrative Law, Procedural Defects and the EIA Directive

Jan H. Jans and Marianne de Jong*

Introduction

In this chapter we shall consider how administrative law courts in the Netherlands deal with procedural defects, and in particular in a European law context. The paper is arranged as follows. First we shall discuss the most relevant provisions of the *Algemene wet bestuursrecht* (General Administrative Law Act hereinafter: *Awb*). For example, Article 6:22 of the Act provides that a decision against which an objection has been made or an appeal has been lodged may, despite an infringement of a procedural rule, be upheld by the authority which rules on the objection or appeal if it is found that the infringement has not prejudiced the interests of the interested parties. We shall then consider more generally how the Dutch administrative courts deal with potential conflicts between national and European law. Here we shall focus especially on environmental law. Finally, and more specifically, we shall consider several judicial decisions involving procedural defects in respect of environmental impact assessment. We shall end the chapter with some concluding remarks and an outlook towards a European solution.

General Administrative Law Act and Procedural Defects

With regard to the effect of procedural errors on the validity of national decisions two provisions of the *Awb*, *namely* Article 6:22 and Article 8:72, paragraphs 3 and 4 *Awb*, are of main importance.[1] The substance and application of these articles

* Paper written for the "Workshop on Member States Administrative Procedural Law and its Impact on the European Harmonization Process" (Florence: European University Institute, 20 November 1999).

1 See the Annex.

will be discussed below. In order to enhance understanding of these articles we will, however, first discuss some general principles of the *Awb*.

Some Tenets of the Dutch Law of Administrative Procedure

In 1994 a new Dutch code of administrative law, the *Awb*, entered into force. Chapters 6 and 8 thereof concern administrative procedural law, harmonising, codifying, simplifying and systemising the large number of existing laws and case law concerning (general) administrative procedure.[2] This uniform procedural law regulates the settlement of disputes between individuals and administrative authorities (and administrative authorities amongst themselves) and applies to the process of decision-making by the administrative courts, as well as to the outcome of judicial proceedings.[3]

Where the character of administrative procedure in the past wavered between "recours objectif" and "recours subjectif", the primary objective of the new procedural law is legal protection of the subjective rights of the individual, and no longer the objective enforcement of the law as such. This focus on legal protection reflects the changed views in the Netherlands on the position of the individual in relation to the administration. In modern legal theory it is maintained that individuals go to court in order to ensure their own individual rights and interests, not merely to obtain a declaration on the legitimacy of measures from public authorities.[4] This entails, for example, that *locus standi* for judicial review is in general limited to interested parties (no *actio popularis*) and that judicial review is confined to the objections made, where specific grounds of review do not exist. Also characteristic for Dutch administrative procedure is that administrative law courts have an active position, being obliged to supplement the legal grounds and being able to supplement legally relevant facts of their own accord, provided they remain within the limits of the dispute (no *ultra petita*). The judge is *dominus litis*, in order to compensate for the inequality between the parties.[5]

Another important consideration underpinning the *Awb* is the effectiveness and the so-called "finality" of the system of judicial protection. An individual is not served with a formal annulment when the outcome would not be any different after redress of the formal defect or when the judgment annulling the decision does not indicate what the substance of the new decision should be. An individual benefits from clarity about his legal status and from substantive (instead of formal) justice.

---

2 Chapter 6 consists of general provisions on objection and appeal. Chapter 8 contains specific provisions concerning appeal before the administrative court.

3 The *Awb* applies to the administrative chambers of the district courts which provide the main part of administrative review. It also applies to cases before the Council of State in first and only instance and in appeal and to cases before some remaining specialist administrative courts.

4 Bolt, "Benaderingen in het bestuursrecht", in: Boxum a.o., *Aantrekkelijke gedachten* (Deventer: Kluwer, 1993), 141-159. Also Handboek Algemene wet bestuursrecht, Samsom Alphen aan de Rijn, II-3, p. 7-10.

5 Handboek Algemene wet bestuursrecht, op. cit. p. 10-13.

However, apart from (effective and final) judicial protection, guaranteeing the legitimacy of administrative action still plays an important role, as application of procedural law has the effect of objective enforcement of the law. The difference is that the changed relationship between the individual and the administration prevents the purpose of objective enforcement of the law from being the single or even primary goal of the law of administrative procedure. The emphasis of judicial control is on the care with which the decision has been taken and on the rationale of the decision, not on its substance. Traditionally, courts may not encroach on policy choices made by the administration, as long as these are within the boundaries of the law.

Fundamentally, the *Awb* focuses on judicial review *ex tunc* of the legality of administrative acts. As this approach may not always suffice from a perspective of judicial protection and effective dispute settlement, the *Awb* includes several provisions allowing for the negative consequences of this approach to be mitigated. This is provided, among others, by the articles regarding the upholding of decisions suffering from procedural defects and the power of the administrative courts to replace annulled decisions with their own judgments: Articles 6:22 and 8:72, paragraphs 3 and 4 *Awb*.[6]

Summing up, the priority of the *Awb* lies with effective judicial protection of the individual. However, objective control of the legality of administrative decisions still plays an important role.

Recently, the so-called juridification (or judicialisation) of public administration and of the relationship between citizens and the administration has aroused criticism. The term "juridification" refers to the increasing number of legal rules generated by the complexity of contemporary society and the increased involvement of the courts in the application of these rules. The *Evaluation Commission Awb*[7] (hereinafter: *Evaluation Commission*) and the *Van Kemenade Working Group* (hereinafter: *Working Group*)[8] have both addressed the issue and the role of the *Awb* therein. The *Evaluation Commission* finds that the negative consequences of judicial interference in substantive administrative issues stem

6 Kleijn a.o., *Rechtsbescherming: bestuursrechtspraak en bestuursprocesrecht* (Monografieen *AWB*, A3b) (Deventer: Kluwer, 1994), 1-5. Cf. also Lubberdink, "De Awb: hoedster van de individuele vrijheid?", in: Boxum a.o., *Aantrekkelijke gedachten* (Deventer: Kluwer, 1993), 131-138. Handboek Algemene wet bestuursrecht, op. cit., 10-11.

7 This *Evaluation Commission* looked into the application and functioning of the *Awb* in light of its objectives, also with regard to the new uniform administrative procedural law. In view of the purpose of unifying and simplifying procedures and enhancing the efficient settlement of disputes, the *Evaluation Commission* found that the *Awb* is functioning satisfactory. There is no reason for major revisions. Commission Evaluatie Algemene wet bestuursrecht, "Toepassing en effecten van de Algemene wet bestuursrecht 1994-1996", 's Gravenhage (18 December 1996), 23-24; 34-37.

8 Van Kemenade, "Bestuur in geding", Haarlem (November 1997). Report of the workgroup on limiting the juridification of public administration. See also Weggeman, "rubriek *Awb*", in: *Nederlands Tijdschrift voor Bestuursrecht*, 1998/1, 16-19.

from modern ideas about effective and definitive settlement of disputes and that as such they can be justified. Society seems willing to accept increased interference by the courts on substantial grounds, besides their performance of procedural checks. The *Working Group*, however, finds that juridification has gone too far. The (administrative) court has become co-executive/administrator. Actions of the administration are increasingly subject to judicial control. Moreover, courts can rule on the basis of general principles of proper administration, besides written rules of law.[9] The application of these principles enables the courts to make judicial policy. As this development is not desirable in view of legal certainty, democracy and the *trias politica* doctrine, the *Working Group* suggests that courts need to restrict themselves to judicial review of objective legitimacy. In its view, courts should only annul a decision on the basis of violation of general principles of law when it would amount to "unreasonable arbitrariness".[10]

Article 6:22 Awb

On the basis of Article 6:22 *Awb* a decision against which an objection has been made or an appeal has been lodged may, despite an infringement of a procedural rule, be upheld by the authority which rules on the objection or appeal if it is found that the infringement has not prejudiced the interests of the interested parties.[11]

Opinions differ as to the ratio of this provision. Most frequently it is maintained that considering the fact that several procedural requirements have been codified and thus have acquired the status of generally binding regulations (such as the principles of careful preparation and motivation), the question arose whether every violation of such requirements would give rise to annulment. The article clearly signifies that the answer is no. However, since the article does not only apply to these codified requirements but also to unwritten general principles of law regarding procedural requirements, this answer may be too limited. Another reason cited lies in the codification of existing practice, which fits the codification purpose that was at the basis of the *Awb*. The purpose of the provision is to assert beyond

9 These principles have been given an important role in the *Awb*, expressing modern views on the reciprocal relation between the citizen and the administration. Cf. Handboek Algemene wet bestuursrecht, op. cit., 7-10.

10 In reaction to both reports a proposal for a first amendment incorporating the technical and minor changes that can be processed simply has been tabled and is scheduled to enter into force this summer. Kamerstuk 1998-1999, 26523, nrs. 1-10, Tweede Kamer. For the position of the government, see Kamerstuk 1997-1998, 25600VI, nr. 46, Tweede Kamer. A second amendment incorporating more fundamental changes, will be submitted in the second half of 2000. Kamerstuk 1999-2000, 26800VI, nr. 7, Tweede Kamer.

11 Cf. De Waard in: Ten Berge (ed.), *Commentaar Algemene wet bestuursrecht*, VUGA Uitgeverij B.V. 's-Gravenhage, commentaar artikel 6:22, 1; Veltman, "Het passeren van procedurele gebreken", in: *Nederlands Tijdschrift voor Bestuursrecht*, 1989/2, 34 and Polak, *Algemene wet bestuursrecht; Tekst and Commentaar*, tweede druk (Deventer: Kluwer, 1997), 222.

doubt that the *Awb* does not entail any substantial changes in existing practice. A third reason cited (contradicting the second) is that the adoption of this provision in the *Awb* has called to a halt an overly formalistic method of dealing with procedural defects occurring frequently in the past.

Thus, In Dutch administrative procedural law a procedural defect does not in all cases lead to the annulment of the decision. This is not to say that the provision obliges the court to uphold the decision; it only gives it the power, the discretion to do so.[12]

The procedural rule in question is understood to be a rule, which does not concern the material substance of the decision, but relates to the procedure leading up to its adoption or the way in which the decision should be taken or laid down. This is why in case of violation of substantive rules the possibility to uphold the decision does not exist. Also, this provision can only be applied when the contested decision has not already been annulled on substantive grounds.[13]

Another condition for the application of this provision is that the contested decision can only be upheld when the interests of the parties concerned have not been prejudiced. This negative standard of proof is downplayed considerably in practice by the wording used in some judgments that it has *not* become apparent that any interests *have* been prejudiced. But, when would this be the case? Interests have not been prejudiced when the decision would not have made any difference to the benefit of the individual had the procedural rule been taken into account. If without the procedural defect another outcome were even *possible* the procedural defect would give rise to complete reconsideration or annulment of the decision. The objective of the provision is to prevent annulment of decisions in cases where no other outcome could possibly be expected had no procedural defect taken place. Also, the provision may be used when the defect did not influence the substantial outcome of the contested decision at all.[14]

The term "interested parties" in Article 6:22 *Awb* should not be interpreted too strictly. It is understood to mean those whose interests the violated provision seeks to protect. Therefore, not only those individuals that have instituted proceedings, but also third parties are included. Even *possible* prejudice to the interests of third parties may preclude the application of Article 6:22 *Awb*. For obvious reasons this may in practice prove a hard condition to fulfil.[15]

Minor procedural defects which may be disregarded under Article 6:22 *Awb* include the lack of a signature under a decision; breach of notification duties; omissions or mistakes in stating legal provisions (on the basis of which the decision was taken); failure to state the possibility and time-limits of appeal and failure to grant leave to inspect certain documents or opinions. Irreparable are violations of the obligation to publish decisions, which is not considered a

---

12 Polak, op. cit., 221-223.

13 Handboek Algemene wet bestuursrecht, Samsom, Alphen aan de Rijn, artikelsgewijs commentaar art. 6:22 (Kleijn), p.1-2.

14 De Waard, op. cit., 10-11; Kleijn in *Handboek*, op. cit., 2; Veltman, op. cit., 34.

15 De Waard, op. cit., 10. Kleijn in *Handboek*, op. cit., 3.

procedural defect which can be remedied under 6:22 *Awb*. This is because the effect of non-observance of the requirement of publication is that the decision does not enter into force.

More serious procedural defects, which are still repairable via Article 6:22 *Awb*, concern the violation of rules pertaining to the hearing of interested parties, a breach of the duty to state reasons and failure to obtain a legally required opinion. Failure to observe the obligation to hear interested parties in the original decision-making process may be disregarded. However, in general, breaches of the obligation to hear interested parties in complaint-proceedings will not be regarded by administrative courts as excusable under Article 6:22 *Awb*.

A defect in the reasoning of the decision will not necessarily lead to annulment. This is the case, for example, if the remaining reasoning was sufficient to carry the decision or if the case files already contain the relevant information or when the grounds can be reconstructed during the procedure or the interested party was not prejudiced because he knew the grounds. However, if there is a problem concerning the substance of the reasoning, this is a substantive flaw and thus does not constitute a procedural defect. This difference in formal and substantive defects regarding the duty to state reasons is reflected in the *Awb* itself. Rules concerning the substantial obligation to state reasons and rules relating to the formal obligation to state reasons are the subject of two separate articles. Only a violation of the formal part of the duty to state reasons may be remedied by Article 6:22 *Awb*.

In general, lack of competence is not considered to be a procedural defect. A decision rendered without the necessary competence cannot be repaired, even if the competent authority subsequently confirms that decision. In administrative case law the lack of a necessary preparatory decision (such as an exemption that needs to be obtained) has not been qualified as a procedural defect either, as it concerns the substance of the decision. Nor are decisions taken within the wrong legal framework or decisions suffering from inaccurate preparation considered to be repairable under 6:22 *Awb*.[16]

So far Article 6:22 *Awb* has been used by the courts rather cautiously, as illustrated above. Several authors have argued that this is rightly so. One author claims that the provision is redundant since it did not bring any innovation to the notice of objection procedures or administrative appeal. The administration deciding in objection or appeal can exercise all powers *ex nunc* it had in first instance. As such it can also repair formal defects. A provision containing the power for administrative courts to uphold the consequences of an annulled decision, such as Article 8:72, paragraph 3 *Awb*, would suffice. The advantage is that the judgment shows that a violation of the law has taken place and that a procedural defect does have some effect.[17] Another author promotes the restrictive application of Article 6:22 *Awb* because procedural rules have generally been adopted to protect and serve substantial interests. Too loose an application might

---

16 Neerhof, "Van effectieve bestuursrechters en geschillen die voorbijgaan...?", in *Jurisprudentie bestuursrecht plus*, nr. 2, dec. 1999, 73-77. De Waard, op. cit., 4-9.

17 De Waard, op. cit., 1-2.

induce the administration not to observe these rules too strictly.[18] Another objection is that the individual has no right to payment of damages after application of Article 6:22 *Awb*, where administrative and civil law concerning compensation require that the appeal was well founded and that the decision was annulled.

Others, however, have argued that the provision should be applied more generously.[19] The *Working Group* has recommended to no longer limit the scope of Article 6:22 *Awb* to "procedural defects", but to extend it to include substantive defects and defects relating to rules of competence, as these defects can be of minor importance. According to the *Working Group*, especially with regard to these defects, which stem from the general principles of administrative law, a toning down of the violation is often justified. Only in cases where a violation would amount to "unreasonable arbitrariness", the court should annul the decision.[20] The government partially endorsed this opinion when it declared it wanted to widen the scope of the provision to include "substantive defects of minor importance".[21]

The scope of application one desires to grant to Article 6:22 *Awb* may relate to the dual character, be it with primary focus on judicial protection, of the *Awb*. If protection of individual rights is the only objective, Article 6:22 *Awb* could have a much broader scope of application. The violation of any written or unwritten rule or general principle of law could always be excused when the interests of the interested parties were not prejudiced. However, since Dutch administrative procedural law also aims at ensuring the legality of administrative action and the observance of legal norms reflecting the general interest, the administrative court has to be able (from an objective perspective) to confront the administration when it violates rules of procedure. This calls for a stricter scope of application. In this context Article 8:72, paragraph 3 *Awb* provides the courts with an important instrument. Where some corrective action with regard to the administration is necessary, but too harsh an approach is not in the interest of the individual or the administration, the upholding of the legal consequences of the contested decision may prove to be a balanced solution.[22] Also, when a defect cannot be disregarded under Article 6:22 *Awb*, courts may try to avoid a second procedure after a formal annulment by including substantial considerations *obiter dictum* in the judgment and thus direct the substance of the new decision to be taken.

---

18 Smit, "Een doorbraak van de formele bbb in het belastingrecht", in *TvO*, 1987, 405.

19 Van der Meulen/Koning, "Pardonnering van vormverzuimen: artikel 6:22 *Awb*", in *Jurisprudentie Bestuursrecht* (18 november 1994), afl.12, nr. 270, 727-733. Ten Berge a.o., *Ervaringen met de Awb, Het bestuursprocesrecht,* Kluwer Deventer, 1996, 250. Commission Evaluatie Algemene wet bestuursrecht, op. cit. 61, 101.

20 Van Kemenade, op. cit., Weggeman, "rubriek *Awb*", in: *Nederlands Tijdschrift voor Bestuursrecht*, 1998/1, 18-19.

21 Kamerstuk 1998-1999, 26360, nr.1, Tweede Kamer, 26. Cf. Hirsch Ballin, "Controversieel bestuursrecht", in: *Nederlands Tijdschrift voor Bestuursrecht*, 1999/3, 54.

22 *Jurisprudentie Bestuursrecht* (29 januari 1998), afl. 1, nr. 5, 36-37.

Article 8:72, Paragraphs 3 and 4 Awb

The first paragraph of Article 8:72 *Awb* states that if the court holds the appeal to be well founded, it shall quash all or part of the disputed decision. The legal consequences are nullified retroactively according to paragraph 2. However, as we have seen above, not in all cases in which the court holds the appeal to be well founded, the effect will be that the decision is annulled; Article 6:22 *Awb* is an example of this. Moreover, the effect of an annulment of a decision, which would normally entail the annulment of its legal consequences *ex tunc*, can be mitigated by the application of paragraph 3 of Article 8:72 *Awb*. This paragraph provides that the court may direct that all or part of the legal consequences of the quashed decision or the quashed part thereof shall be allowed to stand. This so-called "declaration to cover" (covering the annulment) therefore is not as far-reaching as Article 6:22 *Awb* which prevents the decision from being annulled.

The court may use this power for reasons of "judicial economy" or legal protection of the individual. The provision, like Article 6:22 *Awb*, adds to the number of instruments at the disposal of the administrative court for the enhancement of effective dispute settlement. In some cases annulment may suffice from the perspective of objective legitimacy but will not amount to the effective settlement of the dispute.[23] Often the administration will have to take a new decision (taking the court's judgment into account), but in other cases it is more effective if the judge were to make arrangements. One of the possibilities open to the court is to determine that the legal consequences of a decision shall be allowed to stand. Another possibility is offered by Article 8:72, paragraph 4 *Awb* stating that if the court holds that the appeal is well founded, it may direct the administrative authority to make a new decision or to perform another act in accordance with its judgment, or it may direct that its judgment takes the place of the quashed decision or the quashed part thereof. These powers (or supplementary *dicta*) may be combined with annulment. They will be discussed below.

The Application of Paragraph 3 According to the third paragraph of Article 8:72 *Awb* a court may direct that all or part of the legal consequences of the quashed decision or the quashed part thereof shall be allowed to stand. Article 8:72, paragraph 3 *Awb* supplements the powers granted by Article 6:22 *Awb*. As indicated above some defects may not be excused under Article 6:22 *Awb*, causing the annulment of the decision. In those cases, Article 8:72, paragraph 3 *Awb* may provide a less stringent solution. However, also in other cases that do not concern procedural defects, this instrument can be used.[24]

Above we have stated that a lack of competence is not excusable under Article 6:22 *Awb*. One may wonder whether the legal consequences of the decision concerned may, however, still be upheld. In principle the answer would be no. The

---

23 Polak, op. cit., 286-287.

24 Neerhof, op. cit., 77-80. Michiels, in Ten Berge, a.o., Commentaar Algemene wet bestuursrecht, VUGA Uitgeverij B.V., 's-Gravenhage, commentaar artikel 8:72, 8-10.

legal consequences of such decisions cannot be upheld. Such a violation of the rules on competence is considered to be too serious. In some cases however, subsequent confirmation by the competent organ may justify the application of paragraph 3, provided the decision is flawless substantially. Moreover, the applicable provisions should not leave any room for policy discretion. Also of importance is the extent to which doubt could exist as to who is competent.

Three categories of situations in which 8:72, paragraph 3 *Awb* may be applied can be discerned:

In cases where the factual situation has changed since the disputed decision was taken, and the interests of third parties or of the appellant might be prejudiced disproportionately by a plain annulment, application of paragraph 3 may ease the tension. The retroactive effect of an annulment may jeopardise legal certainty and justified expectations, *e.g.*, in case of unjustified dismissal. Also, the provision is applied in cases where a decision has to be annulled because of reasons lying in the past, but where the decision would be lawful if it were to be taken at the moment of review. Annulment would not make much sense in such a scenario. Obviously, this power may only be used if it is beyond any doubt that the decision is substantially correct.

In cases relating to a breach of the duty to state reasons falling outside the scope of Article 6:22 *Awb*, or an inaccuracy in the preparation of the decision, which did not influence the outcome of the procedure, Article 8:72, paragraph 3 *Awb* may also offer a solution. In this type of cases the individual would not be better off with an annulment. For reasons of efficiency and "judicial economy" new procedures leading to the same practical outcome must be avoided. However, when the administration has failed to provide sufficient information about the weighing of interests that has taken place, it is not within the powers of the court to take the place of the administration and determine that the legal consequences of the decision can be upheld.

In cases where the court foresees that the new decision would be unfavourable for the appellant it may apply paragraph 3 to prevent such *reformatio in peius*.

All in all, paragraph 3 of Article 8:72 *Awb* is only applied in a limited number of cases. The scope of application is not very wide, also because of the doctrine of division of powers.

The Application of Paragraph 4 The fourth paragraph of Article 8:72 *Awb* provides that if the court holds that the appeal is well founded, it may direct the administrative authority to make a new decision or to perform another act in accordance with its judgment, or it may direct that its judgment takes the place of the quashed decision or the quashed part thereof.

The application of paragraph 4 is not much wider than that of paragraph 3. The text of the provision does not give any restrictions or conditions for its application except for previous annulment. Courts have, however, applied the criterion that the discretion of the administration should not be violated. This will be the case when the law or the applicable policy rules in combination with the general principles of administrative law lead to the conviction that in the circumstances of the case there can only be one outcome. The courts have applied this criterion strictly, which has resulted in the restrictive application of this provision.[25]

In case of a formal defect it is not possible to determine which decision is substantially correct. Violation of the duty to state reasons or the duty of care, for example, does not allow the judge to consider the substantive issues and decide on the merits. The competent court therefore cannot replace the decision with its own judgment. There are exceptions however. If the court discovers, for example, that a notice of objection has wrongfully been found admissible and unfounded, it can settle the dispute by annulling the decision and still declaring the notice of objection inadmissible. Decisions taken without competence will have to be annulled and cannot be subject to the application of paragraph 4. The division of powers doctrine demands that the proper organ take the decision.

However, many cases concerning substantive defects are not suited to the application of paragraph 4 either. There is room for application of paragraph 4 when it is clear that there is no more room for discretion, the judge has knowledge of all relevant factual and legal issues and the decision replacing the annulled decision is available in concept (*e.g.*, in case of standard licences) or easily realised (possibly with the help of the administration). This can be the case where the administration does not have any discretion one way or the other. But the application of paragraph 4 may not be limited to this. It could also be applied, for example, when policy rules determining the effectuation of the power have been laid down. But paragraph 4 may also be applied, when the administration has incorrectly qualified the facts and it is clear which decision should have been taken had the right qualification been made. The fact that an administrative judge has to make further inquiries to be able to make a decision on the merits does not prevent the application of paragraph 4.

In light of the doctrine of division of powers the administrative court must be cautious not to take the place of the administration weighing the interests and formulating the decision, especially since the court is not the designated organ, nor has the expertise or aptitude. Restrictive use of this power is therefore recommended. Moreover, apart from problems of a (theoretical) constitutional nature, practical considerations may preclude the application of paragraph 4, such as the necessity of elaborate research as to the facts, difficulties in formulating the new decision and also because the interests of third parties may be overlooked. Sometimes it may be better to include some extra "guiding" considerations in the judgment for the administration to take into consideration when taking a new decision in order to prevent a second round of procedures.[26]

In the first years of application of the *Awb*, paragraphs 3 and 4 have not been used very often, despite the expectations of the legislature. Both powers may be used only when there is no more room for discretion and only one outcome is possible. The application of the strict criteria and the restricted use of these

---

25 Michiels, op. cit., 16-21. Neerhof, op. cit., 80-83.

26 Handboek Algemene wet bestuursrecht, Samsom, Alphen aan de Rijn, artikelsgewijs commentaar art. 8:72 (Korteweg-Wiers), 3.

paragraphs may be explained by the fact that administrative courts wanted to "educate" the administration by annulling wrong decisions, but the heavy caseload may also have contributed to this. The practical application and effect of these paragraphs should therefore not be overestimated. Moreover, there is considerable danger that judges might trespass on the territory of the executive powers. Especially with discretionary powers, the legislature deliberately decided to award a large degree of decision-making freedom to the administration. Another method that has been used, however, as mentioned before, is to include considerations *obiter dictum* in order to direct the substance of the new decision to be taken after the annulment.

Although complaints about juridification might suggest otherwise, the *Evaluation Commission* and the *Working Group* both find that the courts have only used these new powers sparingly and recommend a more frequent application of Article 8:72, paragraph 3 and 4 *Awb*.[27]

Conclusion

Since the entry into force of the *Awb*, administrative law courts have three instruments at their disposal to ensure the effective settlement of disputes. They may annul (in part or in whole) contested decisions *ex tunc* with or without allowing legal consequences to stand, uphold decisions excusing some procedural defects, or replace the contested decision with their own. The ratio of these powers is to avoid unnecessary second rounds of procedures, supplementary procedures before the civil and administrative courts (*e.g.*, regarding damages) and to discharge the administration of taking decisions the substance of which is given with the annulment. Moreover, legal certainty is served, as individuals will not have to wait until the administration takes a new decision. The negative effects of the *ex tunc* annulment approach are thus mitigated. Each instrument performs its own function with regard to procedural defects. Decisions suffering from a procedural defect may be annulled on the basis of Article 8:72, paragraph 1 or upheld via Article 6:22 *Awb*, when some specific minor defects are at stake. The annulment may be supplemented by the *dictum* of paragraph 3 when more serious defects are at stake and, in case of still other defects, paragraph 4 may offer a solution.

However, the scope of application of these instruments (Articles 6:22 and 8:72, paragraphs 3 and 4 *Awb*) should not be overestimated. It is limited to a restricted number of cases only. A repairable procedural defect is a well-defined and limited concept. Moreover, several rules of a procedural nature are considered to be (so) essential for ensuring sound decision-making that their violation cannot be excused. An important theoretical restriction for the application of Article 8:72, paragraphs 3 and 4 *Awb* is the theory of division of powers. The objective of effective settlement of disputes needs to be balanced against the principles of

---

27 Commission Evaluatie Algemene wet bestuursrecht, op. cit., p. 36-37, 61, 101. Van Kemenade, op. cit.; Weggeman, op. cit., 18-19.

legality (the "rule of law") and the fundamentals of the division of functions between the administration and the courts. Discretionary powers of the administration in general prevent courts from using their special powers under the *Awb*. In most cases, the court will limit itself to annulling the decision (Article 8:72, paragraph 1 *Awb*). It is then up to the administration to reconsider and take a new decision, also in case of procedural mistakes.

The Influence of EC Law on Dutch Administrative Law

General Observations

In recent years a growing number of publications have shed light on the complex question of the influence of EC law on the general principles and fundamental structures of Dutch administrative law.[28] The general opinion is that there is indeed a growing influence of EC law on Dutch administrative law. This influence is of a "creeping" character, brought to bear by, in particular, the case law of the Court of Justice. It is regarded as a dynamic process of which the outcome will be hard to predict. The general feeling is that this development will continue. Despite this growing importance of EC law, the leading view in the Netherlands is also that the *fundamental* structures and principles of Dutch public law are not significantly affected by it. "Institutional autonomy", as a general principle of EC law, respects the basic structures of the various national legal orders. In essence, European law leaves the national legal orders sufficient discretion in this. Within the boundaries set by European law we still find various very different national systems of administrative law. The differences between English *public law* ("if any") on the one hand and German *Verwaltungsrecht* on the other are substantial. But it is still possible for these systems to operate together with Dutch, Danish, Greek, etc., administrative law within an integrated and shared European legal order.

European law has ensured that the Dutch legal system has become, more so than it already was, open to external influences. The windows of Dutch administrative law are open now and a fresh wind is blowing. Dutch administrative law has become both more and less "provincial" than it was. More provincial, because the general structure of it finds itself within a European setting and confined by European conditions. Less provincial, because European law triggered the import of new ideas on the role, function and content of administrative law. Public authorities, at both the central and regional level, have had to broaden their outlook. An exclusive orientation on national law alone is no longer sufficient.

---

28 Cf. Jans, de Lange, Prechal and Widdershoven, *Inleiding tot het Europees bestuursrecht* (Nijmegen: Ars Aequi Libri, 1999).

Methods of Judicial Review

Before we can consider how Dutch administrative courts deal with procedural defects in a European law context, we must first address a more general issue. And that is: how does the Dutch Council of State, the highest administrative court in respect of environmental issues, deal in general with questions concerning the compatibility of administrative law, individual decisions and European environmental law. Basically, it employs four different techniques, referred to as:

- Concrete review.
- Abstract review.
- Limited abstract review.
- Indirect review.

These require further explanation.

Concrete Review It is clear from the decisions of Dutch administrative courts, and in particular those of the Council of State, that a permit violates provisions of environmental directives, will be annulled. The court will consider directly whether the permit or any other decision complies with the provisions of the directive.

A good example is provided by a decision of the Council of State concerning the relationship between legislation on the prevention of water pollution and Article 3(4) of Directive 76/464.[29] Under that directive discharges into surface waters of "Black List" substances, such as mercury and cadmium, are permissible only on the basis of *temporary* permits. Although any discharge of such substances into surface waters is prohibited in the Netherlands, the temporary permit requirement does not apply to substances, which manifest themselves merely as *traces* in other substances. In other words, Dutch law does not *require* the authorities to grant only a temporary permit in such cases. The Council consequently ruled that permits, which are not granted temporarily, had to be annulled.

This decision indicates that the courts require public authorities to examine whether their *individual* decisions accord with the directive in question. If the public authorities are shown to have failed to take Community law into account in the exercise of their powers, the permit will be annulled. In Dutch literature this method, in which the individual decision is directly examined for compatibility with European law, is referred to as "concrete review".

Abstract Review In addition to concrete review, the Dutch courts have also applied a method known as "abstract review". This type of review does not involve the direct examination of the compatibility of the permit in question with European law, but rather the interpretation of the national *legislation* on the basis of which the permit was granted. If the national *legislation* does not comply with the requirements of Community law, then that *legislation* will not be applied. The permit will subsequently, more or less automatically, be quashed on the ground of

---

[29] Council of State 25 September [1992] *MR* 1992/46.

breach of statutory requirements. This is because once the contravening provisions of national law have been set aside, there is no longer any legal basis for the permit.

A good illustration is provided by the *Brent Geese* case where a permit was annulled as being in breach of the Wild Birds Directive.[30] Dutch hunting legislation prohibited the hunting of Brent geese. However, under section 53 of the *Jachtwet*, at the time providing for completely unfettered powers, the Minister for the Environment had granted a permit to hunt the birds. Under the Directive the Brent goose is a protected bird. Hunting them is prohibited by Article 7, unless the conditions of Article 9 have been fulfilled. Hunting may, for example, be authorised if there are no other satisfactory solutions to prevent serious damage to crops. In its judgment the Court concluded that the Dutch derogation was much more extensive than allowed under the Directive. Under those circumstances the authority to issue permits contained in the Dutch legislation must be set aside and replaced by the unconditional prohibition contained in Article 7 of the Directive. This meant that the hunting of Brent geese was prohibited, because the Dutch criteria on the strength of which the permits had been granted were too mild in comparison with the Directive, even where the permit in question *did* in fact comply with the criteria of the Directive.

In Dutch legal theory this method of review is known as abstract review, because the Council of State does not consider whether a specific decision is compatible with European law, but instead considers the compatibility of national legislation *in abstracto*. The practical difference between these methods of review is the following. Where the concrete method is applied the decision will be annulled only if it is itself in breach of Community law. This means that where the legislature has failed to implement a directive properly, this will not automatically result in decisions based on that legislation being annulled. If the administrative authority is able in a specific case to apply the legislation in conformity with the directive, that decision will stand. Of course this does not diminish the responsibility of the legislature to ensure the legislation is repaired.

On the other hand, where the abstract method is applied, the results are far more drastic, at least for the legislature and for the implementing administrative authority. In this case, where national legislation is examined in the light of directly effective Community law and found to be in breach of that law, the consequence is that there is no longer a legal basis for administrative acts based on that legislation. In other words, because of the defective legislation the authority is deprived of any possibility to take decisions. Whereas in the case of concrete review the authority retains the possibility of taking decisions, which are in conformity with Community law, in the case of abstract review it does not. The administrative authority is then wholly dependent on the speed with which the legislature is able to repair the defective legislation. Only after the legislation has been repaired can the authority again take decisions.

---

30 Council of State 6 March 1986 *Brent Geese* [1987] *M and R* 16-19, with case note by J. H. Jans.

Limited Abstract Review Recently, however, there have been several examples of judicial decisions in which the Council of State has applied a third method: abstract review resulting in the *partial* setting aside of the infringing national legislation. In the *Tholens Livestock Farmer* case, which will be discussed below in more detail, the Council of State applied the abstract method but only set aside the national legislation *to the extent* it was in breach of European law.[31]

In these cases the Council of State, as it were, splits up the national legislation into a part that is void, namely to the extent the national legislation permits activities which are not permitted under Community law and a part that is effective, namely to the extent it permits activities which are permitted under Community law. In terms of its effect this is virtually the same as that of concrete review. After all, the specific decision will only be quashed if the administrative authority takes a decision in breach of Community law. If it takes a decision within the limits of Community law, it is entitled to do so under that part of the national legislation that is considered effective. The difference between this variant and concrete review is that the court assesses the national legislation and, if part of that legislation is in breach of Community Law, sets it aside.

A fairly lively debate has been conducted in the literature on the question what, from a European law point of view, is preferable: abstract review or concrete review.[32] Although this discussion, particularly given the lack of case law, is to some extent theoretic, it is nevertheless useful for a better understanding of the subject matter to consider the main arguments pro and contra.

The main argument in favour of abstract review is the pressure it places on the legislature to repair the legislation quickly. After all, as long as the legislation has not been amended, it cannot be implemented and applied. That pressure is less in the case of concrete review: as long as the administrative authority does not take any decisions, which are contrary to Community law, it does not itself have much of a problem. Of course the legislature is still under a duty from European law to amend the legislation, but the pressure is clearly less. On the other hand, it must be said, there is really no need for additional pressure on the legislature, as Community law has other methods of producing results. Relevant in this respect are, for example, infringement proceedings, financial sanctions, such as a penalty or a fine under Article 228 EC and *Francovich* liability.

The main argument against abstract review is that the courts in fact take a decision, which extends beyond what is strictly necessary to settle the conflict at hand and whose effects are therefore too far-reaching and disproportionate. Abstract review not only prevents administrative authorities from taking decisions which are contrary to Community law, but also from taking decisions which are in conformity with Community law. However, this argument, which is also relevant in a purely national context, has lost a great deal of its importance as far as European law is concerned now the Court of Justice in *Kraaijeveld* has so

31 Council of State 8 August *Tholens Livestock Farmer* [1997] *M and R* 1997/11, no. 126.

32 Cf. Jans, de Lange, Prechal and Widdershoven, *Inleiding tot het Europees bestuursrecht*, Nijmegen 1999, in particular Chapter 3.

emphatically directed the national courts to examine national legislation to see whether the legislative authorities have remained within the limits of their discretion under Community law.[33]

Another important argument in favour of concrete review concerns what might be termed the "integrated legal order". In this view, national and European law are regarded not as separate entities but as a single, interrelated legal order. This view, which has a certain ideological attraction, implies that conflicts should be avoided as far as possible. Abstract review prevents decisions, which do in fact meet the requirements of Community Law, from being upheld, whereas upholding them would be possible using concrete review. In this sense concrete review is a less "blunt" instrument than abstract review.

As to the question whether there is a preference in European law for either of the two methods, there are no unambiguous indications one way or the other in the decisions of the Court of Justice. In principle this seems to be a matter for domestic law, in accordance with the principles laid down in *Rewe* and *Comet*.[34] Nor do the Dutch administrative courts seem keen to provide information on this point. Only rarely are reasons to be found in their decisions, which justify either concrete or abstract review. The criteria applied by the administrative courts when choosing between abstract and concrete review apparently include the nature and extent of the defect in implementation, the object and scope of the directive, the consequences of the decision and the interests at stake.

Indirect Review Indirect review is what we would like to call the situation where the Council of State does not rule on the question of compatibility with EC law as such, but annuls a decision because the public authority did not even consider the question of compatibility with EC law. In these cases the Council of State will quash the decision because it finds the reasoning insufficient or the decision not prepared with due care.

A good example of this is the *Urenco* case.[35] Permits had been granted to Urenco under nuclear energy legislation allowing, among other things, the possession and disposal of nuclear material. In the course of legal proceedings it was argued that the permit violated Article 6 of the Euratom Directive concerning radiation levels. Under Article 6 a permit may only be granted if the "ALARA" ("as low as reasonable achievable") and "justification" principles have been taken into account. The court considered that the relevant administrative authority should have examined the permit in the light of the provisions of the Directive. Since there was no evidence that any such examination had taken place, the court annulled the permit as being in breach of the principle that administrative decisions must be prepared "with due care". The substantive issue of whether there had been a breach of either the ALARA or the justification principle was not, however, considered.

33 Case C-72/95 *Kraaijeveld* [1996] *ECR* I-5403. Cf. on Kraaijeveld also J. H. Jans, *European Environmental Law* (Groningen, 2000).
34 Cf. case C-120/97 *Upjohn Ltd.* [1999] ECR I-223
35 Council of State 27 March 1991 [1991] *M and R*, 424-428, with case note by Nijhoff.

The mere fact that the authority granting the permit had failed to carry out the examination was sufficient ground for nullification.

This method has also been applied with respect to the EIA Directive. Several permits have been annulled by the Council of State by reason that the public authority issuing the permit did not consider whether there was a significant impact on the environment.[36]

This method of judicial review is of course particularly interesting in cases where there is considerable room for discretion for public authorities. It enables the court to exercise its duties without trespassing on the prerogatives of the administration.

Dutch Case Law on Procedural Defects and the EIA Directive

In light of the above the question we will now address is how the Council of State deals with the issue of procedural defects in a European environmental law context, in particular in relation to environmental impact assessment proceedings. The relevant Dutch case law will be discussed below.

In the first place it should be noted that there is established case law of the Council of State concerning what should be done when a public authority has taken a decision without the prescribed environmental impact assessment having been made. We are not aware of any judgment of a Dutch Court where the failure to submit an EIA did not lead to the annulment of the contested decision. Without exception these administrative decisions were quashed. As far as Dutch administrative law is concerned, the question to what extent an impact assessment, if it had been made, might have affected that decision is irrelevant. The case law can best be illustrated by the *Kraaijeveld* and post-*Kraaijeveld* decisions.

In the *Kraaijeveld* case one of the questions at issue was to what extent certain construction work on the dykes was subject to prior environmental impact assessment under Articles 2(1) and 4(2) of the "old" EIA Directive. Article 2(1) contained the general requirement that "projects likely to have significant effects on the environment" are made subject to environmental impact assessment. This general obligation was further specified in Article 4(1) in combination with Annex I of the Directive, which lists which projects must be made subject to an assessment in any event. There is no question of policy discretion here. Article 4(2) in combination with Annex II clearly gives the national legislature, which has to implement the Directive, greater discretionary power. So much, in fact, that the Council of State denied the direct effect of the provision.[37] This was because the national legislative and administrative authorities were able to specify certain types of projects, which had to be made subject to an assessment and fix criteria and/or thresholds to determine whether or not an environmental assessment was required.

---

36 Cf. Council of State 13 July 1999 [1999] *AB* 441, with case note of ChB and Council of State 31 March 2000, to be published in [2000] *M and R*, with case note by J. H. Jans.

37 Council of State 3 August 1993 [1994] *AB* 287.

Construction work on the dykes, which the Court of Justice in this case held to constitute an Annex II project, was subject to an impact assessment in the Netherlands if the dyke in question was 5 km or more in length, with a cross-section of at least 250 m^2. The Court concluded that Article 4(2) did indeed confer on Member States a "measure of discretion", namely the discretion to fix further specifications, thresholds and criteria. However, that discretion was in turn limited by the obligation set out in Article 2(1) that projects likely to have significant effects on the environment are to be subject to an impact assessment. The national court was instructed to examine whether the legislative or administrative authorities had remained within their limits of discretion and was thus required to examine whether the national legislation, in this case the Environmental Impact Assessment Decision, was compatible with Article 2(1) of the Directive. The Court did not require the national court to examine whether in the individual case of *Kraaijeveld* there was a project with significant environmental effects. The Court observed that the question whether a Member State has exceeded the limits of its discretion in setting the criteria and thresholds cannot be determined in relation to the characteristics of a single project. On the contrary, it depends on an overall assessment of the characteristics of projects of that nature. The Court lent the Council of State a further helping hand by observing that where a Member State establishes the criteria or thresholds necessary to classify projects relating to dykes at a level such "that, in practice, all such projects concerning dykes are exempted in advance from the requirement of an impact assessment", it is exceeding the limits of its discretion.

In this case the Council of State held in favour of the authorities. It held that there was no question of their exceeding the limits of their discretion. At the hearing the Ministry of Transport, Public Works and Water Management informed the Court that projects were being carried out which were defined as "construction of a dyke" within the meaning of the Delta Act, for which an impact assessment had been carried out in connection with the exceeding of the thresholds. The Council of State concluded "that as far as the construction of Delta dykes is concerned the situation referred to by the Court of Justice did not arise that the thresholds have been established at a level such that, in practice, all such projects are exempted in advance from the requirement of an impact assessment".

And in response to the question what the consequences are when the legislature has indeed exceeded the limits of its discretion under European law, the Council of State has given a decision in a similar case to *Kraaijeveld*, namely that of the *Tholens Livestock Farmer*.[38]

In that case the Council of State, referring to the judgment of the Court of Justice in *Kraaijeveld*, arrived at the conclusion that the legislature had exceeded its powers under Article 4(2) of the EIA Directive by entirely exempting businesses with pig rearing installations, mentioned in Annex II of the Directive as projects subject to Article 4(2), from the obligation of an impact assessment. The Council of State then declared the Environmental Impact Assessment Decision not

---

[38] Council of State 8 August 1997 [1997] *M and R* 126.

applicable and examined whether the plant which had been granted a permit might, in particular given its nature, size or location, have a significant effect on the environment as referred to in Article 2 of the Directive. In this case the Council of State constructed an EIA obligation via Article 2(1) of the Directive.[39] This approach seems to be in line with the judgment of the Court in the recent *Bozen* case.[40]

A different situation concerns the question what should be done where the public authorities have failed to examine whether the project in question is subject to an environmental impact assessment or not. This was the case in a recent decision of the Council of State.[41]

In that case the public authority had failed to examine whether the existence of a Special Protection Area within the meaning of the Wild Birds Directive implied that the project was subject to environmental impact assessment. Because the authority had failed to examine this sufficiently, the Council of State declared the permit void on the ground that administrative decisions must be prepared with due care. The Council of State did not answer the question of whether a pig rearing installation – this case also involved a permit to keep pigs – is subject to environmental impact assessment or not and did not at all address the question whether, if an assessment had been carried out, this would have affected the grant of the permit.

A next category of court judgments concerns the possibility allowed by the Directive to grant an exemption from the obligation to carry out an environmental impact assessment. On this issue, too, the judicial decisions are unambiguous. Where an exemption is granted on grounds, which are not covered by the Directive, this will inevitably lead to the administrative decision being declared void.[42] In the case of *Rosmalen v. Geffen* the authorities granted an exemption from the obligation to carry out an impact assessment in connection with the construction of a motorway. The exemption was granted on the strength of national legislation, which was formulated much more widely than Article 2(3) of the Directive permitted. In this case the court did not examine the decision to exempt the project from environmental impact assessment in the light of the Directive but instead ascertained whether the Dutch legislation was in conformity with the Directive's requirements. As it appeared that the grounds for exemption applied more widely in the Dutch legislation than the specific and exceptional cases required by the Directive, the court judged the legislation to be inapplicable. The

---

39 Cf. also Council of State 23 December 1997, E01.94.0457. In this case a zoning plan relating to the widening of the A16 motorway was adopted without an environmental impact assessment having been carried out. The court, taking the view that the legislature had exceeded the limits of its discretion under European law, concluded that the municipal council should not have adopted the zoning plan without a prior environmental impact assessment and that the provincial executive was thus unable to approve it.

40 Case C-435/97 *World Wildlife Fund v. Autonome Provinz* [1999] ECR I-5613.

41 Council of State 13 July 1999 [1999] *MR* 50.

42 Council of State 11 November 1991 *Rosmalen/Geffen* [1992] *AB* 50.

decision to exempt the project from an impact assessment was subsequently quashed.

Concluding Remarks on Dutch Law

This study can be summarised as follows. When, either in a specific case, or based on a general consideration of the national legislation in question, it turns out that a required environmental impact assessment has not been carried out, an administrative court will quash the permit. The question whether the lack of an environmental impact assessment would have resulted in a materially different decision is irrelevant in the Dutch context and is not examined by the courts. The administrative courts do not regard the lack of an environmental impact assessment as a procedural defect, which can be remedied by application of Article 6:22 or 8:72 of the *Awb*. It makes no difference whether the obligation to carry out an impact assessment is based on European law or not. Even the failure to fulfil "purely" national environmental impact assessment obligations (after all, the Directive leaves it open to Member States to take more stringent measures) cannot be repaired with the aid of the General Administrative Law Act. Under the non-discrimination principle laid down in the *Rewe* and *Comet* cases, Article 6:22 or 8:72 *Awb* cannot be used in respect of EIA obligations based on European law either.

Dutch Law in a Comparative Context

The way in which a directly effective provision can be invoked in the national legal system and the form in which this occurs depend largely on national law. According to the established case law of the Court of Justice it is for the national legal order of each Member State to designate the competent courts and to lay down the procedural rules for proceedings designed to ensure the protection of the rights, which individuals acquire through the direct effect of Community law.[43] Hence, private individuals are first and foremost dependent on the legal procedures established by national law. Because national procedural law also varies from one country to the next (e.g., differences in time limits for appeal,[44] standing requirements, access to legal aid, intensity of judicial review,[45] court fees, etc.), comparable proceedings may produce very different outcomes. Moreover, it is not

43 Case 45/76 *Comet* [1976] ECR 2043 and case 265/78 *Ferwerda* [1980] ECR 617.

44 Cf. English Court of Appeal 12 April 2000 Regina v. North West Leicestershire Country Council, East Midlands International Airport Ltd. ex parte Moses, n.y.o.r. Reasonable time limits have been upheld as being compatible with the requirements of Community law; case C-188/95 Fantask [1997] ECR I-6783. In the Fantask case the Court more or less retracted from its earlier decision in case C-208/90 Emmott [1991] ECR I-4269.

45 Case C-120/97 *Upjohn Ltd.* [1999] ECR I-223.

always easy to determine whether or not a rule of national procedural law can be applied. The other reports in this volume, in particular the German and UK reports, make it quite clear that according to their legal orders there is a discretion for courts to decide that the failure to submit an EIA does not necessarily lead to the annulment of the permit. How does this divergent national case law relate to European law itself, in particular to the EIA Directive?

Focusing on the Dutch situation, this question leads us to the question what would be the consequence if, hypothetically speaking, Article 6:22 *Awb* would have been applied in respect of EIA obligations based purely on national rules? Would it then also be possible to apply Article 6:22 *Awb* in respect of European EIA obligations? Again based on the non-discrimination requirement of *Rewe* and *Comet*? We see some problems in that respect. It is clear from the *Kraaijeveld* and *Bozen* cases that the obligation to carry out an environmental impact assessment is directly effective and that the Directive itself provides very clearly that no project will be carried out unless there is an EIA submitted. In other words, the Directive has harmonised the issue and provides for a directly effective answer on what to do when no EIA has been submitted. This means that the public authorities cannot take a valid decision without a prior impact assessment. In our view the directly effective provisions of the Directive stand in the way of application of national law, such as Article 6:22 *Awb*, which might repair the breach of its procedural requirements. Also, one can say that applying national procedural rules like Article 6:22 *Awb* to remedy the failure to submit an EIA would run counter to the objective of the Directive and would therefore be in violation of the *bona fide* principle enshrined in Article 10 EC.[46] Under these circumstances, it is the authors' view, that the *Rewe/Comet* doctrine cannot be applied.

From this, the more general conclusion can be drawn that the non-discriminatory application of national procedural law is only possible in those cases where its application does not infringe directly effective procedural standards of European law and thus affects the central objective of the Directive.[47] The EIA Directive is essentially a procedural directive and its key objective is that certain procedures are being followed. Application of Article 6:22 *Awb* to make up for the lack of a required EIA would however, in our view, impair the objective of the obligations resulting from Article 4 juncto Article 2 of the EIA Directive and seems therefore not to be permitted.[48]

The Directive thus seems to harmonise the administrative procedure *and* the legal consequence of non-effectuation of an EIA (annulment) since this is a central requirement of the Directive. This implies also that minor procedural mistakes, which do not affect the central objective of the Directive, may be accepted.

---

46 Cf. House of Lords 6 July 2000 *Berkeley v. Secretary of State for the Environment*, n.y.o.r. According to the House of Lords, a court exercising its discretion to uphold a planning permission which has been granted contrary to the provisions of the EIA Directive, would seem to conflict with Article 10 EC Treaty.

47 See for instance in the area of public procurement case 103/88 *Fratelli Costanzo* [1989] ECR 1839.

48 This would probably also apply to Article 8:72 *Awb*, see below.

A good example of the above may be found in the judgment of the Swedish Supreme Administrative Court regarding the cessation of the right to operate the nuclear power reactor Barsebäck 1. In response to the question what to do when a non-technical summary has not been produced in violation of Article 5(2) of the Directive the court considered: "... *it is evident in the view of the Supreme Administrative Court that a publication of a non-technical summary would not have contributed anything new to the matter and that accordingly the defect that can be considered as having existed in relation to the requirements of the Directive lacked significance for the Government decision*".[49]

In a Dutch case before the Council of State on the EIA Directive the court found that the violated provision lacked direct effect. In this case the Commission had not been notified of the decision to grant an exemption of an EIA.[50] Projects within the scope of the EIA Directive do not always have to be assessed if they come under the exception of Article 1(5) or Article 2(3). The condition is, however, that the Commission should be notified of the reasons for granting the exemption before the licence was granted and that it should be supplied with all relevant information. The Dutch court states that the absence of notification does not automatically entail the illegality of the exemption and/or the licence. The provision does not require the Commission's previous approval for granting an exemption or a licence. The provision only regards the relationship between the Member State and the Commission and does not grant any rights to individuals, which Member States would violate in the absence of notification.[51]

Moreover, even if the central obligation has been violated there may be room for application of national rules of procedure, provided this does not undermine the objective of the directive. An example would be national time limits, which must be observed by applicants for judicial review. It goes without saying that the observance of these national procedural rules does not affect the objectives of the EIA Directive. So even if a permit has been granted without a required EIA having been submitted, the "standard" national time limits must be observed.

An example is provided by the *East Midlands International Airport* case before the English Court of Appeal.[52] In this case a renewed application for permission to move for judicial review was made in connection with the extension of the runway at East Midlands International Airport. The proposed ground of challenge was that the consent for the extension had been granted without first considering "the environmental information" and to that end requiring an environmental statement. An earlier application had been refused for reasons of delay. In this case the court recognised the direct effect of Article 4 of the Directive, but stated:

---

49 Swedish Supreme Administrative Court on 16 June 1999, case no. 1424-1998, 2397-1998 and 2939-1998, n.y.o.r., *Barsebäck 1*.

50 Council of State 16 June 1995 [1995] *M and R* 93.

51 Cf. case 380/87 *Balsamo* [1989] ECR 2491.

52 English Court of Appeal 12 April 2000 *Regina v. North West Leicestershire Country Council, East Midlands International Airport Ltd. ex parte Moses*, n.y.o.r.

> I see nothing in Kraaijeveld that would deprive the Court of its discretion in relation to time limits. The fact that there exists an arguable breach of Community law does not mean that normal procedural safeguards, including those that are there to protect legal certainty, have to be thrown out of the window. National time limits apply, reasonable time limits have been upheld as being compatible with the requirements of Community law.

The condition is that these rules satisfy the *Rewe* criteria of non-discrimination and effectiveness. Since the court found that the criteria were fulfilled the application was dismissed.

Some separate remarks may be made about Article 8:72 *Awb*. One may wonder whether the Directive allows the application of paragraph 3. Could we consider the application of paragraph 3 as entailing a sort of voidability, upholding legal consequences even after setting aside the decision, and does the Directive leave room for voidability (or does it demand that the decision is void without an EIA)? In our opinion, paragraph 3 does provide a sanction for non-compliance but will just as well jeopardise the objective of the Directive, as it does not ensure the effectuation of an EIA either. The practical result would be the same, be it that the legal qualification would be different. Therefore the application of paragraph 3 does not seem to be permitted. Paragraph 4 could probably not be applied either. It does not seem to be a matter for the court to take a decision regarding EIA's, but for the administration.

Summing up, the EIA Directive provides a very good example of how EC Directives can influence national rules of procedural administrative law. In particular where the directive, like the EIA Directive, is primarily of a procedural nature, the room for applying "standard" national rules according to the *Rewe/Comet* doctrine, can be very limited indeed.

Annex

General Administrative Law Act (unofficial translation)

Article 6:22

A decision against which an objection has been made or an appeal has been lodged may, despite an infringement of a procedural rule, be upheld by the authority which rules on the objection or appeal if it is found that the infringement has not prejudiced the interests of the interested parties.

Article 8:72

1. If the court holds the appeal to be well founded, it shall quash all or part of the disputed decision.

2. The quashing of a decision or part of a decision entails the nullification of the legal consequences of that decision or the quashed part thereof.

3. The court may direct that all or part of the legal consequences of the quashed decision or the quashed part thereof shall be allowed to stand.

4. If the court holds that the appeal is well founded, it may direct the administrative authority to make a new decision or to perform another act in accordance with its judgment, or it may direct that its judgment takes the place of the quashed decision or the quashed part thereof.

3. The court may set the administrative authority a period for the making of a new decision or the performing of another act.

4. The court may determine that a provisional remedy will cease to have effect at a later time than the time at which it has given judgment.

6. The court may determine that if or as long as the administrative authority does not comply with a judgment, the legal person designated by the court shall owe a penalty prescribed in the judgment to a party designated by it. Articles? 611a to 611i inclusive of the Code of Civil Procedure shall apply *mutatis mutandis*.

Algemene wet bestuursrecht (Original Text in Dutch)

Art. 6:22

Een besluit waartegen bezwaar is gemaakt of beroep is ingesteld, kan, ondanks schending van een vormvoorschrift, door het orgaan dat op het bezwaar of beroep beslist, in stand worden gelaten indien blijkt dat de belanghebbenden daardoor niet zijn benadeeld.

Art. 8:72

1. Indien de rechtbank het beroep gegrond verklaart, vernietigt zij het bestreden besluit geheel of gedeeltelijk.

2. Vernietiging van een besluit of een gedeelte van een besluit brengt vernietiging van de rechtsgevolgen van dat besluit of van het vernietigde gedeelte daarvan mee.

3. De rechtbank kan bepalen dat de rechtsgevolgen van het vernietigde besluit of het vernietigde gedeelte daarvan geheel of gedeeltelijk in stand blijven.

4. Indien de rechtbank het beroep gegrond verklaart, kan zij het bestuursorgaan opdragen een nieuw besluit te nemen of een andere handeling te verrichten met inachtneming van haar uitspraak, dan wel kan zij bepalen dat haar uitspraak in de plaats treedt van het vernietigde besluit of het vernietigde gedeelte daarvan.

5. De rechtbank kan het bestuursorgaan een termijn stellen voor het nemen van een nieuw besluit of het verrichten van een andere handeling.

6. De rechtbank kan bepalen dat een voorlopige voorziening vervalt op een later tijdstip dan het tijdstip waarop zij uitspraak heeft gedaan.

7. De rechtbank kan bepalen dat, indien of zolang het bestuursorgaan niet voldoet aan een uitspraak, de door haar aangewezen rechtspersoon aan een door haar aangewezen partij een in de uitspraak vast te stellen dwangsom verbeurt. De artikelen 611a tot en met 611i van het Wetboek van Burgerlijke Rechtsvordering zijn van overeenkomstige toepassing.

Chapter 5

Judicial Control of Administrative Procedural Mistakes in Germany: A Comparative European View of Environmental Impact Assessments

Karl–Heinz Ladeur and Rebecca Prelle*

Introduction

Procedural administrative law in Germany is characterised by its strong orientation around the protection of subjective rights.[1] This is an ambivalent basis for a conception of administrative procedure in complex cases, and I will focus on it exclusively.

The centrality of subjective rights excludes all kinds of interests from having an input into administrative decision-making. Even when they are given the opportunity to be heard this might not be due to a right in a strict sense, but might instead be based purely on administrative logic. That is, it might seek to assist an administration that might find it difficult to take all aspects of a case into consideration. So participation in administrative processes is granted either in support of individual rights or as an "objective" contribution to the improvement of fact finding.

This conceptualisation has important consequences for the judicial protection of procedural participation. It is not regarded as an acknowledgement of the necessity of a pluralistic process for *constructing* a factual basis for decision-making and a bargaining element. Whereas in the case of a procedural right to participation linked to a substantive right (property, right to health care, etc.) the procedural element is taken to be just a secondary element which is subservient to the guarantee of the substantive right as such: it may only be invoked as an argument in defending one's right before the court but not for its own sake.

---

* Translated by Iain L. Fraser, European University Institute, Italy.

1 E. Schmidt-Aβmann, in F. Schoch / id. / R. Pietzner, *Verwaltungsgerichtsordnung* (München: Beck, 1999), Introduction No. 18 ss.

Moreover, this conception implies a considerable restriction of the potential for defending a substantive right because it is ultimately the administration that is expected to be able to take into account all facts in an objective way; the individual, by contrast, only pleads his limited subjective position. This might even limit the range of control of the arguments given by the public authority because the right to health and other rights defined by the laws (as opposed to property) can only be invoked on the basis of facts related to this individual right (and not protection of health as such). The administrative court will examine administrative procedure and fact finding only on this condition.

This short remark shows that one has to be careful when establishing conceptual schemes of European administrative systems. The notion of a confrontation between a rights-based conception and a conception centred around protection of the executive might be misleading because the German legal system regards the administration as the interpreter of the public interest as well. It perhaps does so no less than systems that respect the rationality of the executive more openly. The main difference is instead to be found in the type of discourse. The German system is much more "legal-deductive" than focused on specific administrative discretionary rationality. One of the side-effects of the German conception is the devaluation of the creative and constructive element of decision-making, as far as fact finding and the design of the procedure is concerned. This also has consequences also for the intensity of the protection of procedural rights before the courts.

The most striking difference between the German system and others in Europe is the fact that *discretion* is not accepted with reference to fact-finding in Germany, and nor is it relevant for assessing the weight of conflicting interests. In Germany, discretion's only role concerns the preference attributed to conflicting interests and the choice of possible alternatives. For instance, administrative discretion concerning the design of a road would be legitimate. There are only a few contrary examples of a type of discretion in evaluating facts which are limited to cases of a very specific expertise (such as concerning art or the examination of students) which in environmental cases normally cannot be referred to. Only in cases where the precautionary principle is at stake (such as those involving air pollution, as opposed to protection of health as an individual right), is it possible to use a kind of discretion concerning facts. A hard look at all the facts with the potential to affect the administrative decision-making process might greatly increase the risk that an administrator's decision will be struck down by a judge (in spite of the reservations I indicated previously). The is because the court sees itself as on a par with the administration as a guardian of the public interest. This situation led to different legislative approaches that were intended to limit the tendency of courts to overrule the administration (for quite some time, courts regularly overruled the administration, particularly in cases concerning town planning by local governments). One measure taken by the legislator was the extension of the possibility of awarding compensation for procedural and factual errors after the fact (Heilung, § 45 Verwaltungsverfahrensgesetz). Another method was to limit the possibility of invoking procedural infringements and errors in fact-finding to cases in which a causal link could be identified between errors and the decision (§ 46 VerwVerfG in particular). According to the dominant position in literature, this introduces – into administrative law the possibility that the revocation of an illegal act may be denied. This is functionally equivalent to allowing discretion in fact-finding.

Both models have provoked intense discussion as to whether this tendency conforms with the rule of law.[2] There are two alternatives in the case of a requirement of causality between procedural and factual mistake. One concerns the *legal* alternative that is often possible when the administration has a leeway of discretion. Errors in fact finding might have "infected" the use of discretion. Much more problematic is the supplementary test to determine whether there was *a practical alternative*. This is problematic evaluation is the role of a judge who must second-guess the administrative strategy. What difference would it have made to the outcome if a certain fact omitted from the evaluation of a natural resource had been evaluated in the administrative process?

Some authors consider that this kind of administrative behaviour lies beyond the duties of a judge,[3] and I would support this line of argument. The Federal Administrative Court's approach in these cases again raises a question about the consequences of the general approach to administrative procedure in Germany. It is quite consistent with the assumption that fact finding (and evaluation) has an objective character. This leads to a down-playing of the separation between courts and administrators but there is also the administrative domain of "balancing" conflicting interests. This separation is not accepted in most other European countries and leads to difficulties, especially in complex cases. Some problem-solving has been inconsistent, such as the choice of methods or the range of facts to be included in the decision-making process. Courts have thus allowed a certain "leeway" without defining it as administrative discretion. They have accepted methods as equivalent or accepted a dependence of fact-finding on the "situation" to be evaluated or the planning approach taken by a local government. But this not openly regarded as "administrative discretion".

Before demonstrating the consequences of this German approach with reference to environmental impact assessments and the consequences for the implementation of European law, I would like to draw attention to some crucial differences between German, French and English law.

In addition to the limitations of standing, one must be aware of the ambivalence of a conception requiring "one and only correct" objective legal decision. On the one hand, this allows an "illegal" decision (in the case of a procedural infringement) that is ultimately irrevocable because the legal "substance" (the decision as a product) was not affected. This presupposes that the "substance" can be separated from the process of decision-making, and that the judge is able and competent to distinguish between cases in which procedural infringement would

---

2 Cf. F. Hufen, "Heilung und Unbeachtlichkeit von Verfahrensfehlern", *Juristische Schulung* 1999, 313 ss.

3 Cf. Hufen, *Fehler im Verwaltungsverfahren* (München: Beck, 1998), 31.

influence the outcome and those in which it can be excluded. On the other hand, the Federal Administrative Court tries to simplify this task by a presumption that the factual basis set up by the administration was sufficient despite procedural shortcomings if the claimant cannot plausibly invoke a practical alternative that the administration might have chosen (for instance, in a town planning case).

The question may be raised whether this conception of procedure is compatible with the requirement of the "*effet utile*" to be guaranteed by Member States' general administrative law in the process of implementation of the specific European norms such as environmental law. Which standard should be derived from European law? Are Member States more or less free? Or does the principle of "*effet utile*" force Member States to guarantee a common framework for the general administrative law? Do we even need a common European administrative code? Or is it possible to find some common ground for administrative law that would give Member States more freedom in the interpretation of the "*effet utile*"? Is it possible to compensate between different effects? The German case would be a potential example of a contradictory effect as administrative law allows for a hard look at fact finding but court control is limited to cases where a practical alternative to the illegal decision cannot be shown.

The Example of the Environmental Impact Assessment

The application of European Environmental Impact Assessment law ("EIA") in Germany over the last eight years has disclosed some problems regarding the incompatibility of the EIA provisions with the underlying administrative-law structures of the respective Member States. There are fewer concerns about how to implement the EIA directive correctly. The procedural structure and the integrative assessment approach of EIA is not automatically effective in legal systems in which substantive questions are subject to intense supervision by the administrative court and procedural errors are less important (as in Germany). In application of the "*effet utile*" principle, it can therefore be asked whether national legal structures need to be adapted in order to secure effective application of the EIA provisions, or if the EIA objective could perhaps be reached using flexible, innovative, comparative-law methods. Observations drawn from various Member States' systematic approaches to administrative court monitoring and the resulting consequences for EIA application could perhaps be applied in Germany.

We shall now present the German case law regarding EIA errors. This is followed by American, British and French laws' approaches to determining the consequences of error and the absence of EIAs. Finally, possible conclusions concerning the further development of German law and its harmonisation with European law will be put forward.

German Case Law on EIA

Most judicial decisions on EIA and the consequences of its absence or defectiveness in the context of technical licensing decisions have occurred in relation to highway planning decisions. It is not important that the judgments of some second instance regional administrative courts (such as the Bayrische Verwaltungsgerichtshof and Oberverwaltungsgericht Koblenz) have not accorded with the Bundesverwaltungsgericht as this outcome resulted from a differing evaluation of the status of EIA in the context of permit procedure.

BVerwG Decisions

From the outset, the BVerwG (Federal Administrative Tribunal) equated the absence or defectiveness of EIA with other procedural errors. The consequence was that simply establishing non-compliance with EIA provisions did not give an entitlement to those affected by expropriation[4] to have the decision establishing a highway set aside.[5] Highway law §17 VI (c), first sentence, Bundesfernstraßengesetz applies in that regard, so the error must have been obvious and must have influenced the decision. As with other procedural errors, and in accordance with the BVerwG's traditional causality case law developed on the basis of § 46 Verwaltungsverfahrensgesetz (concerning procedural infringements), this sort of relevance of an EIA defect is asserted where there is a practical possibility that the decision – the highway planning order – would have been different but for the error.[6] Where there is no EIA, the BVerwG investigates whether the environmental interests raised in the reasons for the decision require an EIA. The BVerwG does not see the introduction of EIA as substantively intensifying the requirements to be weighed into the decision-making process; environmental interests that were hitherto regarded irrelevant remain irrelevant, and environmental interests are not awarded priority treatment.[7] For the planning authorities, the EIA is a formalised, intermediate step intended to dissipate, in the examination of interests that would otherwise be centralised, discovery and assessment of the effects of the project on the environment. It is only because it is "tak[en] into account" pursuant to § 12 UVPG (EIA-Statute) in the context of the

---

4 Only those affected by prior expropriation can, on the prevailing view, criticise objective errors, meaning also errors in EIA procedure, in the decision. On this cf. the judgments of the BVerwG of 18.03.1983, Deutsches Verwaltungsblatt 1983, 899 ss.; OVG Koblenz, of 29.12.1994, DBVl (1995), 146, 147.

5 Cf. only BVerwG judgments or orders of 23.02.1994, DVBl. 1994, 763; of 21.07.1994, BVerwGE 96, 239; of 18.05.1995, NuR 537, 542; of 8.06.1995, DVBl. 1995, 1012 ss.; of 25.01.1996, DVBl. 1996, 677; of 28.02.1996, UPR 1996, 270, 271; of 21.03.1996, NVwZ 1996, 1016 ss.; of 17.02.1997, NuR 1998, 305 ss.; of 21.2.1997, NuR 1997, 353, of 19.5.1998, NVwZ 1998, 961 ss.

6 For §17 VI c FStrG no other criteria apply in this connection; cf. BVerwG, judgment of 16.8.1995, UPR 1995, 445.

7 BVerwG, judgment of 21.03.1996 (Fn. 5) 1018.

planning decision, that the EIA receives substantive importance. However, this does not mean that some other way of introducing the same information about environmental effects to the decision-making process would always be inadequate.[8] Thus, in cases in which an EIA was not performed, the BVerwG has held that adequate environmental interests are raised to reject the possibility of another planning outcome.

Decisions of the BayVGH and OVG Koblenz

The BayVGH and the OVG Koblenz have a different approach because they perceive EIA more as an instrument for information procurement. In both courts, the EIA inspired new procedural and balancing structures that lead to better information about the likely environmental effects of a project. Like the BverwG, the BayVGH and the OVG Koblenz have both refused to intensify the substantive criteria used to assess environmental interests through EIA, although they do accentuate the autonomous importance of the formal EIA. Individual EIA provisions thus create an extremely close connection between the procedural law and the actual substantive requirement for the procedural and substantive balancing of conflicting interests in the establishment of a plan.[9] The judgments see the function of EIA as "guaranteeing correctness through procedure" or as "proceduralising environmental interests".[10] In addition, the EIA is viewed as a formal procedure that is intended primarily to compensate for factual uncertainties in relation to the likely environmental impact of a project.[11] Particularly after the explicit regulation of § 17 I FStrG, the courts therefore take the view that the constitutional requirement for balancing can only be satisfied by a balancing that takes the EIA into account. The relevance of an EIA defect can therefore be denied only if the possibility the error might have affected the decision can be ruled out.[12] Absence of the requisite formal EIA thus points to a defect in the balancing, and this presumption has to be refuted. In the few cases in which significantly different variants were offered, both courts affirmed the relevance of the absence of an EIA. And, in applying § 17 VI c, second sentence, the FStrG either set the decision aside or referred it back to the authorities for supplementation.[13] However, these decisions were not sustained by the BVerwG.

The courts – particularly the BayVGH – have placed great importance on the substantive quality of EIA. They therefore require comprehensive investigations of

---

8 BVerwG, judgment of 8.6.1995 (Fn. 5), 1015; of 25.1.1996 (Fn. 4) 680.

9 Cf. BayVGH, judgments of 19.10.1993. NuR 1994, 244; of 5.07.1994, DVB1. 1994, 1198, 1200; of 16.03.1993, NuR 1993, 285, 286; of 15.02.1996, A 94.40116; of 16.01.1995, 8 A 94.40083; OVG Koblenz, of 29.12.1994, ZUR 1995, 146 ss.

10 Cf. BayVGH, of 19.10.1993 (Fn. 9), 245; of 5.07.1994 (Fn. 9), 1198; OVG Koblenz (Fn. 9), 149.

11 Cf. BayVGH, of 5.07.1994 (Fn. 9), 1201; OVG Koblenz (Fn. 9), 150.

12 Cf. BayVGH, of 19.10.1993 (Fn. 9), 245; OVG Koblenz (Fn. 9), 149.

13 BayVGH, of 5.07.1994 (Fn. 9), 1200; of 15.02.1996, 8 A 94.40116; OVG Koblenz (Fn. 9), 150.

environmental effects. And, with questions that extend beyond the general state of knowledge, missing standards are expected to be discussed methodically through dialogue between experts on both sides.[14] However, the BVerwG has rejected this view on the ground that EIA is "not a search procedure in which all conceivable effects of a project on environmental values and their evaluations have to be studied in all details and the finest ramifications, or even answers to be found to questions still not clarified by science".[15]

Difficulties of Implementing European Environmental Law in German General Administrative Law: The Example of EIA

The controversy between the BVerwG and OVG Koblenz on the one hand, and the BayVGH on the other, shows that German law's difficulties with EIA did not end with the statutory adoption of the EIA directive into German environmental law. Instead, the debate continues as the directive is applied, and this is not surprising in light of the complex administrative procedures its application entails. The problem forms part of the transformation process associated with the necessity of decision-making in conditions of uncertainty (particularly in environmental and technical law). This is a major problem for a legal system hitherto used to either one-off decisions on the basis of general statutory commitments or the situational logic of decisions involving administrative discretion. The problem seems more worrying because the doctrinal search for possible links to the pre-existing regulatory pattern, or to its tentative further development, feels irritated by references to the European law requirements underlying the EIA Act.[16] This feeling is entirely justified because of the unavoidable acknowledgement of the existence of a European administrative law doctrine (at least in rudimentary outline) that offers an "ordering idea" for adapting the law to new requirements comparable with those

---

14 BayVGH, of 5.07.1994 (Fn. 9), 1201.

15 Cf. BVerwG, of 21.03.1996 (Fn. 5) 1018.

16 On this cf. only B. Becker, "Einführung in künftige Rechts- und Vollzugsprobleme des neuen Bundesgesetzes über die UVP" *Bayerisches Verwaltungsblatt* (1990), 353 ss.; J. Cupei, UVP (Köln u.a.: Heymann, 1986); E. Gassner, *Die medien- und verfahrensübergreifende UVP*, UPR 1990, 361 ss.; H.D. Jarass, *Auslegung und Umsetzung der EG-Richtlinie zur UVP* (Baden-Baden: Nomos, 1989); K.H. Ladeur, *Die Umsetzung der EG-Richtlinie zur Umweltverträglichkeitsprüfung in nationales Recht und die Koordination mit dem allgemeinen Verwaltungsrecht*, UPR 1996, 419 ss.; H. Soell and F. Dirnberger, *Bestandsaufnahme und Bewertung der Gesetze zur Umsetzung der EG-Richtlinie über Umweltverträglichkeitsprüfung*, UPR 1992, 212 ss.; R. Steinberg, "Chancen der Effektivierung der UVP durch die Gerichte?", *Die öffentliche Verwaltung* (1996), 221 ss.; A. Schink, Die UPV – eine Bilanz, NuR 1998, 174 ss.; W. Erbguth, Das BVerwG und die UVP – einige Anmerkungen ausgehend vom BVerwG-Urteil v. 21.03.1996 – 4 C 19/94 – NuR 1996, 589, in NuR 1997, 261 ss.; K. Lange, "Rechtsfolgen der UVP für die Genehmigung oder Zulassung eines Projekts", *DÖV* (1992), 780 ss.

of national administrative law.[17] The particular provisions of European environmental law have a more transnational, heterogeneous nature that is oriented towards cooperation and can be attributed to the rather unsystematic linkage of elements of various national administrative legal systems.[18] Accordingly, the solution to the problem of Europeanising administrative law[19] lies in the development of a comparative transnational doctrine that incorporates mutual observation,[20] the "transplantation" of individual regulatory components,[21] and the competition of rules.[22]

The Development of EIA in the US: Administrative Freedom in Establishing the Facts

EIA was developed by the US legal system[23] and then introduced into French and British law. However, looking closer, each of these legal systems displays considerable uncertainties regarding the procedural requirements for the conduct of EIAs. This is particularly noticeable in relation to the demarcation of responsibility between the administration and (administrative) courts. In these countries, administrations traditionally have relative freedom in the gathering and

---

17 Cf. E. Schmidt-Aßmann, Das allgemeine Verwaltungsrecht als Ordnungsidee (Berlin/Heidelberg: Springer, 1998), esp. 1 ss.

18 On this cf. again Schmidt-Aßmann, op. cit. (Fn. 17), 307 ss.; and in general J. Schwarze, Europäisches Verwaltungsrecht, 2 vols. (Baden-Baden: Nomos, 1988); idem (ed.), *Das Verwaltungsrecht unter europäischem Einfluß* (Baden-Baden: Nomos, 1996); B.S. Markesinis (ed), *The Gradual Convergence: Foreign Ideas, Foreign Influences and English Law on the Eve of the 21st Century* (Oxford: Clarendon, 1994).

19 On this cf. only F. Schoch, Die Europäisierung des Allgemeinen Verwaltungsrechts, Juristenzeitung 1995, 109 ss.; idem, *Die Europäisierung des verwaltungsgerichtlichen Rechtsschutzes* (Berlin/New York: de Gruyter, 2000), 45; E. Schmidt-Aβmann, "Allgemeines Verwaltungsrecht in europäischer Perspektive", *Zeitschrift für öffentliches Recht* (2000), 159 ss; D. H. Scheuing, Europarechtliche Impulse für innovative Ansätze im deutschen Verwaltungsrecht, in W. Hoffmann-Riem/E. Schmidt-Aßmann (ed.), *Innovation and Flexibilität des Verwaltungshandelns* (Baden-Baden: Nomos, 1994), 289 ss; idem, "Die Europäisierung des verwaltungsgerichtlichen Rechtsschutzes", *Die Verwaltung* (2001), 107 ss.

20 Cf. on the importance of practical "legal comparison" within the EC, E.A. Kramer, *Juristische Methodenlehre* (Bern/München: Stämpfli, 1998), 191 ss.

21 Cf. G. Teubner, "Legal Irritants: Good Faith in British Law or How Unifying Law Ends up in New Divergence", *Modern Law Review* (1998), 11 ss.

22 Cf. V. Vanberg and M.C. Kerber, "Institutional Competition among Jurisdictions", *Constitutional Political Economy* (1994), 113 ss.

23 From the literature cf. only S. T. French, "Judicial Review of the Administrative Records in NEPA Litigation", *California Law Review* (1993), 929 ss.; W. A. Tilleman, "Public Participation in the Environmental Impact Assessment Process – A Comparative Study of Impact Assessment in Canada, the U. S. and the EC", *Columbia Journal of Transnational Law* (1995), 337 ss.

assessing of the facts underlying administrative decisions.[24] By contrast, European EIA is intended to structure the administrative procedure more tightly in an immanent perspective focused on administrative rationality and intrinsic to administration, and an external perspective focused on informing the public.[25] That is, EIA is intended to limit the administration's "discretion as to the facts". Meanwhile the supervisory density of the case law recognising the primacy of the administration's expert knowledge in gathering the facts is recognised in principle.[26] Judicial definition of the legal limits of administrative action (including the administrations freedom to find the facts), is a doctrinal preoccupation that has not yet been solved.[27] It is therefore important to understand that the incorporation of EIA into German administrative law cannot occur simply through the adoption of European or American standards.

US case law on EIA holds that the extent of investigation must be determined "in proportion to significance". Otherwise, the "record rule" applies, according to which the courts are guided primarily by the administrative "record" (the *de facto* basis for the decisions). Particularly in connection with National Environment Protection Act ("NEPA") requirements, additional information and viewpoints are tendered in cases in which "serious environmental consequences" or the existence of a "reasonable alternative" are alleged. These extra viewpoints become relevant where the investigation is found to have been "clearly inadequate".[28]

It is also required that widespread opinions of the "scientific community" are taken into account. Beyond this, the "burden of analysis" lies with the administration which is primarily responsible for the actual investigation and its

---

24 Cf. French, op. cit. (Fn. 20), 956; J. Alder, "Environmental Impact Assessment – The Inadequacies of English Law", *Journal of Environmental* (1993), 203 ss.; B. Hough, "Relevance and Reasons in Planning Matters", *Journal of Planning and Environmental Law* (1998), 625, 629; on France cf. only A. de Laubadère and J. C Vénézia, *Traité de Droit Administratif*, vol. 3 (Paris: LGD, 1993), 324; G. Knaub, "Le contrôle par le juge administratif français de l'appréciation des faits" in J. Burmeister (ed.), *Die verfassungsrechtliche Stellung der Verwaltung in Frankreich und in der Bundesrepublik Deutschland* (Köln: Heymann, 1991), 129 ss.

25 This is why the introduction of EIA is assessed more positively by the administration in Britain than in Germany, where the technical level of environment decisions was already higher even before the introduction of EIA; cf. K. Marr, *Environmental Impact Assessment in the U.K and Germany* (Aldershot: Ashgate, 1997), 270; in the US too, the "educative effect" of EIA is stressed, French, op. cit. (Fn. 23), 965.

26 Cf. e.g. on France Knaub, op. cit. (Fn. 24), 144

27 Cf. G. Richardson and H.Glenn, *Administrative Law and Government Action* (Oxford: Clarendon, 1994), 146 f.; S. Ball and S. Bell, *Environmental Law* (London: Blackstone, 1991), 208 ss.

28 Cf. French, op. cit. (Fn. 23), 950 ss; Tilleman, op. cit. (Fn. 20), 382 ss; similarly in French law: here all that is verified is whether a manifest error of evaluation ("erreur manifeste d'appréciation") is present. Cf. de Laubadère and Vénézia, op. cit. (Fn. 21), 324 f,; similarly in the USA: "clear error of judgment" (Overton Park, 401 U.S. 402, 416 (1971); on English law cf. Richardson and Glenn, op. cit. (Fn. 24), 128; 146 ss.

extent.[29] The next stage requires appropriate balancing of the relevant facts, and consistent explanation and justification of the conclusion.[30] This is similar to the decision-making process of German planning law. However, American law administrations have discretion in both "gathering material for the balancing" and in weighing the interests.

In other respects, the American requirement of consistent justification of planning decisions differs from German law. The American requirement of explanation and justification serves primarily to inform the public rather than to protect individual rights. This is intended to improve the quality of the administrative decisions while also informing the public of environment protection requirements. The same goals are reflected in the fact that a plaintiff alleging the incompleteness of an EIA demonstrate that the project would "significantly" affect a relevant environmental factor.[31] The case law is not uniform in this respect[32] and the literature draws attention to cases insisting on the "completeness" of the basis for the decision; this because all information must inevitably be incomplete.[33] However, American law offers no clear criteria for this differentiation.

By contrast with the German legal position, the causality of a procedural error plays only a secondary role regarding the outcome in American law.[34] Once an essential procedural defect has been established, the decision will almost certainly be set aside or a new investigation ordered. This is quite consistent with a stronger distinction between administrative and judicial functions: the administration has primary responsibility for composing the decision and the court is limited to checking that the administration did not bypass its legal limitations. The American and German outcomes will often be similar, but the justificatory approaches are different. Watching procedural limitations is different to assessing substantive lawfulness.

Legal Limits on Administrative Establishment of the Facts in German Planning Law

German planning law[35] is strict in relation to the establishment of the facts. Although planning law cases occasionally speak of the administration's "creative freedom" , this creative power has not developed a doctrinal approach. The same

---

29 Cf. French, op. cit. (Fn. 23), 945 f., 956 f.; 977 f.

30 Cf. French, op. cit. (Fn. 23), 976 f.

31 Cf. French, op. cit. (Fn. 23), 985.

32 Cf. in general US Supreme Court 435 U.S. 519, 551 (1978) – Vermont Yankee, as well as on the verification of alternatives in EIA, decision 472 F 2 d. 693 (2d Circuit) 1972; cf. also Tilleman, op. cit. (Fn. 23), 392.

33 Cf. M. Shapiro, "The Giving Reasons Requirement", *Chicago Legal Forum* (1992), 179 ss.

34 English law is different here (see below).

35 Cf. only W. Hoppe and S. Grotefels, *Öffentliches Baurecht* (München: Beck, 2000), § 7 Rnr. 44 with further references.

can be said of checks on forecasts, which are frequently necessary in planning decisions.[36] Some discretion is accepted in the choosing of forecasting methods, but otherwise – especially regarding economic forecasts ("transactional requirements") – the narrow concept of "discretion in evaluation" is used. This does not recognise freedom in selecting the underlying facts themselves (at least, not explicitly).[37]

To the extent to which it may take its objectives into account in selecting the facts to consider, the administration has certain creative freedom in "gathering the material for the balancing" in planning law. In principle the relevance of facts is otherwise regarded as accessible to judicial control,[38] although the case law is not free from ambiguities in this respect. The collection and composition of material for balancing leads to a type of examination of open legal concepts which can only give a vague orientation to administrative decision-makers for the evaluation of complex situations, e.g. in planning law. Here the case law recognises limitations on guidance through legal concepts, though – in contrast to American, British and French law – without the giving the administration that degree of discretionary power.

This case law has received little criticism.[39] Only with the recent influence of European and comparative law has a sharper distinction been called for between the administration's creative tasks and judicial review in accordance with general rules in German law.[40]

---

36 From the earlier case law see only BVerwGE 34, 301; 45, 309, 56, 110; and Hoppe and Grotefels, op cit. (Fn. 35), § 7 Rnr. 56 ss., 108 ss.; K.H. Ladeur, "Die rechtliche Kontrolle planerischer Prognosen", *NuR* (1985), 81 ss.

37 A certain discretion in evaluating facts over and above the narrow limits of the discretion in assessment has for some years now been accepted in the case of general administrative measures in the variant of the "discretion in standardisation"; cf., from the case law, BVerwGE 72, 300 ss., 316, 320; and from the literature, R. Wahl, "Risikobewertung der Exekutive und gerichtliche Kontrolldichte – Auswirkungen auf das Verwaltungs- und das gerichtliche Verfahren", *NVwZ* (1991), 409 ss.

38 But see W. Hoppe, who has with good reason postulated stronger creative freedom for the administration in "gathering material for the balancing" in German law too, in Hoppe/Grotefels, op. cit. (Fn. 35), § 7 Rnr. 48 ss.; BVerwGE 59, 87, 103: the focus is on an objective criterion of the value of interests and their cognizability.

39 Cf. W. Hoppe, Die "Zusammenstellung des Abwägungsmaterials" und die "Einstellung der Belange" und die Abwägung "nach Lage der Dinge" bei der Planung, DVBl 1977, 136, 138; idem, Die Bedeutung von Optimierungsgeboten im Planungsrecht, DVBl 1992, 853 ss.; idem, Die Beimessung eines besonderen Gewichts nach § 7 Abs. 4, 1 Nr. 2 ROG 1998, DVBl 1998, 1008, 1010; cf. also M. Beckmann, W. Hoppe (ed), *UVPG-Kommentar* (Köln u.a.: Heymann 1995), § 12 Rnr. 108; cf., on the reviewing of evidence in a balancing between conflicting values, BVerwGE 56, 230, 283, 290.

40 Cf. C. Classen, Das nationale Verwaltungsverfahren im Kraftfeld des europäischen Gemeinschaftsrechts, Die Verwaltung 1998, 307 ss.; idem, Strukturunterschiede zwischen deutschem und europäischem Verwaltungsrecht, NJW 1995, 2457 ss.; Th. v. Danwitz, Rechtliche Optimierungsgebote oder Rahmensetzungen für das Verwaltungshandeln?, DVBl 1998, 928 ss.; F. Ossenbühl, DJT-Gutachten (50.DJT),

The requirement for structured assessment of environmental impact does not change anything here. Graduated assessment is also dependent on prior methodological and objective decisions as to the essentiality of environmental factors and the appropriateness of taking them into account. But the inherent problem lies in the modelling and design of administrative procedure; the apparently objective reference to the evaluation of the "state of things" ("Lage der Dinge") or assessment of effects on the environment, tends to suppress the unavoidable creative and subjective component of decision-making. The dependence of this "state of things" on a circumstantial evaluation does not, in principle, present an obstacle to legal control through the courts. Similarly, the testing of alternatives[41] is legally relevant only to the extent that alternatives must "impose themselves". This involves nothing other than a demonstration of procedural discretion, which is reduced only where an alternative seems to "impose itself". Conversely, this does mean that the administration *may* also examine further alternatives. It is not helpful to avoid a clear statement that the administration is exercising discretion in this situation, even though legal limits on the intensity of supervision through the administrative courts are noted.

EIA and the Administrative Freedom of Fact Finding in Britain and France

The Example of Britain

The statements we have made about American law's general "discretion as to facts" and particularly its EIA procedure can, in principle, also be applied to French and British procedural law.

English courts are very reluctant to acknowledge *legal* errors when reviewing alleged "errors of fact".[42] While review of procedure also covers "all relevant

---

München 1974, S. B 186; idem, *Gedanken zur Kontrolldichte in der verwaltungsgerichtlichen Rechtsprechung, Festschrift Redeker* (München: Beck, 1993), 55 ss., which calls for conceptualizing administrative court supervision not in terms of the concept but of the decision; cf. also E. Schmidt-Aßmann, Die Kontrolldichte der Verwaltungsgerichte – verfassungsrechtliche Vorgaben und Perspektiven, DVBl 1997, 281 ss.

41 Cf. only the BVerwG decision discussed here; and in general, G. Winter, *Alternativen in der administrativen Entscheidungsbildung* (Düsseldorf: Werner, 1997), 108 ss., 141 (on the EU-EIA).

42 Cf. Richardson and Glenn, op. cit. (Fn 27), 116 ss., 143; Hough, op. cit. (Fn. 24); the crossing of the legal boundary was formerly handled in accordance with the "Wednesbury" Test: the administration's decision could be set aside only where "no reasonable authority could ever come to it" (Ass. Prov. Picture Houses Ltd. v. Wednesbury Corp, 1948), 1 KB 223; most recently the case law has changed, though without taking on any clear shape; cf. Richardson and Glenn, 133, 150; S. De Smith, M. Woolf, J. Jowell and A. Le Sueur, *Judicial Review of Administrative Action* (London: Sweet and Maxwell, 1995), 284 ss.; cf. also Schmidt-Aßmann, op. cit. (Fn. 40).

facts" and the adequacy of evaluation, a technical "specialisation" gives the administration (by contrast with judges) greater scope to investigate factual questions. The testing of alternatives in English law also tends to adopt an immanent approach to the control of administrative consistency. The need to investigate the influence of procedural errors on the outcome is apparently not assessed uniformly. The case law initially assumed that an administrative activity based on defective facts is not to be set aside where an additional facts adduced by the administration support the outcome, even though the decision was not based on these secondary facts. However, in individual cases it has also been asked whether the error "caused" the outcome.[43]

The same problems also emerge in reviewing EIAs. One particular difficulty regarding EIAs is the absence of quality standards, making their legal limits hard to define.[44] The British literature contains a very pertinent reference[45] suggesting that reticence in assessing the factual basis for a decision is justified because the administration, on the basis of its expert knowledge, must develop a "coherent pattern" of decision-making into which the individual decision can be fitted.

The mere absence of an EIA does not make a decision unlawful in English law. It is only when this shortcoming amounts to an "essential" defect in the collection of facts that the decision is deemed to be unlawful. However, there is doubt in the literature as to whether European law requires a change to this position in Britain.[46]

These doubts are supported by a recent decision of the House of Lords in which the Court made a remarkable step towards a reasonable approach to the coordination of the administrative law of Member States, European environmental law, and the Environmental Impact Assessment Directive (*Berkeley v. Secretary of State for the Environment* and others, 6 July 2000). In contrast to the decision of the Court of Appeal and in accordance with the ECJ,[47] the Lords decided that the Directive's procedural requirements grant directly enforceable rights to individuals. The Court did not consider whether the outcome of a decision might have been influenced by an infringement.

The idea of the "inclusive and democratic procedure" of the EIA is preferred over the assumption that the facts and analyses compiled by the administrative

---

43 Cf. Hough, op. cit. (Fn 24), 628; Alder, op. cit. (Fn. 24), 214; on EIA in general cf. also Ball/Bell, op.cit. (Fn. 27), 208; V. Moore, *Planning Law* (London: Blackstone, 1992), 198 (specifically on the quality of the investigation); C.E. Jones and C.H. Wood, "The Impact of Environmental Impact Assessment on Public Inquiry Decisions", *Journal of Planning and Environmental Law* (1995), 890 ss., P. Kunzlik/B. Jacobson, "Environmental Impact Assessment: The British Cases", *European Environmental Law* (1995), 336 ss.

44 Cf. Richardson and Glenn, op. cit. (Fn. 27) s. 133, 150; Ball and Bell, op. cit. (Fn. 24), 208.

45 Richardson and Glenn, op. cit (Fn 27), 116 ss.

46 Cf. Moore, op. cit. (Fn. 43), 198; Jones and Wood, op. cit. (Fn. 43)

47 Case C-72/95 [1996] E.C.R. –5403, 5427 para 70., Opinion of the Advocate General Elmer, Kraaijeveld v. Staaten van Zuid Holland; Case C-435/97 [2000], CMLR 149 at 178, para. 70; WWWF v. Bozen.

authorities (but not the applicant seeking permission to undertake the project) might have given sufficient information to the administrative decision-makers. A "disparate collection of documents" which may be traceable only by "a person with a great deal of energy and persistence" cannot satisfy the requirement "to make available to the public the ... information which should have been produced by the developer". This is not only an important decision on the relationship between European and English administrative law, but it might become a cornerstone in the process of setting up a common European transnational legal order. It should also influence discussion in Germany. French court practices follow similar reasoning. However, the English decision is much clearer and more explicit. In addition, it is frequently uncertain in the French cases whether biased or incomplete information provided to decision-makers coincides with lack of transparency for the public, or whether the latter argument might be sufficient for the annulment of a decision made in contravention of the EIA Directive. The Lords have also made an important contribution to the role of procedure in administrative law, and this is all the more crucial once decisions become increasingly complex and deviate from shared experience.

The Example of France

French law also introduced EIA (known as the "*étude d'impact*") in a similar attempt to legally limit the administration's discretion as to the facts. And it did so even before the EC directive entered into force. It similarly separates errors of law ("*erreur de droit*") and factual errors ("*erreur de fait*"); the latter are subject to only limited review, especially where expert knowledge is required in order to determine the factual position.[48] The French case law also has to face the problem that factual errors and legal errors cannot always be clearly separated.[49] In relation to EIA, the investigation of the position must have been appropriately differentiated and be otherwise directed at completeness and "seriousness". However, this allows for quite substantial creative freedom.[50]

Both general administrative law and environmental law require that a procedural error has been "*déterminant*" before an action will be set aside, and this carries through to EIA procedure (Annulation).[51] Unlike the German practice of focussing on the causality leading to the decision, French case law tends to seek an intrinsic procedural standard, even if that might be unclear. The absence of an EIA is "*déterminant*" when this has impaired the consistency and utility of the factual material available as a basis for decision. The decision must be comprehensible to the public. In principle, the absence of an EIA is accordingly regarded to be a legal

---

48 Cf. de Laubadère and Vénézia, op. cit. (Fn. 24); on the effect of an error on a decision see Ch. Debbasch and C. Ricci, *Contentieux Administratif* (Paris: Dalloz, 1990), nos. 818, 830.

49 Cf. Knaub, op. cit. (Fn 24), 131.

50 Cf. Prieur, *Droit de l'environnement* (Paris: Dalloz, 1996), no. 97.

51 Cf. Debbasch and Ricci, op. cit. (Fn. 47), no. 830.

defect that leads to the administrative decision being set aside. Appropriate differentiations are made when an EIA is incomplete.[52] The more important the project, and the greater its potential consequences for the environment, the more serious and strict will be the requirements for a complete EIA.[53] For example, the Conseil d'État and the administrative courts have asserted the defectiveness of EIAs and set aside administrative decisions where serious before/after consideration of the environment was missing,[54] where the EIA was carried out too summarily,[55] where flora, fauna and biological equilibrium were not studied at all,[56] and where no peculiarities specific to the site were considered or analysed.[57]

It is very likely that these defective EIAs would have been set aside in accordance with the BVerwG's case law too; each case involved important environmental factors and the defective EIAs would have been regarded as "causative" in German law. However, there is a tendency to determine the completeness and appropriateness of the EIA according to more procedural issues, namely their suitability for informing the public and the requirement that the administration adhere to particular investigative standards.[58] The effect on the material outcome is irrelevant.[59] The Conseil d'État[60] also regards the testing of alternatives as unnecessary in principle.[61]

Omission of the cost calculation required by French law from the documented reasons for the decision may lead to the administration's decision being setting aside. This demonstrates the procedural reference of the decision-making criteria in

---

52 Cf. Conseil d'Etat (C.E.) of 23.03.1994, *Revue Juridique de l'Environnement* (1995), 328; C.E. of 29.07.1994, RJE, 328; Cour d'Appel Administrative (C.A.A.) Nantes of 19.02.1997, RJE 1997, 438.

53 C.E. of 24.10.1984, RJE 1984, 334; C.E. of. 14.10.1988, Cahiers juridiques de l'électricité et du gaz 1989, 189.

54 C.E. of 11.2.1983, Rec., 57; C.A.A.Nancy, of 2.4.1997, req. n° 94NO00798, RJE 1997, 438.

55 C.E. of 10.6.1983, Rec., 255; T.A. Caen, of 9.7.1996, req. n° 95, 601; T.A. of Rennes, 25.8.1989, RJE 1990, 113.

56 T.A. Limoges, of 1.2.1983, RJE 1984, 150.

57 T.A. d'Amiens, of 20.11.1992, RJE 1993, 577.

58 Cf. C.A.A. Lyon of 31.01.1995, RJE 1996, 155; Tribunal Administratif Nice of 20.04.1995, RJE 1996, 158 (set aside because the EIA was not a component part of the procedural documents); C.A.A. Nantes of 04.10.1995, RJE 1996, 160, C.E. of 27.03.1995, RJE 1996, 159.

59 The autonomy of the procedural reference framework can also be seen where the Dijon administrative court focuses on the EIA's suitability for informing the public. Cf. T.A. Dijon of 18.03.1997, RJE 1997, 439; C.A.A. Nantes of 19.02.1997, RJE 1997, 438.

60 Cf. C.E. of 24.02.1997, RJE 1997, 440.

61 The view is present in the literature that particularly the amendment of 03.03.1997 to the EC directive has to lead to a change in this case law, since now Article 5 (3) requires presentation of the major alternatives tested by the project presenters. On this cf. in general W. Sheate, "The Environmental Impact Assessment Amendment Directive 97/11/EC – A small Step forward?", *European Environmental Law Review* (1997), 235 ss; M. Prieur, note on C.E., op. cit. (Fn. 59), RJE 1997, 441.

French administrative courts, although the German approach would suggest the effect on the outcome is doubtful.[62]

What is the "Guiding Idea" of European Administrative Law?

This cursory survey of American, French and British law has confirmed that problems implementing EIA in German law are not simply related to adopting a European "transplant". They are instead transnational problems about how to make complex decision through new procedural forms, and they are common throughout the affected legal systems. It thus follows that EIA cannot be regarded as a European-law institution with clear outlines[63] to which German law would have to adjust. Recourse to the ECJ's "*effect utile*" case law cannot provide any further assistance, particularly with incorporation into and underpinning by national general administrative law. In particular, the unfair competition that then arises between economic agents in different Member States seems to be a barrier to this "effet utile". It is therefore important for Member States to be granted more room for coordinating national and European law, and for the development of a greater focus on a transnational learning process by mutual observation and practical comparison. In Germany, for example, this would include the possibility of developing separate ways of incorporating EIA into existing environmental law. More precisely, the question would have to be asked whether – following the approaches of foreign legal systems – the autonomy of procedural rationality and its linkage with rationality of outcomes ought to be improved.

The Importance of the Procedural Idea in a Comparative Perspective

The Need for a Distinction between "Essential" Procedural Errors and Causality

Let us merely sketch the German implementation approach. It can be stated that "learning" cannot occur by German law merely adopting a model developed

---

62 It is only because of special circumstances that the administration's decision *In re C.E.* of. 27.03.1997, RJE 1996, 159 was not set aside.

63 J. Schwarze's work tends to exaggerate *de facto* existing procedural "convergence" of European administrative legal systems into a relatively uniform European administrative law; cf. also idem, "The Convergence of the Administrative Laws of the EU Member States", *European Public Law* (1998), 191 ss.; this is presumably going too far, since it neglects the continuing considerable differences, which can very well also be used productively for learning by the various administrative legal systems (cf. also von Danwitz, op. cit. (Fn. 40); for a British view C. Harlow, "European Administrative Law and the Global Challenge", European University Institute, Florence *WP/RSC 98/23*, which rightly draws attention to the differing perception of the relationship between administration and judicial review in Europe; cf. also M. Chiti, "Towards a Unified Judicial Protection in Europe", *European Public Law Review* (1997), 553 ss.

elsewhere. In order to verify the issues, it would first have to be asked (initially without considering the outcome), whether the investigative strategy nonetheless showed a conception allowing appropriate establishment of the environmental impacts. That is, would the public and the administration both have received consistent information though the chosen procedure? The consequence cannot be that infringement of formal requirements of the EIA procedure would automatically (without regard to § 46 VwVfG) allow the administrative act to be annulled in accordance with European law. Nor could it establish a barely refutable presumption as to the influence of the defect on the outcome of the decision, as OVG Koblenz and BayVGH assume. Such a position is based on a misunderstanding of the procedural function: "proceduralisation" is not the same as a "guarantee of correctness" through procedure (compare this with the way in which a procedural infringement would reduce substantive unlawfulness). This evades the point that – as the BVerwG rightly states – EIA neither leads to a substantive increased valuation of environmental interests,[64] nor is a search procedure different in principle from other administrative planning procedures intended to produce a usable basis for decision under conditions of uncertainty.[65] Due to the absence of standards for a multimedia testing approach, specifically different investigative strategies have to be developed for various different types of EIA in order to specify and flesh out individual procedural elements. However, conducting an EIA cannot guarantee the correctness of a decision.

The Autonomy of the Test for Procedural Errors

In the absence of an EIA, the procedural error should be regarded as immaterial if the environmental interests have been appropriately considered and presented so that their importance in the "planning" procedure can be recognised both by the administration and by the public. In shaping the plan EIA in detail, for the administrative discretion should be recognised explicitly, and an appropriate theory of error developed.[66] This also meets the provision of Article 173 TEC for EC administrative law by introducing a relevance threshold for procedural errors.[67]

---

64 Cf. M. Schmidt-Preuß, Veränderungen grundlegender Strukturen des deutschen (Umwelt)Rechts durch das "Umweltgesetzbuch I", DVB1. 1998, 857 ss.

65 Cf. for a differentiatian between "action"- and "result"-oriented procedural norms R.Breuer, "Verfahrens- und Formfehler der Planfeststellung für raum- und umweltrelevante Großvorhaben", *Festschrift* (Köln: Heymann, 1996), 357ss.; cf. Generally K. H. Ladeur, "Umweltverträglichkeitsprüfung und Ermittlung von Umweltbeeinträchtigungen unter Ungewißheitsbedingungen", *Zeitschrift für Umweltpolitik und Umweltrecht* (1994), 1 ss.

66 For considerations on a unitary "discretion as to facts and as to legal consequences" see M. Herdegen, "Beurteilungsspielraum und Ermessen im praktischen Vergleich", *Juristenzeitung* (1991), 771 ss.; in general cf. also Danwitz, op. cit. (Fn. 41).

67 Cf. on review of procedures ECJ 1994, 1829 (1849 f.), nos 32-36 (PCP); in general cf. E. Pache, "Kontrolldichte in der Rechtsprechung der Gerichte der europäischen

In other respects, the administrative courts can and must develop their own procedural requirements based on their experience with the establishment of plans. Examples include how to take alternatives into account in relation, say, to the stage at which they have to be developed, with how much differentiation, and how long they have to "run together". The administration must itself develop practicable strategies oriented to learning and differentiation. Within the framework of its procedural discretion, it must be obliged to differentiate its strategies beyond the individual case and "pay" for its creative freedom itself through tighter procedural self-control.[68]

One should nevertheless ask how the courts can monitor the correctness of the choice of methods, or what criteria the developer should use to select the method. Especially where methods of investigation have not yet been tested, the developer must be entitled to some freedom in shaping the procedures. As provided in Article 16 II of the IPPC directive for emission limitations on new installations, EIA findings could also be collected in technical documents known as BVT leaflets.[69] This could give rise to practice guidelines requiring developers and authorities to orient themselves in researching environmental effects and courts in their substantive supervision.

Granting an assessment prerogative to developers and authorities in the selection of evaluative methods, should be linked to limited court control referring to a meta-level of methodological consistency in opening the models and the design chosen in a case according to standards of best administrative practices. Strengthening procedural control as a framework for method selection might guarantee more effective application of the EIA provisions, and might even make a more homogeneous application of EIA law possible in the European Community.

Only later would one have to ask whether the decision would also have affected the outcome. A presumption might certainly help once it has been established that the procedure no longer fits the basic requirements demanded of the decision-makers regarding the provision of information.

The BVerwG's case law is thus similar to that of the US, Britain and France. The BVerwG is also correct in its criticism of the careless linking of procedure with questions about the "guarantee of correctness". But procedural rationality necessarily implies a certain creative freedom for the administration, with the consequence that it must first be asked: having regard to the administration's

---

Gemeinschaften", *DVBl.* (1998), 380, 382; especially on the orientation to French standards in general administrative law, in relation to the test of discretion too.

68 These approaches to a room for manoeuvre free of judicial control for the project presenter or authority in selection of methods can also be found in Article 5 (1) of the EIA directive taken together with Annex III no 4/7, stating inter alia that project presenters should describe the "methods used" for preliminary estimation of the environmental effects, as well as any difficulties (technical lacunae or lack of knowledge) in gathering the requisite data.

69 Cf. also the presentation in K.-H.Zierock and N.Salomon, "Die Umsetzung des Art. 16 Abs 2 der EG-IVU-Richtlinie auf internationaler und nationaler Ebene", *ZUR* (1998), 227, 228.

creative freedom, can the factual position discovered be regarded as consistent and adequate?

Summary

German administrative law must – and not only in the area examined here – abandon some myths about the function of administrative court procedure in protecting individual rights.[70] It must also pay more attention to the rationality of administrative procedure (without, however, impulsively linking procedural law with a "guarantee of correctness"). A similar problem also arises from the IPPC directive;[71] the problems of implementation cannot simply be attributed to the influences of alien "transplants" into German administrative law. Here too it can be seen that the compulsion to "account for" various environmental impacts in permit procedures must ultimately lead to abandonment of the fiction of "strict legal binding" (of the sole correct decision) in permit procedures. This need not lead to administrative arbitrariness. The room for manoeuvre in decision-making can, and must, be shaped according to the type and level of decision at hand. This would simultaneously constitute an alternative to the more or less *ad hoc* recognition of "exceptional cases". The administration's freedom could then be narrowly limited (in permit procedures, for example). This is also necessary if of administrative legal doctrine is to adapt to the requirements of complicated administrative decisions that no longer fit the pattern of the application of legal norms to facts.

70 Cf. Danwitz, op. cit. (Fn. 37); it may be doubted that § 43 UGB-KomE will help here; but cf. R. Breuer, "Tendenzwende des Rechtsschutzes?" Betrachtungen zu §§ 43 ss. UGB-KomE, "Jahrbuch des Umwelt- und Technikrechts" (1998), 161 ss.; cf. also Schmidt-Preuß op. cit. (Fn. 63).

71 Cf. K. H. Ladeur, "Integrierter Umweltschutz im Genehmigungsverfahren", *ZUR* (1998), 245 ss.

Chapter 6

Administrative Review of Complex Decisions: Litigation on the Declaration of Public Utility in French Law

René Hostiou

Many administrative law decisions are subject to "complex"[1] procedures. They involve various participants, require a succession of different consultations, oblige the administration to associate those administered with its projects, and they require the public authorities to justify choices that are very often result from trade-offs between opposing legal principles, contrary claims and opposing interests. These decisions most often occur in particular contexts – participation, acting in concert, or even negotiation or co-decision – though, strictly speaking, they can be categorised as administrative decisions of a unilateral nature.

An example can be found in the "declaration of public utility" ("DUP"). This is a proclamation of by the State authorities (Prime Minister, Ministers or Prefects) on the general interest in an operation regarded as being of public utility. It follows a procedure of public consultation (public enquiry) after an opinion from the Commissioner of Enquiry and after consulting the *Conseil d'Etat*, where

---

1 The concept of a complex operation has a special meaning in French law associated with strictly LITIGATION-related considerations. There is a complex operation whenever, in a continuing process, a series of intermediate decisions taken in the framework of a given piece of legislation leads to a final decision, with the administrative judge then stating that in this case any appeal against these intermediate decisions is inadmissible, while authorising the petitioner to make use, on the occasion of an appeal against the final decision, of irregularities affecting these previous decisions. This is the case, for instance, with inadmissibility of an appeal against a decree opening a public enquiry, since this act is regarded as "not adverse", with the petitioner instead entitled to invoke irregularity of this act in support of an appeal against the declaration of public utility. Cf. M. Distel, "La notion d'opération administrative complexe", Rev. Adm. 1981, 370 ; F. Chevalier, "La fonction contentieuse de la théorie des opérations administratives complexes", A.J.D.A. 1981, 331 ; P. Chrétien, "De la belle carrière promise à la notion d'opération complexe", A.J.D.A. 1982, 20.

appropriate. It most often authorises the authorities to employ the procedure of expropriation in the performance of this operation.

Accordingly, the DUP is the compulsory "checkpoint" for any major planning operation (motorways, railway lines, power stations, etc.). It gives rise to quantitatively and qualitatively significant litigation, the scope of which is worth analysing.

A DUP can be appealed against on the ground that it is *ultra vires*, and success on appeal allows for cancellation of an administrative decision on grounds of illegality. It is generally accepted that the administrative judge hearing such an appeal should confine himself to verifying that the challenged decision confirms – or is compatible – with the law in the broad sense. That is, does it conform or is it compatible with the variety of established legal norms that bind the author of the decision due to the hierarchy of decisions. In these circumstances, a judge deciding whether there has been any breach of power is entitled to check only whether the administrative decision challenged is regular in law. He is not entitled to inquire into the "advisability" of the choices made by the administration. Nor may he ask how the decision might injure subjective rights of the applicant. He is instead confined to checking the administration's conduct against "objective" legality[2] and cancelling the decision if it is found to have been affected by unlawfulness.

This juridical check investigates both external legality (competence of the decision maker, and the form and procedure of the decision) and internal legality (error in law, illegality of grounds, purpose outside the notion of general interest). "External legality" relates not to what has been decided but to the regularity of the process of decision, the ways in detail according to which the challenged decision was taken. "Internal legality" concerns the content of the decision. In both cases, however, it is understood that the administrative judge confines himself to checking the legal regularity of the decisions by testing it against a set of pre-established rules; this analysis is independent of any subjective assessment or any value judgment relating to the nature of the interests at stake.

However, this classic, rather theoretical view of *ultra vires* litigation must be relativised. Only the physical or legal persons who can show a relevant interest have standing to challenge the legality of a decision, even though logically speaking this ought not to be necessary were an *ultra vires* appeal totally "objective".[3] However, a finer and more realistic analysis of such disputes demonstrates that the administrative jurisdiction does not totally abstract from the rights and interests of petitioners. More precisely, and contrary to what the classic

---

2 Cf. the works of F. Melleray: "Essai sur la structure du contentieux administrative français. Pour un renouvellement de la classification des principales voies de droit ouvertes devant les juridictions administratives à compétence générale" (Thése. Pau. 2000) and "Déclaration de droits et recours pour excès de pouvoir", Rev. Dr. Publ. 1998, 1089.

3 Even if the notion of "interest in play" is generally understood broadly, it will be noted that someone living in a municipality not directly affected by a decree declaring the public utility of motorway construction does not have such an interest. CE 29 January 1992, Poujol, G.P. 1992, 2, pan.dr.adm., 128.

theory might have us believe, it could be argued that in assuming the legality of a decision, the administrative courts sometimes tend to balance these interests against the infinitely more general ones upheld in the original decision. I shall seek to show this by, first, exploring verification of the external legality of the DUP and, second, exploring its internal legality.

Verification of the External Legality of the Declaration of Public Utility: Problems raised by Procedural Error

Procedural error is present *a priori* when any irregularity affects the process of production of a unilateral administrative decision (the "*negocium*"). It is obvious that the more complex the procedure leading to an administrative decision is, the more participants it involves, the more it contains safeguards to protect the administered and the more it is associated with delays, the greater the risk of omissions, errors and irregularities, be they voluntary or otherwise. In these circumstances, the sophistication of the procedures appears as a "fragility" factor in litigation concerning unilateral administrative decisions, an irregularity in French law (even if simply formal or procedural, or without any direct consequences for the content of the decision) may result in the cancellation of a decision. What does this mean for DUP?

Submission of the Project to Public Enquiry

i. The DUP follows a complex process in which the public enquiry procedure plays a central part. This is particularly reaffirmed by the law of 12 July 1983 that extends this requirement to any planning project likely to have a significant affect the environment.[4]

The DUP is a procedure prior to the decision that enables the public (owners, tenants, neighbours, various associations and all interested persons in general) to submit, on the basis of a dossier produced by the administration, their assessments, suggestions and counter-proposals on the carrying out of the projects, works or actions planned. The aim is to enable the competent authority to have available all the information necessary for making its decision. This dossier must contain details about the object and location of the operation, its technical features, its financial cost and its environmental impact (an Environmental Impact Assessment).

The public enquiry is conducted by a commissioner of enquiry – subject to the principle of independence and impartiality – designated by the president of the territorially competent administrative tribunal under the law of 12 July 1983.[5] This commissioner of enquiry, having considered the background, heard

4 Cf. R. Hostiou and J.-C. Hélin: "Droit des enquêtes publiques", Ed. du Moniteur 1993.

5 Cf. R. Hostiou: "Le commissaire-enquêteur nouveau est-il arrivé ?" : Rev. Fr. de Dr. Adm. 1998, N° 6, 1147.

the various parties and analysed the public reactions, is bound to draw up a personal, reasoned opinion of the operation in question. This opinion does not have the nature of a binding decision. However two essential consequences are to be noted if the enquiry commissioner's conclusions are unfavourable to implementation of the proposal:

(a) On the one hand, the DUP in this case requires a decree in *Conseil d'Etat* (taken by the Prime Minister after consulting the *Conseil d'Etat*), regardless of the nature of the project.

(b) On the other hand, should an action be brought against the DUP, securing a stay of execution is greatly facilitated. (A stay aims to block the directly "executory" nature of administrative decisions through its corollary that appeals do not have the effect of suspending the activity. It thus secures a provisional halt to the project.)

Any possible irregularities regarding the organisation and conduct of the public enquiry give rise to an action for procedural error,[6] and this has traditionally been regarded as separate from actions for substantive error.

ii. One can thus distinguish two hypotheses that raise difficulties of different natures when examined in light of the intensity of the administrative judge's supervisory powers and his discretionary powers.

There might be a simple omission of a requirement laid down by the texts, such as when a project has not – contrary to the provisions of the Act – been submitted to public enquiry, or the legally required Environmental Impact Study is not in the file. Then the answer is easy. If an appeal is lodged by any person with an actionable interest, the administrative judge's discretion is practically nil and the irregularity results in cancellation of the challenged activity.

Alternatively (and an infinitely more frequent type case), there might be various irregularities affecting the organisation or conduct of the procedure. Examples include the giving of inadequate publicity regarding the decision to open the enquiry, the identity of the commissioner of enquiry or the formulation of his opinion, or the composition of the file, the duration of the enquiry or non-respect for certain deadlines. Such irregularities lead the administrative judge to ask whether they have been sufficiently well characterised to justify cancellation of the impugned act, and to consequently distinguish "substantial" irregularities (that will bring about cancellation of the impugned activity), or whether they have an "accessory", "non-substantial" character that does not justify this sanction.

Nonetheless, it remains rather problematic to determine which criterion should decide whether procedural irregularities are "substantial". Various suggestions have been offered. These include the effect of the irregularity on

---

6 It will be noted that an action relating to the interpretation of the enquiry commissioner's conclusions has, since the prefect is empowered to make the DUP only if these conclusions favour the project, to do with incompetence rather than procedural flaw.

the actual content of the decision challenged, and the nature of the guarantees implied for those administered by of this procedure. If the irregularity is presented as "insubstantial", should the judge consider that it has had no affect on the content of the decision, or that it has failed to meet the expectations or attached to these formal requirements? Or, that it is "substantial" if there is a contrary finding, and "insubstantial" if the judge reaches the opposite conclusion?[7] This "simplistic" explanation does not exhaust the theme. The administrative judge uses this argument infinitely more subtly. And it is used differently depending on whether the challenged decision will be confirmed or overturned.

It is obviously particularly risky to seek to establish the effect of any irregularity committed in the course of carrying out a public enquiry, since the formality involved is purely consultative by definition. In general terms, there is no way of absolutely affirming that scrupulous respect for the texts would have led to adoption of any notably different decision. Similarly, unless it is considered that the ignored provisions were merely guidelines rather than binding laws, it is equally risky to ask about the effect of the alleged irregularity in relation to the guarantees that would be attached to the procedure.[8]

One should therefore have no illusions as to the explanatory value of these criteria. If the administrative judge makes reference to them, it is generally in negative terms. That is, the judge justifies his refusal to cancel an act for an excusable or venial irregularity by showing that the alleged irregularity had no adverse affect on the petitioners. For example, the justification might be that, despite the fact that the duration of the prior enquiry did not meet the law's prescriptions or that the publicity given to the opening of the enquiry seems insufficient, the petitioners were nonetheless able to present their observations so that the alleged irregularity was without effect for them.[9]

This does not however allow us to affirm *a contrario* that only irregularities of such a kind as to affect the sense of the decision or notably alter the guarantees attached to the proper conduct of the enquiry procedure are substantial in nature. When he intends to cancel the DUP, it is enough for an administrative judge to take note of the breach of the applicable text without having to show the effects of the irregularity committed or having to establish proof that scrupulous respect for the texts would have led to adoption of a different decision. Thus, one cancelled DUP had been taken following a public enquiry procedure organised on the basis of the provisions of the law of 12 July

---

7 Cf. our observations on CE 7 March 1975, Association des amis de l'abbaye de Fontevraud, AJDA 1976, II, 208.

8 This is what the administrative judge very classically does in finding that certain deadlines, in particular deadlines imposed on the commissioner of enquiry for submitting his conclusions following the public enquiry, have not been laid down for purposes of nullity, and that in consequence their breach need not lead to sanctions.

9 See e.g.: CE 3 July 1998, Association de défense et de protection de l'environnement de Saint-Côme-d'Olt, Rec. 283.

1983, even though the challenged project (creating sport, cultural and leisure infrastructure) came under the enquiry "by ordinary law". It was therefore impossible to consider whether this irregularity had affected the content of the challenged activity, nor whether it infringed any guarantees, as the procedure that was ultimately followed might appear to have been infinitely superior in this respect.[10]

It must be acknowledged that the multiplication of procedures, with the resultantly inevitable risk of irregularities, thus confers on the administrative judge an implicit "arbitration" function among the various interests involved. This is the source of many misunderstandings.[11]

The Surge in Actions Concerning External Legality: Consequences

i. The rise in the number of actions for external legality intrinsically associated with the very concept of a complex administrative decision is directly connected with some of the techniques for checking legality used by administrative judges in French law.

When administrative judges must hear appeals directed against a DUP relating to a controversial planning operation, and when those against the project concurrently invoke grounds of external and internal legality, the courts frequently apply a principle known as "economy of means". This enables them to adopt only one reason that they consider to be sound and capable entailing cancellation of the challenged decision, and it is not necessary for them to also analyse the other grounds of illegality raised by the petitioners.[12] It is therefore enough for administrative judges to note a ground of external legality (even where the scope of this procedural irregularity would seem entirely minor in relation to the issues at stake) in order to cancel the decision. They do not need to confront the basic problems raised by the petitioners.

For instance, the project for building a bridge between the mainland and the Ile de Ré was very strongly challenged by ecologists. An administrative judge cancelled the DUP on the basis of irregularities affecting the conduct of the enquiry, as well as failure to respect deadlines for convoking the municipal council.[13] The DUP relating to the building of the Somport tunnel in the Pyrenees was cancelled on the basis of inadequacy in the content of the Environmental Impact Study.[14] And administrative judges cancelled the

---

10 C.E. 8 March 1991, ville de Maisons-Lafitte, Rec. 85 ; C.J. E.G. 1991, J., 287, concl. M. de Montgolfier.

11 Cf. the numerous reactions of incomprehension towards C.E. 8 March 1991, ville de Maisons-Laffitte v. Comité de défense intercommunal de Maisons-Laffittee, Rec. 85.

12 R. Chapus: "Droit du contentieux administratif", 8th ed. 1999, 840.

13 R. Hostiou: "Le droit vu pont". Anuaire de Droit Maritime et aérien, T.X., 1989, 123.

14 TA Pau, 2 December 1992, France-Nature Environnement, Rev. Fr. de Dr. Adm. 1998, N° 2, 277, concl. J.-L. Rey, note R. Hostiou.

challenged DUPs concerning the building of a metro at Rennes[15] and an airport in Angers[16] due to the inadequacy of the socio-economic assessment appearing in the file for the public enquiry in both cases.

It should however be noted that since each of these cases was a litigious cancellation founded on external illegality of the DUPs in question, there is nothing to prevent the administration from making identical decisions while ensuring that the procedures are followed as required.

ii. This position presents a number of drawbacks. It gives the impression (particularly to decision-makers) that administrative judges are being unduly "legalistic" and impeding the completion of socially useful projects for inadequate reasons. It is, moreover, often poorly understood by petitioners – especially non-lawyers – who find it hard to accept that cancellation of a decision does not definitively prevent the project. Finally, to the extent that it calls into question the utility and efficacy of litigious mediation, this procedure provokes many court actions,[17] and it is indubitably harmful to the image of the administrative judge.

Checking the Internal Legality of the Declaration of Public Utility: the Soundness of the Operation Challenged.

We can recall that French administrative law is built around two great principles:

i. The opposition between general interest and private interest. This assumes that public action fundamentally obeys different canons from those corresponding to actions between private parties.
ii. The opposition between legality and expediency. This implies that the administrative judge's review of decisions taken by the administration is confined to verifying their legal regularity.

However, the contemporary evolution of litigation on the DUP leads us to relativise the scope of this presentation.

---

15 C.E. 4 Dec. 1995. District urbain de l'agglomération rennaise, Rev. Jur. De l'Env. 1996, N° 1-2, 152, obs. R.H.

16 TA Nantes, 4 March 1991, Assoc. de défense contre l'aéroport d'Angers-Seiches-sur-le-Loir, Rev. Jur. de l'Env. 1991, N° 3, 389, note R. Romi ; Rev. Jur. de l'Ouest, N° 4, 1991, 538, note R. Hostiou.

17 Without ruling out the possibility, after a first cancellation of the DUP for procedural flaws, of cancellation in a second stage for basic reasons. See e.g. the planning operation at Port-Fréjus, where the Conseil d'Etat, having initially cancelled the DUP because of the composition of the file for the public enquiry (CE 27 July 1990, ville de Fréjus, Petites Affiches 28 October 1991, N° 129, 6, Obs. A. Holleaux), in a second stage cancelled it on the ground of the project's incompatibility with the provisions of the Littoral law (CE 25 February 1995, Association de Défense des quariers de Fréjus, Fréjus-Plage, Villepey and Saint-Aygulf et autres, A.J.D.A. 1995, 468, concl. B. du Marais; Rec. 110).

The Notion of General Interest and the Theory of Misuse of Powers Two points can be made:

i. It is classically accepted that the administration's actions must have the exclusive goal of promoting the general interest, with every administrative decision that supports private interests being automatically tainted with illegality.

This is a rather "simplistic" conception with the general interest on the one hand and private interests on the other. It is hard to defend in light of the frequency with which public and private interests (particularly in relation to planning decision) are very closely interwoven and the public interest does not necessarily exclude financial considerations.[18]

In the Ville de Sochaux judgment, the administrative judge took note of this position and accepted that an expropriation operation was not tainted with illegality on the sole ground that it might serve the private interests of automobile manufacturer Peugeot. In this case, the motive in question was not "determinant". So, although it had flow-on benefits for private interests, the challenged activity (a project to deviate a road) could be accomplished at less cost to the public and was therefore not incompatible with the public interest.[19]

ii. This "realistic" analysis that requires administrative judges to weigh the various interests attaching to completion of planning operations helps to "demystify" a basic datum of French administrative law. Balancing of issues is, by definition, extremely delicate and highly subjective, and the "realistic" analysis is thus responsible for highly controversial decisions that in fact reflect the uncertainties of contemporary law in this area.[20] In the Municipality of Lauterbourg case, the *Conseil d'Etat* had first cancelled the proposed creation of an artificial lake, on the ground that the operation favoured the interests of a private company[21] and was therefore a misuse of powers. In a counter suit by the municipality, the same court ultimately decided that the municipality had intended to serve the public interest "at least cost", and that the challenged DUP was therefore not tainted with by illegality.[22]

These divergences in analysis clearly show that the administrative judge has no landmarks when faced by joint operations that closely associate public and private persons, and the general interest and private interests. This position has led to the introduction of various monitoring instruments by administrative judges.

---

18 Cf. C. Teitgen-Colly: "La légalité de l'intérêt financier dans l'action administrative", Paris 1981.

19 CE 20 July 1971, ville de Sochaux, Rec. 561.

20 Cf. our observations on CE 7 December 1983, commune de Lauterbourg, D. 1984, J., 583, and on CE 17 September 1999, commune de Castirla, A.J.D.I. 2000, 131. Also, R. Hostiou : "Utilité publique du projet et utilisation privée du bien exproprié", Petites Affiches 20 July 1992, N° 87, 21.

21 CE 3 October 1980, Schwartz, AJDA 1981, 205, note J. Lemasurier.

22 CE 7 December 1983, prec.

The Opposition Between Legality and Expediency, and the "Cost-benefit Balance" Theory Again, two points are made:

i. Having no normative reference available able to supply it with a legal framework enabling it to fix the notion of public utility, in 1971 the *Conseil d'Etat* adopted the "cost-benefit balance" theory.[23]

According to this jurisprudential theory, the public utility of a planning operation is subject to a comparative analysis of its advantages and disadvantages. To assess whether a DUP is legal, the administrative judge draws a balance between the positive aspects of the challenged operation (transport convenience, road safety, energy independence, industrial development, etc.) and its negative aspects (damage caused to private property, financial costs, social costs, impact on the environment, impact on other public interests). Thus the legality of the act is ultimately the outcome of the balance between these various advantages and drawbacks. This case law has thus contributed to making a project's "expediency" a condition of its "legality", or at least to restricting – in the administrative judge's favour – the freedom of assessment traditionally allowed to the administration in this area.

This sort of analysis was initially challenged for its lack of legal density and the fact that it would improperly transfer powers from the administration to the administrative judge.[24] The limitations of the new theory were soon apparent as it led to a very clear differentiation between projects coming from the State's central authorities and those from non-State bodies., The balance in the case law is systematically positive with regard to the former type of project, even if the recent cancellation of a project for a motorway link due to its excessive financial cost has led some to challenge this presentation.[25] Projects proposed by non-State bodies are the only ones in which the cost-benefit balance is likely to lead to a negative assessment by the administrative judge. In the French context of competition resulting from jurisdictional dualism, the theory of the balance contributes to upholding the idea of the administrative judge as a guarantor of private property[26] who will not hesitate to extend the concept of legality to the extreme if doing so will better to protect property rights. However, a survey of the case law shows that this type of check has never fundamentally challenged the action of the State authorities.

ii. It should be added that the creation of administrative appeal courts through a reform introduced by the law of 31 December 1987, considerably altered the organisational structures of French court actions. While continuing to play the part of judge of first (and last) instance in a number of cases, the *Conseil d'Etat*

---

23 CE 28 May 1971, Ville nouvelle-Est, Rec. P. 409, concl. G. Braibant. See R. Hostiou: "L'évolution du contrôle juridictionnel de la notion d'utilité publique", AJPI 1973, 877 and "Deux siècles d'évolution de la notion d'utilité publique" in "Un droit inviolable et sacré : la propriété", ADEF 1991, 30.

24 Cf. note J.K. under CE 26 October 1973, Grassin, AJDA 1974, 37.

25 CE 28 March 1997, Association contre le projet de l'autoroute transchablaisienne, Rec. 120. See our observations on this : Rev. Gen. des Proc. N° 1, January-March 1998, 136.

26 J.-P. Gilli: "Le rôle du juge administratif en matière d'expropriation", AJDA 1973, 13.

now intervenes most often as the final appeals judge for decisions handed down by the seven interregional administrative courts. However, the role of a final appeals judge is to "judge the judgment" and not the case that gave rise to the judgment. This implies that the "evaluation" of the facts handed down by the judges in the main case is traditionally regarded as sovereign (unless it has been "perverted"). By contrast, the "legal description" is a matter to be monitored by the final appeals judge. In reality the dividing line between these two legal categories arises from considerations of jurisprudential policy, and it is noted that the *Conseil d'Etat* recently decided – contrary to the conclusions of the government commissioner – that the "balance" drawn up by the underlying jurisdictions regarding the public utility of an operation fell to the final appeals judge rather than to the courts in the main case.[27] Some commentators presented this as a mark of the highest jurisdiction's attachment to protecting the right of private property and this extensive analysis enabled the *Conseil d'Etat* to take on the position of a court of third instance. As such, it is able to assert the same power as final appeals judge as it does regarding claims that an action is *ultra vires*. It is consequently to impose its conception of the notion of public utility on the lower courts by, for instance, cancelling a highway plan felt to cause excessive aesthetic nuisances, or by accepting an operation to reorganise municipal services "more rationally".[28]

Legal actions surrounding the DUP provide an excellent example because they involve conflicts of values, oppositions of interests, divergences of views concerning the future of the car, the railway, nuclear energy and the environment, public and private property, and national and local planning. In particular, they testify to the highly delicate nature of relations between public authorities and the administrative jurisdiction.

The shortcomings of the legal framework for the notion of public utility and the ambiguities regarding the nature, modalities and limits of administrative litigation have led administrative judges to take on a role that has more to do with the logic of arbitration than with the traditional understanding of verifying legality.

However, this transfer of power to the administrative judge is not satisfactory, as is stressed in a recent report on the matter.[29] The *Conseil d'Etat* found that evaluation of the notion of public utility by the judge is "increasingly delicate" and that it involves "the balancing of elements hard to weigh against each other". The *Conseil d'Etat* deplored "the increasing cumbersomeness of more and more procedural litigation that renders the legal stability of decisions taken fragile". One could not better highlight the limits of litigation in this area.

---

27 CE 3 July 1998, Mme Salva-Couderc, D. 1999, J., 101, note R. Hostiou ; Rec. 298; Rev. Fr. de Dr. Adm. 1999, N° 1, 112, concl. P. Hubert, note A. Bourrel ; CE 15 March 1999, Mme Canonne, Rev. Jur. de l'Env. 1999, 477.

28 See our observations under CE 2 July 1999, commune de Volvic, R.F.D.A. 1999, 1185.

29 "L'Utilité publique aujourd'hui", Documentation française, 1999, 41.

Chapter 7

A Theoretical Approach to the Tension between Form and Substance in English Judicial Reasoning

Leonor Moral Soriano[*]

Introduction

The subject of this book is to elucidate how far procedural mistakes in decision-making do not invalidate administrative acts. This presupposes that procedural mistakes are sometimes irrelevant in determining whether the validity of an administrative act can be challenged before the judiciary.[1] In this sense, it is argued that the irrelevance of some procedural errors should not be interpreted as a loss of confidence in the virtues of procedures; it should rather be understood as a sign that a complex notion of rational decisions is being embraced. This notion of rationality aims to reconcile form and substance in law.

Procedures play an overwhelming role in decision-making: they promote rationality and consequently avoid arbitrariness. Indeed, procedures – policy-making, legislative, judicial, etc. – aim to reach rational decisions. Rationality is a very complex notion (or ideal). However, given the dominance of practical philosophy, it would be uncontroversial to say that "giving reasons" to justify a decision is an essential component of rationality. The decision-maker is required to spell out the reasons that support a particular policy choice, a particular regulation, or a particular judicial decision. "To give reasons" seems to be an essential requirement of rationality and also a barrier against arbitrariness. However, to ask

---

* This chapter was written during my stay at the Centre for Law and Society (Edinburgh University) as Marie Curie Fellow.

1 For example, delay in making representations in EIA procedures does not invalidate the representations as far as the public administration aims at gathering all relevant information and public participation in the decision-making. In Italy, the tension between form and substance in administrative decisions leads to inconsistent results: in some cases, the omission of the duty to give notice of the opening of an administrative file invalidates the act; whereas in other cases, this omission does not invalidate the act, if the administration pleads that participation was of no use.

for reasons can become an irrational activity. Why? There are essentially two explanations: either because the demand for reasons is infinite[2] and makes it impossible to reach a decision, or because the giving of reasons is interrupted by a reason which claims not to require further justification,[3] making the decision irrational and arbitrary. This situation is known as the Münchausen trilemma and can be avoided by introducing the notion of procedure. Procedures can be thought of as compromises between the need to make rational decisions and the need to reach decisions. This compromise is achieved by ruling who is competent to make a decision, which aspects or reasons have to be taken into account, who can participate, and so on. Hence, procedures provide an important barrier against arbitrariness. This is not because the discretion of the maker might be limited by rules, but because procedures guarantee that decisions can be reached and justified.

Procedures are neutral tools by which rational decisions can be reached. This is true since procedures say nothing concerning the content of the rules that determine the requirements of justification (who is competent, who can participate, what has to be considered, what deadlines should be established, etc), and nor do they determine the content of the final decision. Indeed, the rules of the procedure – the content of the procedure – are a matter very much related to the notion of democracy. In Europe, for example, the notion of pluralist democracy influences the content of decision-making procedures; this is reflected in the great concern about participation and justification. Participation (getting information, presenting pleas, affording hearings, recognising the right to access to courts, etc.) guarantees that all relevant interests, facts and arguments are taken into account by the decision-maker, whose function is to strike a balance between colliding interests. The greater the participation, the more information can be gathered, and the more rational the final decision.[4] In addition, participation also promotes the legitimacy of the final decision, providing that parties effectively take part in the procedure (and not only as a formality). Justifying final decisions – the second characteristic of a pluralist decision-making procedure – promotes both the transparency and accountability of the public body. Reasons are essential tools by which to ensure that those charged with the exercise of official power exercise it rationally. Reasons are a valuable instrument for controlling the exercise of discretionary power.

In the same way that procedures do not determine their own content, they do not determine the content of the final decision. This statement requires further explanation, for procedures guarantee the validity of the final decision in terms of formal validity. That is, if a particular decision is the outcome of a procedure, the decision is valid: the public officer will implement it and citizens will comply with

---

2 As a child who endlessly asks "why" – asking for justification.

3 Keeping the metaphor of children asking for reasons, in this case rational activity would be interrupted by appealing to the authority of parents upon the children.

4 There is, or course, a danger of pushing too far the requirement of participation. This will increase the costs of time and resources, which are necessary to afford a hearing to all interested citizens and to answer their arguments in an appropriate way.

it. If a particular decision is challenged before the judiciary, the judicial review will focus on the legality of the decision and possible procedural mistakes, leaving aside questions concerning the substance (merits) of the decision.

The formal validity of decisions, in terms of decisions being the outcome of procedures, will be enough if a pure formalist theory of law (which focuses on the form rather than on the substance of decisions) were to be embraced. However, something that characterises the understanding of law in Western societies is the concern for substance without renouncing form.[5] The challenge of this understanding of law is that it neither focuses on substance and renounces form, nor focuses on form and renounces substance. On the contrary, the tension between form and substance is recognised, and there is no point in trying to solve it in a conclusive way. This unresolved or inconclusive tension between form and substance explains a complex notion of validity that tries to combine both formal validity and the acceptability of the final decision; this is the so-called "axiological validity".[6]

Does the procedure determine the substance of a decision? The answer is "no". However, this does not mean that the substance of the decision is irrelevant, or that the procedural correctness of the decision is sufficient ground for demonstrating its validity. Only once it is understood that there is a tension between the (correct) form and the (sound) substance of a decision, can the question of how far procedural mistakes are irrelevant to an assessment of the validity of a decision be fully perceived and properly answered. The question is not of an "either/or" nature, but it is rather a matter of finding a balance between procedure and substance.

Going back to the subject of this book – namely, procedural mistakes in environmental decision-making – the tension between form and substance can be reformulated as the tension between environmental protection being a matter of "wrongs" (formal mistakes) or "rights" (substantive protection). It will be argued that the question is not "either/or" but a matter of balance.[7]

Focus on Environment and Legal Reasoning

When a judicial action is brought against an administrative act on the basis of errors of form, the judiciary has the last word as to how the tension "wrongs"/rights (form/substance) should be solved. For this reason, attention has to be paid to judicial reasoning, by which we mean the way in which judges justify how the tension form/substance or "wrongs"/rights has to be dealt with and solved.

---

5 The outcome is what Wróblewski calls a legal and rational ideology of law (1992).

6 J. Wróblewski, *The Judicial Application of Law*, Z. Bankowski, N. MacCormick and J. Wróblewski (eds), The Judicial Application of Law (Dordrecht: Kluwer, 1992), 80.

7 According to Section 6:22 of the Dutch General Administrative Act (1994), the judiciary should solve the tension between form (procedural mistakes) and substance, taken into account that no prejudice of the interests of the parties is caused. Hence, the tension form/substance has to be solved bearing in mind that the role of the judiciary and the content of procedural law is the protection of subjective rights.

This is crucial for one reason: coherence. Indeed, since judges have to weigh form against substance in law, the final balance is justified if the judge succeeds in connecting the legal system with political and constitutional theories.

The legal reasoning of English judges in environmental cases is analysed here. The interest in English judges stems from their rather formal understanding of judicial review, which collides with the substantive claims of environmental protection. The interest in environmental cases is justified by the fact that they provide excellent vehicles by which to analyse how English judges justify decisions, and how they contribute to the generation of coherence in the legal system by striking balances between form and substance (that is, between formal and substantive reasons).

Justifying is the activity of supporting a statement with good reasons. Legal justification is particular because it involves two kinds of reasons: authority reasons (legal norms, precedents and legal doctrine) and substantive reasons (values and principles which, according to Summers, include both rightness reasons and goal reasons).[8] Environmental cases are complex because they involve both formal authority and substantive reasons: principles of the legal system (the supremacy of European law, Parliamentary supremacy, self-regulation of the judiciary, the doctrine of separation of powers), environmental principles (precaution, polluter pays, remedy of environmental damages at source), protection of rights (substantive right to a healthy environment, procedural rights to access to justice, information and participation), and policy considerations (environmental protection, economic sustainable development, nature conservation, energy policy, etc.). Both authority and substantive reasons must be taken into account when justifying a decision; failure to do so can be interpreted as a failure to generate coherence in adjudication.[9] The question in this sense is: do English judges take account of authority and substantive reasons? That is, how far does the model of legal reasoning embraced by English judges generate coherence in legal adjudication?

The potential contribution of the judiciary in making sense of the legal system as a whole (generating coherence) is also exemplified by environmental cases. Environmental law is a relatively novel branch of public law that receives the crucial influence of European law and European environmental law principles. This means that, when dealing with environmental issues, English judges have to bring alien law and principles together with domestic law. To do so is a matter of generating coherence in the legal system. In particular, cases of judicial review in environmental matters show how European (environmental) law and the

8 R. Summers, "Two Types of Substantive Reasons: the Core of a Theory of Common-Law Justification", *Cornell Law Review* 63: 716-724.

9 Coherence in adjudication is understood as connecting all relevant considerations which come up in a particular case. A judicial decision is not more coherent if a major number of considerations are taken into account, but rather if the premises taken into account are strongly connected. In this sense to leave aside values or principles because "they are no business of the judges" who are concerned with the text of the law is a failure to justify rationally and coherently a decision.

recognition and protection of (environmental) rights challenge the basis of judicial actions, and to some extent the legitimacy of the judiciary. The outcome – the "new system of judicial review" – is a way of making the legal system coherent.

The question of whether the judiciary generates coherence in adjudication and in the legal system when dealing with environmental cases should be differentiated from the question of whether English judges are concerned with protection of the environment. In many judgments about ecological matters, an environmentally aimless approach is adopted.[10] However, this does not mean that judges are the enemies of the environment;[11] it instead means that some difficulties have to be overcome in order to achieve a higher level of protection by the judiciary. These difficulties include the absence of appropriate scientific and technological support that would facilitate a better understanding of environmental cases by the courts,[12] the dominance of a model of legal reasoning that makes it difficult to take appropriate consideration of substantive factors such as rights and policies, and the predominant understanding that the judiciary is the guardian of legality rather than mainly a defender of citizens' rights against public actions. The environmental compromise taken by courts and tribunals can be evaluated only once appropriate instruments have been provided to the judiciary and these obstacles have been overcome.

Perspectives in Judicial Review

There are two approaches to judicial review: either it is about "wrongs" or it is about rights.

i. As a matter of "wrongs", judicial review concerns misuse of the law. This is the dominant approach in public law and it is said to be fundamentally about neither rights nor principles. "Wrongness" was initially interpreted narrowly as "illegal": the prime English constitutional principle of the supremacy of Parliament instructs the judiciary to ensure that those charged with the exercise of official power exercise it according to Parliament's will. The judiciary is the guardian of legality. A broader understanding of the basis of judicial actions was introduced by Lord Diplock in the *GCHQ* case;[13] in addition to illegality, he referred to procedural impropriety and irrationality as grounds of judicial

10 Judges are reluctant to recognise rights connected to environmental protection; in other situations, they are reluctant to evaluate the level of protection pursued by a public action.

11 As Steyn LJ said in the Lappel Bank case, "[W]e all share the instincts of the Bird Man of Alcatraz" (*R v. Secretary of State for the Environment, ex p Royal Society for the protection of Birds* [1995] *JEL* p. 245).

12 Woolf suggests that a multi-faceted tribunal which combines the services of existing courts, tribunals and inspectors in the environmental field should be created (H. Woolf, "Are the Judiciary Environmentally Myopic?" [1992] *Journal of Environmental Law* 14).

13 *Council for Civil Service Unions v. Minister for the Civil Service* [1985] AC 374.

review. By making such a distinction, Lord Diplock "exploded the fiction that all judicial review is concerned with the interpretation of the Parliament's will".[14] Indeed, procedural impropriety is based on the democratic principle that individuals should participate in decisions that affect them; irrationality ("Wednesbury reasonableness") is based on the acceptance of logic and moral standards as the minimum requirement of rationality.[15] What Lord Diplock did not defeat is the notion that public law, and particularly judicial review, is an instrument by which to scrutinise how the state exercises public power, rather than an instrument to recognise and protect individual rights. Judicial review and actions of appeal established in legislation embrace the notion of "wrongs" as the basis of judicial actions.

ii. As a matter of rights, judicial review is about the recognition and protection of individual rights. This approach is gaining force as Community law gives rise to individual rights, and the Human Rights Act 1998 introduced the ECHR into domestic law in 2000. This approach justifies "new" grounds of judicial review such as legitimate expectations and proportionality.[16] It is in this framework that environmental protection and especially environmental rights (either substantive or procedural) challenge the traditional role and legitimacy of the judiciary.

Both approaches represent two degrees of judicial scrutiny depending on the subject-matter of the particular case. If the measure is a matter of policies (environmental protection verses economic development) it requires political decisions that the judiciary will rarely be willing to challenge. Then, the judicial action has a concrete target: finding illegalities such as taking account of irrelevant considerations. Legality, procedural propriety, and the "high standard" of Wednesbury rationality[17] fit into this category. If the activity of the public body affects individual rights, then the judicial action has a different target: determining whether the justification of the intrusion is well and sufficiently founded (legitimate expectations and proportionality belong to this category).[18]

---

14 J. Jowell, "Restraining the State. Politics, Principle and Judicial Review" [1997] *Current Legal Problems*, 189-212, 203.

15 Lord Diplock in the *GCHQ* case defined irrationality as "a decision which is so outrageous in its defiance of logic or accepted moral standards that no person who had applied his mind to the question to be decided could have arrived at it".

16 It could be held that, rather than new grounds of judicial review, legitimate expectations and proportionality are more elaborate forms of procedural impropriety and irrationality.

17 According to Irvine of Lairs, there are two standards of Wednesbury irrationality: the high standard which applies in the field of policy making; and the low standard which applies in the field of individuals rights (Irvine of Lairs, "Judges and Decision-Makers: the Theory and Practice of Wednesbury review" [1996] *Public Law* 59).

18 Neither the "wrongs" approach nor the "rights" approach allow the judiciary to enter into the merits of the challenged decision. Indeed, the judge or the court is concerned with the manner in which the decision of the executive is reached rather than with the substantive merits of the decision itself. It must be right enough that the doctrine of the separation of powers is one of the pillars of the Rule of Law. Judges are not policy-makers.

How do English judges approach environmental cases? Are they a matter of "wrongs" or a matter of rights? To embrace one approach or the other depends on a number of issues: the content of judicial activity (either the control of misuses of the law or abuses of individual rights), the legitimacy of the judiciary (either the guardian of the Parliament's will or the protector of citizens rights), and the attitude of the judiciary (either self-restraint or individual rights activism).

The choice of approach affects the content of the legal reasoning. Whether an environmental case is dealt with as a matter of "wrongs" or rights does not determine which method of interpretation must be adopted (literal, historical, teleological interpretation, or evaluation of consequences), although literal and historical methods are among those preferred by English judges. The interest depends on whether or not judges take substantive reasons into account (such as individual rights and policy considerations), whether or not they reconstruct cases as conflicts of reasons (the right to a healthy environment verses energy policy) and, if they do, whether or not they strike a balance between the colliding reasons. To take account of substantive reasons, and to solve a conflict of reasons by striking a balance should not be interpreted as a sign of the judiciary acting as decision-maker It instead signifies that the judiciary is generating coherence in adjudication and in the legal system.

A Matter of "Wrongs"

Relevant Considerations in Environmental Cases

It is crucial to identify the relevant considerations that must be taken into account in decision-making processes. This limits the discretion of the decision-maker and provides an instrument of judicial scrutiny; taking account of irrelevant considerations or disregarding relevant considerations are grounds for judicial review. Indeed, in the *Wednesbury* case,[19] Lord Greene MR said that "[the decision-maker] must call his own attention to the matters which he is bound to consider. He must exclude from his consideration matters which are irrelevant to what he has to consider" (229). Wednesbury – relevance/irrelevance questions – has been identified as the third ground of judicial review stated by Lord Diplock: irrationality. Irrationality in the Wednesbury sense is consistent with the idea that judicial review is a matter of "wrongs" (misuses of the law by the decision-maker).

Wednesbury irrationality is a crucial ground of judicial review in cases where environmental protection is at stake, such as applications to discharge radioactive waste, planning permissions, and the granting of Environmental Impact assessments. Judicial scrutiny in these cases focuses, first, on whether environmental protection and related issues (such as protection of health) are relevant considerations to be taken into account in the decision-making process, and second, on whether the decision-maker took account of them. These questions

[19] *Associated Provincial Picture Houses Ltd v. Wednesbury Comp.* [1948] 1 K.B. 223

are answered by an orthodox understanding of Wednesbury. According to this interpretation, what amounts to a relevant consideration depends on the statutory provision: wrongly identifying relevant considerations makes the decision illegal.[20]

In cases of judicial review based on irrationality (in the Wednesbury sense), legal reasoning focuses on the interpretation of the statutory provision that confers power on the decision-maker. Judicial scrutiny focuses on questions of *which* are the relevant considerations according to the law, leaving aside questions of *how* relevant these considerations are.[21]

A wider or stricter approach to the relevance of considerations will be very much determined by the method of interpretation.

In the *Newport BC* case,[22] Newport Borough Council refused to grant permission to Browning Ferris to develop a waste treatment plant. Its refusal was based on the ground that the local community believed that there would be unacceptable risks to public health and safety if the development were to be implemented. The Secretary of State for Wales made an award of costs against Newport BC because its decision was founded on an unreasonable consideration as the public perception was based on fear rather than on scientific evidence. When the case arrived at the Court of Appeal, it was asked whether it is irrational (in Wednesbury terms) to take account of unreasonable considerations (such as public fear). Are unreasonable considerations *relevant* to the making of a decision?

The Court of Appeal focused on the interpretation of paragraph 9 of Circular 5/87 containing the Secretary of State's policy on the issue:

> Planning authorities are expected to take into account the views of local residents when determining a planning application. Nevertheless, on its own, local opposition to a proposal is not a reasonable ground for the refusal of the planning application, unless that opposition is founded upon valid planning reasons which are supported by substantial evidence.

Two Lords of the Court of Appeal interpreted the aforementioned provision in a way that differentiated unreasonable considerations from unreasonable grounds for the perception. The Court of Appeal considered that although the public's perception of risk was unfounded, it is a material consideration relevant to the granting (or refusing) of a planning permission. By rejecting the consideration of

---

20 As such, the contravention of the principle of rationality involves an error of law, since the decision of the policy-maker has gone beyond the legal limits of discretion. The distinction between rationality and legality collapses.

21 A *how* question on relevant considerations is thought of as an open door for the judiciary to enter into the domain of the executive and the legislature, that is, into the domain of policy-making, by allowing the judiciary to appraise the particular weight of relevant considerations. In this sense, judges can identify two colliding considerations as being relevant; however, they cannot solve the conflict: that is the competence of the decision-maker.

22 *Newport BC v. the Secretary of State for Wales and Browning Ferris Environmental Services Ltd* [1998] *Env. L.R* 174.

an unreasonable perception, concluded the Court of Appeal, the Secretary of State had made a material error in law. However, Staughton LJ gave a dissenting opinion. He held that the appeal should have been dismissed because the Circular established, as a matter of discretion, whether public concern could amount to a reason for refusing a planning permission.

Although there was disagreement among their Lordships, all shared the same model of legal reasoning. Justifying reasons are authority reasons (paragraph 9 of Circular 5/87). The focus is on the plain meaning of the law; that is, on the literal interpretation of a statutory provision. Indeed, the closer the interpretation is to the plain meaning of the law, the better the judiciary plays its role as guardian of legality. However, the fact that the judges achieved opposing conclusions while using the same method of interpretation undermines the correctness and justifying force of the decision. Finally, there is little attention paid to the particularities of the case, which might play a role in determining relevant questions.

A different approach concerning the particularities of the case was taken in the *Bolton* decision.[23] This suggested that the question of relevance in part depends upon its likely causative effect upon the decision:[24] "if the decision-maker would have reached the same decision notwithstanding the defect [on relevant considerations] the court is unlikely to intervene".[25] This method of assessing questions of relevance reveals changes in the understanding of procedural errors and judicial review. First, legality is not the only criterion for assessing the actions of the administration. Other criteria such as the principle of good administration and the protection of individual rights justify judiciary intervention because the consequences of these considerations upon the decision determine their relevance. Second, attention is paid to the particular case: relevant considerations do not only depend on the wording of the law but also on the particularities of the case.

Unfortunately, the causation approach to relevance questions in decision-making procedures has not been welcomed. Hough insists that "relevancy should be determined by the traditional Wednesbury principles. This is dependent on a process of statutory construction to determine the purposes for which power was conferred".[26] Thus legality, rather than causation, should be the criterion to solve questions of relevance. This can also be interpreted as the preference for form over substance.

Since statutory provisions determine which considerations are relevant, what happens if the law remains silent on questions of relevance? Is the judiciary unable to assess such questions? An answer to these queries might be provided by the case of *R v. Secretary of State for the Environment ex p Kingston Upon Hull City*

---

23 *Re. v. Secretary of State for the Environment, ex p. Bolton Metropolitan B.C.* [1991] J.P.L. 32.

24 The German legal position is close to the causation approach: in cases of absence of EIA, the decision is invalid only if the procedural error affects the decision.

25 B. Hough, "Relevance and Reasons in Planning Matters" [1998] *Journal of Planning Law* 625, 628.

26 Ibid. 634.

Council and, ex p Bristol City Council and Woodspring District Council,[27] even though environmental protection was considered in this case (as in the last) to be a matter of "wrongs". The case arose when the Secretary of State for the Environment issued decisions establishing the outer limits of the Humber and Severn Estuaries and designated them as high natural dispersion areas. As a consequence, urban waste-water that is discharged into the estuaries should receive primary treatment, which is less stringent than secondary treatment.[28] The respondent considered the cost of treating waste-water in order to determine the limits of the estuaries. The applicants claimed that the respondent failed to comply with the conditions established by the Directive concerning the designation of estuaries' limits; they also claimed that the Secretary of State took irrelevant considerations into account (namely the cost of water treatment). Harrison J decided to quash both decisions of the Secretary of State. His reasoning starts with the plain meaning of the Directive: it does not establish which criteria should be taken into account in determining the limits of estuaries. It instead means that Member States do have discretion in this matter.[29] However, Harrison J argues that despite the discretion of Member States, there are two criteria that determine "a genuine and rational assessment in each case of what actually constitutes the estuary". These criteria are (i) the characteristics of the area of water in question, and (ii) the purpose of the Directive. These criteria lead Harrison J to the conclusion that consideration of the cost of treating waste-water is not relevant to what constitutes an estuary. Otherwise, Harrison J concluded, Member States would be able to avoid the obligations imposed by the Directive.

Unlike the *Newport BC* case, substantive considerations are taken into account in the *Estuaries* case. Harrison J. brought together a teleological argument (the purpose of the Directive), the circumstances of the concrete case (characteristics of the water), and an argument based on consequences (the possibility that Member States might not comply with the aim of the Directive). There is also an argument oriented at promoting coherence in the legal system; namely, the principle of the supremacy of EC law. Harrison J concluded that the discretion of Member States cannot override the supremacy of EC law. The *Estuaries* case shows that legality cannot be reduced to legalism, even though control of the legality of public actions justifies judicial scrutiny. That is, the interpretation of statutes cannot leave aside justifications based on principles, rights and goal-related reasons. Indeed, taking policy factors into account, consequence considerations, legal principles, and other substantive justifications does not mean relaxing restraints on the judiciary. These considerations should be understood as a method by which to increase the

---

27 [1996] *Env. L. R* 248.

28 According to the Directive on Urban Waste Water, secondary treatment is the norm, while primary treatment is allowed under certain circumstances.

29 This point in the reasoning of Harrison J is very interesting, because judges are reluctant to become involved in decisions taken within the framework of a legally recognised discretion. That is, judges are reluctant to evaluate the merits of the decisions taken by public bodies.

correctness of legal reasoning, and as a way in which to contribute to the coherence of the legal system.

What do the aforementioned cases have in common? Both approach environmental issues as a matter of "wrongs"; that is, as a matter of finding illegalities in the decision making process, rather than ruling upon the correctness or soundness of the decision.[30] This explains why the judicial reasoning in these cases is about *what* matters, rather than *how much* matters. The point is whether public fear (in the *Newport BC* case) or an evaluation of economic costs (in the *Estuaries* case) are relevant. That is, should they have been considered by the public body, rather than how relevant these considerations are when confronted by other arguments such as scientific evidence or environmental damage. Hence, approaching environmental issues as a matter of "wrongs" determines a particular way of constructing cases that excludes evaluations of the weight the decision-maker has attributed to policies or interests involved in the decision. By so doing, the self-restraint of the judiciary is guaranteed and judicial activism is avoided.

"Wrongs" and the Deferential Attitude of English Judges

However, the "deferential philosophy"[31] according to which judges cannot appraise the weight of colliding relevant considerations and, in particular, environmental considerations is being defeated. The *Lappel Bank* case[32] provides an example of this. In that case, the Court of Appeal stated that Member States have discretion to take account of economic and recreational interests along with ecological considerations when designating the limits of Special Protected Areas (a conservation measure established by the Directive on the protection of wild birds). These interests have to be weighed against each other in order to achieve a decision. The weighing is a matter of discretion for the decision-maker that cannot be examined for lack of legitimacy by the judiciary. Hoffmann LJ (then in the Court of Appeal) gave a dissenting opinion that was later upheld by the ECJ. For Hoffmann LJ, Member States do not have such great discretion. According to the Directive on the protection of wild birds, Member States cannot take account of economic and recreational interests, and only the preservation of human life can be balanced against the public interest in bird conservation. Hence, statutory provisions – and EC Law in particular – can considerably limit the discretion of the decision-maker by identifying relevant considerations, and by stating the weight to be given to such considerations.

There are other areas in which the deferential attitude of English judges towards public bodies remains untouched at the cost of attacking the core of pluralist procedures. Judicial control of administrative decisions concerning

---

30 Irvine of Lairs 1996, supra, 60.

31 J. Alder, "Environmental Impact Assessment – The Inadequancies of English Law" [1993] *Journal of Environmental Law*, 203, 212.

32 *R. v. Secretary of State for the Environment, ex p. Royal Society for the Protection of Birds* [1995] *J.E.L.* 245.

whether or not to require an Environmental Impact Assessment ("EIA") is one of these "untouched" areas. As Alder notes, whether a project belongs to Annex II of the Directive on EIA[33] is a matter of law for the courts. However, English judges "have not taken this approach but have treated the matter as one of fact and judgement, thus attracting only a minimal level of review".[34] Judges are not willing to be involved in matters of discretion. However, this deferential attitude affects the pluralistic approach to environmental assessment procedures in two ways. First, EIA does not aim to protect the environment; it instead aims to gather all relevant information. Full knowledge of a situation is a requirement for rational decision-making. In this sense, the more information the administration can gather, the more rationally the discretionary powers can be used. Second, EIA is a valuable participatory channel that aims to gather information and also legitimise the final decision. In this sense, the more the participatory channels are open to the public, the more the project is going to be accepted. Hence, the refusal to review decisions on whether to require assessment at all undermines the gathering of relevant information and participation. And, ultimately, it undermines the rationality and legitimacy of the decision itself.

European law provides a valuable instrument to fight against this deferential attitude in this particular area. In the recent *Marson* case,[35] the Secretary of State decided to grant planning permission to an industrial estate development project without requiring an environmental assessment. The Secretary of State considered that the project would not be likely to have a significant effect on the environment "by virtue of factors such as its nature, size and location". Apart from these words, the Secretary of State did not justify his decision as to why he did not direct the commissioning of an EIA. Indeed, English regulations require that reasons be given when an EIA is required, but they remain silent about when an EIA is refused. The applicant in *Marson* could only use Community law to support his claim. In particular, he argued before the Court of Appeal that public bodies have the duty to give reasons for declining to require an EIA, and this duty arises from Community Law. The argument runs as follows: environmental assessment is a prerequisite of planning permission in some projects, and this derives from Community law. English courts have to protect Community rights, but the right cannot be protected unless reasons are given for a refusal to direct the commission of an environmental assessment. In the absence of reasons, no proper decision could be taken as to whether to apply to the courts. And because there can be no effective recourse to courts, the applicant is deprived of rights. The applicant basically claimed that public administration accountability is impossible if there is

33 The Directive on EIA differentiates two kinds of projects which have a significant effect on the environment. For projects contained in Annex I, assessment is compulsory, whereas for projects under Annex II, assessment is at the discretion of the Member States.

34 Alder, supra, 214.

35 *R. v. Secretary of State for the Environment, Transport and Regions and Parcelforce, ex p Marson* [1998] *JPL* 869.

no obligation to give reasons. Therefore, reasons have to be given, not only when assessment is directed, but also when it is not.

The Court of Appeal focused on whether European law requires reasons. However, there is not such a general requirement when the decision affects rights conferred by the Treaty. In that situation, Community law imposes an obligation to give reasons.The crucial question then became whether there was a Community law derived right to environmental assessment. The Court of Appeal rightly argued that there was no "European" right to reasons for decisions refusing to order an environmental assessment. The Court of Appeal instead concluded that there was a right to a decision from the Secretary as to whether or not assessment is required. This right was not been affected, but rather satisfied, by the decision of the Secretary of State.

Indeed, the Court of Appeal took the right decision as far as "form" (authority reasons) is concerned, for neither English nor European law recognise a right to justify decisions refusing to order a EIA. However, what the Court of Appeal did not consider was whether there was a fundamental right to justify administrative decisions, regardless of whether they reject or accept an application to order an assessment. The rejection of such a right means that there are certain areas of decision-making for which the public administration is not accountable. The Court of Appeal probably did not put the question in these terms because it considers that to ask for reasons is a way of reducing public bodies' discretionary powers (powers that Community law grants to Member States). But this is an incorrect understanding of the function of reasons: reasons are not means of reducing discretionary powers. They are rather means by which to rationalise their use.[36]

A Matter of Rights

An administrative decision (such as a decision not to order an EIA) can be legal, procedurally proper and rational, and yet it can be subject to judicial review. Why? Like the Parliament's will, individual rights are also a tool for governmental accountability. Indeed, the administration must exercise its discretionary powers according to the law and without violating citizens' rights. The protection of individual rights justifies grounds of judicial review that can be seen as the result of collating traditional grounds of judicial review and individual's rights. These grounds are proportionality and legitimate expectations.

---

36 "To ask for reasons" promotes the accountability of public bodies and the rationality of their decisions. However, if pushed too far, this requirement may cause a perverse result: that of making the procedure inefficient. Indeed, if reasons are required for everything, the public administration would collapse because it lacks time, knowledge and resources to justify all decisions. Again, the answer is not an either/or one, but rather a matter of finding a balance between the claim to rational decisions and the claim to efficient procedures.

Proportionality, in public law, has to be understood as the balance between individual's liberties, rights and interests on the one hand, and the purpose of the measure on the other hand. Legitimate expectations refer to the rights of citizens against the decision-makers, and they oblige the latter to afford a hearing to the public in the event of a change of policy. They also require the change be justified by strong countervailing reasons.[37]

Proportionality and legitimate expectations allow the judiciary to examine the substance of the administrative decision. The focus is on whether or not the justification provided by the public authority supports the intrusion into an individual's right. This control cannot be misunderstood as policy-making because it is not the business of the court to substitute the decision taken by the public authorities with the court's own decision. The aim is rather the protection of citizens against abuses (not only misuses) of public power.

These grounds of judicial review have been used in environmental cases with rather unpromising results. A possible explanation is the non-existence of a right to a healthy environment. However, there are two reasons why this is not (or won't be) the true explanation. First, there is a substantial right to health, and the right to enjoy private and family life according to the ECHR that might be at stake in environmental issues.[38] Second, along with substantive rights, there are procedural environmental rights, namely the right of standing before the court in environmental cases, the right of information in environmental matters, and the right of participation in decision-making processes in which environmental protection is at stake. However, although there are environmentally related rights, and grounds of judicial review that allow for the protection of these rights, the dominant opinion that public law is about misuses (not abuses) prevents the judiciary from taking rights and principles seriously.

---

37 In this sense, a policy generates expectations for the citizens; in particular, the expectation that the policy is going to be kept; the expectation that a hearing is going to be afforded in the event of a change of policy; and, finally, the expectation that a strong justification is going to be provided in the event of a change of policy. These expectations are understood as rights of the citizens against public administration.

38 Indeed, the case *López Ostra v. Spain* (Vol. 303.C) provides a ground-breaking precedent in this sense. The European Court of Human Rights ruled that pollution from a waste treatment plant close to the residence of Mrs López Ostra violated Art. 8 of ECHR (private life and family life). The ECHR explained that "despite the margin of appreciation left to the respondent State, the Court considers that the State did not succeed in striking a fair balance between the interest of the town's economic well-being – that of having a waste-treatment plant – and the applicant's effective enjoyment of her right of respect for her home and her private and family life". Spain, the respondent State, was found liable by the ECHR which showed its willingness to treat environmental infringements as human-rights violations.

Proportionality

In the *Duddridge* case,[39] the applicants (three children) sought judicial review of the Secretary of State's regulations on the supply of electricity. The applicants held that the Secretary of State should have issued regulations to safeguard the health of the applicants and to take a precautionary view of the risks of damage to health. By not adopting the regulations in compliance with the precautionary principle contained in Article 130r of the Treaty (new Article 174), the Secretary of State breached European law.

The court could have used the principle of proportionality to solve the conflict between the right to health, and the aim of the administrative measure (energy policy). If it had done so, the focus would have been on the justification provided by the public body; as there was an intrusion into the right to health, the actions undertaken by the administration should have been appropriately justified to back such an intrusion. The evaluation of the justification provided by the public body, and therefore the evaluation of the proportionality of the measure, is not left to the discretion to the judge. Alexy explains that there is a rational procedure to determine whether a measure is proportionate.[40] The first step is the "rule of suitability" in which the focus is on whether a measure is a suitable means by which to achieve the maximal realisation of a principle. The second step is the "rule of necessity" that focuses on whether the means is necessary to achieve particular goals. The last step is the "rule of proportionality" in a narrow sense, according to which the more the intensive interference in one principle, the more important the realization of the other principle must be. It is here that the protection of human health has to be taken into account and weighed against energy policy.

Despite the importance of the principle of proportionality to the solution of this case, the court decided not to embrace this approach. Instead, it followed a rather formal approach by asking "whether the Secretary of State, in declining to take specific measures to limit the level of EMFs (electromagnetic fields) has acted unlawfully". The question referred to neither the proportionality of the measure nor compliance with the precautionary principle. It instead asked whether Article 174 Treaty (ex Article 130r) imposes binding obligations on Member States. The conclusion was negative. To the court, the "ordinary sense of the Article itself shows that it is intended that a policy for the environment will be formulated at some future time".[41] In addition, the interpretation of Article 174 in connection with Article 175 Treaty (ex Article 130s) reveals that the policy contained in Article 174 "shall be brought into effect by the introduction of measures by the various Community institutions".[42]

---

39 *R v. Secretary of State for Trade and Industry, ex p Duddridge and others* [1995] *Env. L.R.* 151.

40 R. Alexy, "Rights, Legal Reasoning and Rational Discourse", *Ratio Juris* 5 (1992), 149 ff.

41 Ibid., 168.

42 Id, 168.

This decision speaks volumes about the reasons for English judges' failure to take rights and principles seriously. English judges are not environmentally myopic. They simply have an understanding of public law that is incompatible with the recognition of rights: what matters is the misuse of the law, that is, whether a public body has acted unlawfully. The question "is the infringement of an individual's right sufficiently justified?" is substituted by the question "does the public body have discretion according to the law to issue a particular decision?"[43]

In addition, English judges have a particular understanding of principles according to which both principles and rules are different from a linguistic point of view, but they are identical from the perspective of their role in legal reasoning. Rules and principles are normative statements that differ in their degree of generality (rules are specific normative statements, whereas principles are general). As far as their roles in legal reasoning are concerned, rules and principles are identical; both are normative statements that apply in an either/or fashion and according to deontological reasoning.[44] This explains why Smith LJ applied the precautionary principle as if it were a statutory norm: he focused on the obligations that the principle established for public bodies, and concluded that no obligations derived from this principle because Community institutions have not implemented it. Smith LJ is right. Or he is right if one accepts (as Smith LJ does) that rules and principles do not have different functions in legal reasoning: both rules and principles have to be followed. Indeed, it is argued that rules apply to legal

---

43 Unlike in the *Duddridge* case, in the case of *R v. The Environment Agency, ex p Dockgrange Ltd and Mayer Parry Ltd* ([1998] *J.E.L.* 146) Carnwath J was not reluctant to apply the principle of proportionality. He turned down a measure of the Environmental Agency regulating the system of authorisation of transfrontier waste shipments, because it was not proportional. Carnwath J did not refer to a non-proportional balance between rights and means; he rather meant that the measure established a too restrictive system of shipments, since substances which were to be found under the green list of the Directive on waste (Directive 75/442/EEC) were subject to a stricter control by the Environmental Agency. The argument on proportionality was accepted: "There is in my view more flexibility within the system than the Agency's current policy allows… I am happy to reach that conclusion, since nothing is more likely to bring disrepute on the systems of control under the European Treaty than over-rigid application of the criteria resulting in needless hardship" (pp. 153-154). The overriding interest in this case is the possibility of controlling the substance of a decision (a policy) by judicial review using proportionality as the ground of the remedy, and as a European principle. Rather than judicial activism, this decision can be interpreted in terms of a contribution to the consistency of legislation on waste treatment, and coherence in the legal system. It shows how easy it is for national judges to strike a balance of means and ends, and to justify it, once proportionality has been understood as having the "cool and dispassionate objectivity of determining the suitability of means to ends" (O'Neil 1993, 192).

44 "Either/or" means that either the normative statements applies, or it does not. There is no possibility of finding a compromise in order to optimise the application of two competing normative statements. Deontic logic is the application of normative statements by deductive logic.

reasoning in an either/or fashion and according to deontological reasoning; however, principles apply to legal reasoning in a more-or-less fashion and according to the logic of optimisation. This means that principles, such as precaution in environmental matters, can be more or less relevant to the decision in an environmental case, but they have to be taken into account since they are elements that make environmental law coherent. In addition, principles cannot be followed: they have to be weighed. This is only understandable if principles are conceived as commands to optimise.[45] This means, first, that they are commands that require the highest degree of realisation and, second, that a greater realisation of one principle will reduce the degree of realisation of other principles.[46]

This interpretation of the role of principles in legal reasoning is more appropriate if the aim is the promotion of coherence. Indeed, the coherence of a set of laws can be expressed in terms of principles: "the coherence of a set of norms is a function of its justificability under higher order principles or values".[47] Principles are *prima facie* reasons that promote the coherence of the legal system by uniting all parts of a given legal system. Failure to take account of this function of principles in legal reasoning amounts to a failure to generate coherence.

Legitimate Expectations

In the abovementioned *GCHQ* case, Lord Diplock defines the concept of legitimate expectations as follows:

> To qualify as a subject for judicial review the decision must have consequences which affect some person (or body of persons) other than the decision-maker, although it may affect him too. It must affect such other person either (a) by altering rights or obligations of that person which are enforceable by or against him in private law; or (b) by depriving him of some benefit or advantage which either (i) he had in the past been permitted by the decision-maker to enjoy and which he can legitimately expect to be permitted to continue to do until there has been communicated to him some rational grounds for withdrawing it on which he has been given an opportunity to comment; or (ii) he has received assurance from the decision-maker will not be withdrawn without giving him first an opportunity of advancing reasons for contending that they should not be withdrawn.[48]

The main criticism of this notion of legitimate expectations is that it focuses on the attitude of the decision-maker rather than on the nature of the interest

---

45 Alexy, supra, 149.

46 A major realisation of a principle does not lead to the exclusion of a competing principle, but rather to its minor realisation. This implies that principles have to be weighed.

47 N. MacCormick, "Coherence in Legal Justification", *Theory of Legal Science*, A. Peczenik *et al.* (eds), Theory of legal science : proceedings of the Conference on Legal Theory and Philosophy of *Science, Lund, Sweden, December 11-14, 1983* (Dordrecht/Boston: Reidel/ Hingham, c.1984), 238.

48 [1985] A.C. 408-409.

affected.[49] The decision-maker creates expectations either by express promise or by a past practice. It means that in the event that the decision-maker grants a planning permission, the decision may affect the interests of the neighbours. However, the neighbours do not have the right to be represented or make representations because neither the practice of the decision-maker nor a promise has been made to afford such representation.[50]

In the event of a change of policy, the notion of legitimate expectations has to be elaborated further. Legitimate expectations do not imply that a policy generates certain expectations to which the decision-maker is bound. It instead means that, in the event of a change of policy, the decision-maker must justify the change by a strong countervailing public interest.[51] Whether that legitimate expectation may be infringed by an overriding public interest must be subject to proportionality. Prior warning is due here: the notion of legitimate expectations does not allow the judiciary to inquire into the merits of the decision; it allows judges to assess the "countervailing" public interest.

A good example of legitimate expectations as a remedy in environmental matters is the case *R v. Secretary of State for Transport, ex p. Council of the London Borough of Richmond and Others.*[52] A number of local authorities from the areas of Heathrow, Gatwick and Stansted airports challenged the decision of the Secretary of State for Transport concerning the number of night flights to and from those airports. Indeed, it was believed that the government's measure would have produced an increase in the number of night flights and, therefore, in the level of noise. The applicants claimed that, in the Consultation Paper of 1988, the Secretary of State created legitimate expectations that noise levels during the night would be reduced. The applicants expected that this policy could not be modified irrespective of any opportunity they enjoyed to complain about new proposals (in particular the new Consultation Paper of 1993 that proposed a new scheme for night flights). For Laws J, the question was not the source of the legitimate expectations, that is, whether the public authority had promised the right to be heard, or whether it had promised the continuation of the policy. The key question was instead "whether the discipline of fairness, imposed by the common law, ought to prevent the public authority respondent from acting as it proposes".[53] The discipline of fairness allows the public authority to change its policy without first giving a fair hearing if an overriding public interest demands it. Thus limitations on a right (the right to be heard) are justified by an overriding public interest. This notion of legal expectations leads towards two alternative conclusions. On the one

49 P. Elias, "Legitimate Expectation and Judicial Review" in J.L. Jowell (ed.), *New Directions in Judicial Review* (London: Stevens, 1997), 37-50, 39.

50 Ibid., 41.

51 In this sense, the foundation of legitimate expectations is the principle of consistency, that is, the idea that citizens expect the public authorities to continue doing what has been done in the past. Were a policy to be changed then, the authorities would be obliged to hold a public hearing.

52 [1994] *Environmental Law Report* 134.

53 Ibid., 156.

hand, one can say – as the applicants did – that the court should examine whether such an overriding public interest exists. But one could also say – as Laws J did – that it is not the business of the court to enter into the evaluation of overriding public interests since such a judgment would lead to the evaluation of the merits of the proposed policy change. To Laws J: "[T]he court is not the judge of the merits of the decision-maker's policy".[54]

The orthodox notion of the separation of powers that Laws J embraces (policy considerations are the domain of the executive and the legislature, whereas the judiciary is concerned with the application of the law) significantly reduces the scope of judicial review based on legitimate expectations. Indeed, if the court is not able to determine whether overriding interests justify not holding a hearing, what is left? The answer is the monitoring of the legality of the decision.[55] Hence, substantive considerations concerning the balance between overriding public interests and the right to be heard are excluded from the reasoning.

But should legality be the only criterion of correctness that informs legal reasoning? Should legality be the only criterion of validity? This question has significant importance in environmental issues, for it is an area in which great legal developments take place, including the recognition of a substantive right, the elaboration of procedural rights, and the reception of EC law. Should the monitoring of legality be the exclusive role of the judiciary, or should it be complemented by the protection of citizens against abuses by public bodies?

Challenges to Face

Judicial review of environmental measures can be approached as a matter of "wrongs" (focussing on monitoring the legality of the measure) or as a matter or rights (focussing on the protection of individuals' rights from administrative actions). In both cases, judicial decisions unveil new challenges that the judiciary is facing (or avoiding) concerning both the model of legal reasoning and the notion of coherence in the legal system.

As to the model of legal reasoning, linguistic methods of interpretation (literal, or ordinary, or obvious, or the plain meaning of the law) and systemic methods of interpretation (matching the legal text to the legal context) are preferred to teleological and evaluative ones. This does not depend on whether or not the case is concerned with "wrongs" or rights. It instead depends on the constitutional

54 Ibid., 157.

55 In particular, Laws J accepts the literal interpretation of section 78(3) of the Civil Aviation Act 1982: the scheme with which the Secretary of State proposed to rationalise the number of night flights does not fulfil the statutory purpose of the aforementioned section because if the Secretary of State implements the scheme "he will not specify the maximum number of occasions on which aircraft of descriptions so specified may be permitted to take off or land… [as section 78(3) requires]. He will specify something entirely different, namely the maximum number of quota points, which… the aircraft operators are not to exceed" (p. 151).

principle of Parliamentary supremacy. As Tridimas explains, unlike Community Treaties that favour principles, English statutes favour precise definitions.[56] Legislative texts are "free of ambivalence or equivocation, so the governmental accountability is ensured by Parliamentary, rather than judicial, control".[57] Principles (such as precaution and proportionality) and rights (such as the right to a healthy environment), challenge the primacy of this linguistic method of interpretation. Indeed, a judgment that holds that there is no obligation on the administration because the precautionary principle has not been implemented by the competent authorities, is an incorrect decision. It is wrong because it fails to take appropriate account of principles. Principles are part of legal systems; they are not just programmatic commands to the legislator. As part of legal systems, principles can be referred to as systemic arguments that have an extremely positive effect upon the legal system as they promote its cohesion.

The primacy of a linguistic method of interpretation is very much linked to a particular model of reasoning: deductive reasoning. There is nothing wrong with deductions. On the contrary, they are crucial in assessing the correctness of judicial decisions. However, legal reasoning is not only a matter of deduction, it is also a matter of making choices. Choices must be made between methods of interpretation, relevant considerations, authority reasons, substantive reasons, and so on. The problem of reducing legal reasoning to deductive reasoning is that these choices are not elucidated by the judge, and they therefore they fall outside the control of rationality. For example, in the *Newport BC* case, linguistic interpretation alone leads to two contradictory understandings of the statutory provision. The absence of so-called secondary arguments (arguments that justify why one interpretation is preferred to another) undermines the rationality of the judgment. From the perspective of deductive reasoning ("internal justification"), the judgment in *Newport BC* is well justified. But from the point of view of the second level of justification ("external justification") the decision is not justified because choices (concerning the meaning of the legal provision) have not been justified. A model of reasoning that competes with justifications for choices requires reference to principles, rights and goals, even if it is based on deductive logic. One interpretation is better than another because it promotes more important values, or principles, rights or goals. The use of these elements of the legal system cannot be seen to cross the line between law and politics.

As to coherence of the legal system, judges do not work in a vacuum.[58] Choices about colliding arguments, rights, interests, goals, and so on, must be considered in connection with moral and political theories. This is especially true when defining the role and legitimacy of the judiciary. The main notion is that the judiciary scrutinises the legality of public actions. To go beyond the control of legality means to break two imperatives that support judicial review: the constitutional

---

56 T. Tridimas, "The Court of Justice and Judicial Activism" [1996] *E.L.Rev.* 199-210, 204.

57 Id.

58 J. Steyn, "Does Legal Formalism Hold Sway in England?" [1996] *C.L.P.*, 43-58.

imperative of the separation of powers and the democratic imperative that suggests that judges lack democratic legitimacy in decision-making. However, this vision is challenged by the protection of individuals' rights as judges have the constitutional role of protecting citizens from abuses of official power. Once this constitutional role was accepted, says Steyn LJ, "there was not much room for formalist techniques".[59] Judges should not relinquish their function as guarantors of legality. They should instead complete this function with the protection of the rights of individuals.

When it is approached as a matter of rights rather than "wrongs", judicial review allows the judiciary a more in-depth scrutiny of governmental actions through an examination that extends to the appropriateness of the justification provided by the public body. This might be an argument for approaching environmental protection as a matter of rights (rather than "wrongs"). However, this new understanding of the constitutional role of the judiciary as a protector of citizens' rights has only just begun. Although the adoption of the ECHR will boost the new role of the judiciary in this direction, judges are still reluctant – or lack the appropriate legal reasoning techniques – to take rights seriously.

Challenges Posed to the ECJ

The legal reasoning of English judges and, therefore, the tension between form and substance in law, is challenged by substantive considerations. This is not the case in the ECJ, but that does not mean that the Court should not face any challenge. On the contrary. Whereas rights (and principles) pose challenges to the "wrongs" approach embraced by English judges, the "wrongs" approach poses challenges the way in which a particular right – namely the right to bring judicial actions – is recognised by Community law.

Section 31(3) of the Supreme Court Act says that "...the court shall not grant leave to make such an application [for judicial review] unless it considers that the applicant has a sufficient interest in the matter to which the application relates". This means that the recognition of *locus standi* in English law is a matter of discretion for the judge. The judge decides on a case-by-case basis whether or not to recognise "sufficient interest".

The fact that the recognition of *locus standi* falls within the discretion of the judiciary is very interesting from a theoretical point of view, as it requires judges to balance relevant considerations and to justify their choices. Two principles of public law collide in matters of the recognition of *locus standi*. On the one hand, there is the constitutional principle of the supremacy of Parliament: "[T]he law does not see it as the function of the courts to be there for every individual who is interested in having the legality of an administrative action litigated. Parliament

[59] Ibid., 51.

could have given such a wide right of access to the court but it has not done so".[60] This approach considerably reduces the number of cases that can be brought before the courts. On the other hand, there is the principle of judicial accountability of executive power. According to this principle, the function of the court is to control the misuse of public power: "Public law is not at base about rights, even though abuses of power may and often do invade private rights; it is about wrong — that is to say misuses of public power".[61] Whereas the principle of parliamentary supremacy supports a narrow recognition of the *locus standi* of those individuals who have a direct right or interest in the case, the principle of government accountability promotes a wider recognition of *locus standi* by allowing environmental groups to bring judicial actions. As public law is about misuses of power, English judges uphold the principle of judicial accountability of the government's actions. The final outcome is the promotion of the role of environmental groups in judicial scrutiny of administrative acts,[62] even though this is not a priority or a crucial feature taken into account by English judges.

The "English" approach to *locus standi* facilitates the access to justice of environmental groups which have both the knowledge and the resources to bring actions in very complex cases.[63] Why does this approach pose a challenge to the ECJ? Like English judges, the ECJ seems to face a tension between principles in the recognition of judicial standing. The misuse of Community law (breaches of Community law or the failure to implement a Directive) generates the right to bring judicial actions against the Member State and at the national level. However, the direct and individual concern established in Article 173 (new Article 230) generates the right to bring judicial actions against Community acts. Unlike English judges, the tension between misuses of power and recognition of individual interest as a basis for recognising *locus standi* is not solved by the ECJ through a process of balancing, but as an "either/or". The *Greenpeace* case[64] provides a good example. In that case, Greenpeace brought a judicial action against a decision of the European Commission that had granted European Regional Development Funds for the construction of two nuclear power stations in Spain.

---

60 Shiemann J's opinion in the *Rose Theatre Trust* case (*R v. Secretary of State for the Environment ex p. Rose Theatre Trust*, [1990] 1 *All ER* 522). In addition, the protection of *individuals'* rights has to be taken into account, especially since the ECHR is part of the British legal system. The right to private life and the right to health are potential vehicles to bring judicial actions against public authorities.

61 Sedley J's opinion in the case *R v. Somerset Council ex p. Dixon*, [1998] *J.E.L.* p. 180. See also Alder 1998.

62 See for example the cases *R v. Inspectorate of Pollution and another ex p. Greenpeace Ltd (No 2)* [1994] 4 I, 329, and *R v. Secretary of State for Trade and Industry, ex p. Greenpeace Ltd* [1998] *Env. L.R* 415. In Italy the situation is different, for Article 9 Administrative Procedure Act (1990) establishes the participation of diffuse interest groups in decision-making.

63 Since individuals lack time, knowledge and resources, either they are not up to the complexity of the case, or they simply give up in bringing judicial actions.

64 C-321/95 [1998] ECR I-1651.

The Court upheld a narrow interpretation of the "direct and individual concern" established in Article 173 (new Article 230) against Community acts, whilst upholding a "wrongs" approach at the national level. By so doing, the Court implemented a dual understanding of the basis of judicial standing depending upon whether the action is brought against a Member State or a Community institution. That is, the notion of accountability of Member States for European law breaches justifies judicial review and the access to courts at the national level, but the individual and direct involvement of a person in a decision justifies judicial review and access to justice at the European level. This incoherence is challenged by English judges[65] who have maintained a consistent approach to both judicial review and *locus standi*. For them, the principle of accountability of the public administration is both the reason for judicial scrutiny and the reason for access to justice.

65 The causes and consequences of this different approach by the ECJ are analysed in another chapter.

Chapter 8

The ECJ and Judicial Review of National Administrative Procedure in the field of EIA

Gráinne de Búrca and Áine Ryall

Introduction

The Community legal order relies to a considerable extent on the national courts to protect rights deriving from Community law. Proceedings in the national courts of the various Member States that involve claims based on Community law take place within a complex framework of diverse jurisdictional and procedural rules. This practical reality leads, inevitably, to a lack of uniformity in the application and enforcement of Community law at national court level. In the absence of general measures harmonising the rules governing national procedures for the enforcement of Community law, the European Court of Justice (ECJ) has attempted to balance the need to ensure the effective application of Community law with respect for the autonomy of national legal systems.

This chapter examines the role of the Court of Justice in relation to national judicial review of administrative discretion in the area of European Community (EC) law. The particular focus will be on environmental assessment law and judicial control of the discretion that the environmental impact assessment directive[1] leaves national administrative bodies. General questions relating to judicial review before the national courts where Community law rights or interests are concerned tend to be subsumed into a broad and developing line of ECJ jurisprudence on what might be called "national procedural or jurisdictional rules which may hinder the effectiveness of EC law". To date however, the ECJ has had little to say on the specific subject of the standard of national judicial review of administrative action, such as its scope and intensity or the appropriate grounds of review.

---

1 [1985] OJ L 175/40. This directive has been the subject of significant amendments pursuant to Directive 97/11/EC [1997] OJ L 73/5. The decisions of the ECJ discussed in this chapter concern the original directive.

The first part begins with a brief overview of the ECJ's general approach to procedure before national courts. To date the Court seems to have adopted a somewhat ambivalent approach, tending on the one hand to appear relatively deferential to the autonomy and primary role of national law in defining procedures, while leaving open the possibility for greater interference and prescriptiveness in this area.

The second part considers the ECJ's recent approach to environmental impact assessment law and, in particular, to the duties that the environmental impact assessment directive imposes on national administrative bodies and the extent of the discretion left to them by the directive. The scope of this has been restrictively interpreted by the ECJ. The Court's approach, in narrowing the extent of the discretion, thus leaves the decisions of these national administrative bodies more amenable to challenge by way of judicial review.

In the final section, we examine whether there is any specific indication of the ECJ's likely approach to the role of national courts which are charged with judicially reviewing the exercise of discretion by national administrative bodies where these bodies are, or ought to be, applying Community law.

The ECJ's Approach to Procedures Before National Courts Concerning the Enforcement of Community Law

The "classic" approach developed by the ECJ in relation to national procedures, including those for national judicial review of administrative bodies, is supposedly contained in the twin principles of "equivalence" and "effectiveness". However, the question of the relationship between substantive Community law and its reception into national law through the prism of national procedural law has never been answered by the ECJ with the same kind of doctrinal absolutism or clarity on which the Court originally insisted when articulating the doctrines of supremacy and direct effect. An analysis of the relevant jurisprudence reveals an initial discourse of deference to the autonomy of national legal systems, which later gave way to an articulation of stricter obligations for national courts when faced with litigants presenting claims based on Community law.

In early decisions such as *Rewe-Zentralfinanz*,[2] the Court held that subject to the twin principles of equivalence and practical possibility, Member States were entitled to apply their own procedural rules to claims based on Community law. According to the Court:

> ... [I]n the absence of Community rules on this subject, it is for the domestic legal system of each Member State to designate the courts having jurisdiction and to determine the procedural conditions governing actions at law intended to ensure the protection of the rights which citizens have from the direct effect of Community law, it

---

2 Case 33/76 *Rewe-Zentralfinanz eG and Rewe-Zentral AG v. Landwirtschaftskammer für das Saarland* [1976] ECR 1989.

> being understood that such conditions cannot be less favourable than those relating to similar actions of a domestic nature
>
> ...
>
> In the absence of such measures of harmonisation the right conferred by Community law must be exercised before the national courts in accordance with the conditions laid down by national rules.
>
> The position would be different only if the conditions and time-limits made it impossible in practice to exercise the rights which the national courts are obliged to protect. (paragraph 5)

Subsequently, in *Simmental*,[3] the ECJ set out a strong statement regarding the effective supremacy of Community law over restrictive national rules:

> ... every national court must, in a case within its jurisdiction, apply Community law in its entirely and protect rights which the latter confers on individuals and must accordingly set aside any provision of national law which may conflict with it, whether prior to or subsequent to the Community rule. (paragraph 21)
>
> Accordingly, any provision of a national legal system and any legislative, administrative or judicial practice which might impair the effectiveness of Community law by withholding from the national court having jurisdiction to apply such law the power to do everything necessary at the moment of its application to set aside national legislative provisions which might prevent Community rules from having full force and effect are incompatible with those requirements which are the very essence of Community law. (paragraph 22)

In *Von Colson and Kamann*,[4] the ECJ went on to articulate the requirement that national remedies must provide adequate and effective judicial protection for Community rights. There followed a series of strong decisions, including *Emmott*[5] and *Factortame (No. 1)*,[6] in which the ECJ emphasised the concept of effectiveness. In both *Emmott* and *Factortame (No. 1)* the Court ruled that the restrictive national rules at issue in those cases should be set aside in order to ensure the effective protection of Community law.

In two later decisions, *Peterbroeck*[7] and *Van Schijndel*,[8] the ECJ expressed an intermediate position, in between that of "equivalence and practical possibility" on the one hand, and a strong requirement of "adequacy and effectiveness" on the

---

3 Case 106/77 *Amministrazione delle Finanze dello Stato v. Simmenthal SpA* [1978] ECR 629.

4 Case 14/83 *Von Colson and Kamann v. Land Nordrhein-Westfalen* [1984] ECR 1891.

5 Case C-208/90 *Emmott v. Minister for Social Welfare* [1991] ECR I-4629.

6 Case C-213/89 *R. v. Secretary of State for Transport, ex parte Factortame Ltd.* [1990] ECR I-2433.

7 Case C-312/93 *Peterbroeck, Van Campenhout and Cie SCS v. Belgian State* [1995] I-ECR 4599.

8 Cases C-430/93 and C-431/93 *Van Schijndel and Van Veen v. Stichting Pensioenfonds voor Fysiotherapeuten* [1995] I-ECR 4705.

other. In *Van Schijndel*, the Court reiterated the basic principle of national procedural autonomy subject to the principles of equivalence and effectiveness. The Court then went on to provide guidance as to how a potentially restrictive national procedural rule should be scrutinised in light of these principles:

> For the purposes of applying those principles, each case which raises the question whether a national procedural provision renders application of Community law impossible or excessively difficult must be analysed by reference to the role of that provision in the procedure, its progress and its special features, viewed as a whole, before the various national instances. In the light of that analysis the basic principles of the domestic judicial system, such as protection of the rights of the defence, the principle of legal certainty and the proper conduct of procedure, must, where appropriate, be taken into consideration.[9] (paragraph 19)

This is not a strongly directive approach from the ECJ. It acknowledges the basic principle of national procedural autonomy and legitimacy while expressing the concept of *effet utile* not as an inexorably overriding doctrine that requires the national legal order to yield in whatever way is necessary to give fullest effect to Community law, but rather as one (albeit very significant) value to weigh in the balance with national procedural rules and the values underlying those rules.

The approach adopted in *Van Schindel* continues to form the cornerstone of recent ECJ jurisprudence in this area. However, an analysis of the recent jurisprudence suggests that the Court's attitude to national procedural rules remains somewhat ambivalent. As the more recent decisions are not in the environmental law field they will not be considered in detail here. Rather the rulings that most clearly illustrate the ambiguity of the Court's approach will be noted.

Applying *Van Schindel*, the Court in *Edis*[10] confirmed that, subject to the twin principles of equivalence and effectiveness, Member States are entitled to set down reasonable limitation periods within which proceedings must be instituted in the interest of legal certainty. The principle of equivalence requires that the contested procedural rule must apply equally to claims based on Community law and similar claims based on national law. The principle does not, however, require Member States to extend their most favourable procedural rules to actions based on Community law rights. Member States are therefore entitled to apply different procedural requirements to different areas of substantive law so long as any less

---

9 Note that the Court has recently provided further guidance to assist national courts in determining whether national procedural rules are equivalent in the context of claims in the field of employment law. See Case C-78/98 *Preston v. Wolverhampton Healthcare NHS Trust and Fletcher v. Midland Bank plc.*, ruling of 16 May 2000, not yet reported, paragraphs 49-63.

10 Case C-231/96 *Edilizia Industriale Siderurgica Srl (Edis) v. Ministero delle Finanze* [1998] ECR I-4951.

favourable procedural rules do not apply exclusively to actions based on Community law.[11]

In *Edis*, the Court took the opportunity to clarify (following *Fantask*)[12] that its earlier strong decision in *Emmott* was justified on the facts of that particular case. The contested time limit in *Emmott* had had the effect of depriving the plaintiff of any opportunity whatsoever to rely on her right to equal treatment under Community law. In *Edis* the Court ruled that subject to the principles of equivalence and effectiveness, national time limits will, in certain circumstances, be compatible with Community law even where time begins to run before the directive in question has been properly transposed into national law. In this context, the Court indicated that it is necessary to consider whether the conduct of the national authority in question, together with the existence of the contested time-limit has the effect of depriving the plaintiff of any opportunity of enforcing his or her Community rights before the national courts. The decision in *Edis* (and subsequent decisions in *Ansaldo Energia*[13] and *IN.CO.GE.'90*)[14] certainly gives considerable weight to the requirement of respect for national procedural autonomy.

However, it is also clear that the Court remains willing to take a more interventionist approach (in different circumstances) to ensure the effective application of Community law at national level. In *Levez*,[15] the Court held that Community law precluded the application of the time limit at issue in that case because the applicant's delay in initiating proceedings was due to deliberate misrepresentation on the part of her employer. The Court took the view that it would be "manifestly incompatible with the principle of effectiveness"[16] to permit an employer to rely on the relevant national rules in the circumstances of the particular case. A more prescriptive approach by the Court is also evident in the *Eco Swiss China Time* case.[17] Here, the ECJ applied its reasoning in *Van Schijndel* to require a national court, to which application had been made to annul an arbitration award, to raise the issue of whether the award was in breach of EC competition law of its own motion. The Court emphasised that Article 81 EC (ex Article 85) constituted "a fundamental provision which is essential for the accomplishment of the tasks entrusted to the Community and, in particular, for the functioning of the internal market".[18] Accordingly, where domestic procedural

11 See also Cases C-279/96, C-280/96 and C-281/96 *Anslado Energia SpA and GMB Srl v. Amministrazione delle Finanze dello Stato and Amministrazione delle Finanze dello Stato v. Marine Insurance Consultants Srl* [1998] ECR I-5025.

12 Case C-188/95 *Fantask A/S v. Industriministeriet* [1997] ECR I-6783.

13 Above Fn. 11.

14 Cases C-10/97 to C-22/97 *Ministero delle Finanze v. IN.CO.GE.'90 Srl* [1998] ECR I-6307.

15 Case C-326/96 *Levez v. Jennings (Harlow Pools) Ltd.* [1998] I-ECR 7835.

16 At paragraph 32.

17 Case C-126/97 *Eco Swiss China Time Ltd v. Benetton International NV* [1999] ECR I-3055.

18 At paragraph 36.

rules require a national court to annul an arbitration award on the grounds of failure to comply with national rules of public policy, the national court was also required to grant such an application where it considered that the award in question was contrary to Article 81 EC. In this case it would seem that the normative weight accorded by the Court to the basic competition rules of the Treaty pointed towards an "effectiveness" approach which did not leave the same degree of choice to the national court in exercising its procedural autonomy.

It remains to be seen how the Court will react when faced with questions regarding restrictive national procedures in the environmental law field. In the meantime, the effectiveness of individuals' rights under EC environmental law remains dependent on the willingness of the national courts to disapply restrictive national procedural rules. Apart from possible future developments in ECJ jurisprudence regarding national procedural rules in the context of environmental protection, the recent Århus Convention on *Access to Information, Public Participation in Decision-Making and Access to Justice in Environmental Matters*[19] should be a critical instrument in sharpening the effectiveness of environmental rights based on both national and EC law.[20]

The ECJ's Approach to the Discretion Left to Member States Under the Environmental Impact Assessment (EIA) Directive

Much of the ECJ's case law on the EIA directive is concerned with interpreting the discretion that the directive leaves Member States in Article 4(2). Article 4(2) provides that Annex II projects must be subject to an assessment "where Member States consider that their characteristics so require". An analysis of the Court's jurisprudence reveals that the Court takes a robust attitude towards the requirements set out in the directive. While it is clear that Article 4(2) allows Member States a certain element of discretion, the Court has ruled that the limits of that discretion are to be found in Article 2 (*Kraaijeveld*,[21] *Bozen*,[22] *Linster*[23]). Article 2 requires that "projects likely to have significant effects on the environment by virtue, *inter alia*, of their nature, size or location" must be subjected to assessment. The Court has consistently held that Member States are not permitted to set thresholds or criteria at such levels as to exempt in advance certain classes of project listed in Annex II from the EIA requirement. (See, for

[19] United Nations Economic Commission for Europe, Århus, Denmark, June 1998.

[20] In this context see also *Complaint Procedures and Access to Justice for Citizens and NGOs in the field of the environment within the EU* (IMPEL, 2000).

[21] Case C-72/95 *Aannemersbedrijf Kraaijeveld BV v. Gedeputeerde Staten van Zuid-Holland* [1996] ECR I-5403.

[22] Case C-435/97 *World Wildlife Fund (WWF) v. Autonome Provinz Bozen* [1999] ECR I-5613.

[23] Case C-287/98 *Luxembourg v. Linster*, ruling of September 19, 2000, not yet reported.

example, *Commission v. Belgium*,[24] *Kraaijeveld*, *Commission v. Germany*,[25] *Commission v. Ireland*[26] and *Bozen*.)

In *Kraaijeveld* (discussed further in the final section of this chapter) the ECJ emphasised that the directive had a wide scope and broad purpose. In light of this analysis, the Court ruled that even though the directive did not refer expressly to modifications to Annex II projects, this did not justify the conclusion that they were not covered by the directive. The Court was firmly of the view that the purpose of the directive would be undermined if the expression "modifications to development projects" was construed in such a way as to allow works which were likely to have significant effects on the environment to escape assessment. The Court also clarified that the directive may be invoked by "those concerned" before the national courts where it is alleged that the national legislature or administrative authorities have exceeded the limits of the discretion conferred on them by the directive. This aspect of the *Kraaijeveld* ruling is discussed in greater detail in the final part of this chapter.

The recent decision in *Bozen*[27] sheds further light on the Court's approach to the directive. *Bozen* concerned a challenge to a decision approving a project for the restructuring of Bolzano airport. The applicants in the main proceedings before the national court argued that the procedure followed in approving the project did not comply with the requirements of the directive. The project had been subjected to what the national court described as "simplified environmental assessment" but it was uncontested that the procedure which had been followed was not that set down by the directive.

The Court held that Article 2(1) and (2) of the directive permits a Member State to use an alternative assessment procedure to that introduced by the directive. However, any such alternative procedure must meet the aims of the directive and satisfy the requirements of Article 3 and Articles 5 to 10. The Court specifically mentioned that any alternative procedure which purports to be sufficient to satisfy the terms of the directive must comply with the public participation requirements set out in Article 6. This ruling also confirms the importance the Court attaches to public participation in the development consent procedure.

In *Bozen* the Court was also called on to interpret Article 1(5) of the directive. Article 1(5) exempts certain projects falling within the scope of the directive from the assessment procedure. However, exemption is subject to two conditions. First, the details of the project in question must be adopted by a specific legislative act. Second, the legislative process must achieve the objectives of the directive, and these objectives include the supplying of information. The Court relied on the sixth recital in the preamble to the directive in interpreting Article 1(5). According to the sixth recital, development consent for projects which are likely to have significant effects on the environment should only be granted after prior assessment of the

---

24 Case C-133/94 *Commission v. Belgium* [1996] ECR I-2323.

25 Case C-301/95 *Commission v. Germany* [1998] ECR I-6135.

26 Case C-392/96 *Commission v. Ireland* [1999] ECR I-5901

27 See Fn. 22, above.

likely significant environmental effects of those projects. This assessment must be conducted on the basis of the appropriate information supplied by the developer, which may be supplemented by the relevant national authorities and by "the people who may be concerned by the project".

The Court held that Article 1(5):

> [did not apply] to a project, such as that at issue in the main proceedings, which, while provided for by a legislative provision setting out a programme, has received development consent under a separate administrative procedure. (paragraph 63)

In order to benefit from the exemption envisaged by Article 1(5), the specific legislative act must include all the elements which may be relevant to the assessment of the impact of the project on the environment. Any alternative interpretation would result in the objectives of the directive, including the supplying of information, being undermined. On that basis the Court concluded that the project in question did not fall within the scope of the exemption in Article 1(5), tightening, once again, the potential areas of discretion left by the directive.

Most recently, in *Linster,* the Court confirmed that although Article 5(1) of the directive allows Member States an element of discretion in implementing the requirement that the developer supplies certain specified information about the project into national law, this discretion:

> [did] not preclude judicial review of the question whether it has been exceeded by the national authorities… it follows that the provisions of the Directive may be taken into account by national courts in order to review whether the national legislature has kept within the limits of the discretion set by it. (paragraphs 37-38)

Linster concerned a challenge to the legality of the expropriation of plots of privately owned land (in the public interest) to facilitate the construction of a motorway. The Court was again called upon to interpret Article 1(5) of the directive. As noted above, this Article provides that the directive does not apply in the case of projects whose details have been adopted by a specific legislative act. The Court noted that as this Article potentially limited the application of the directive it was to be interpreted restrictively. Accordingly the Court (following *Bozen*) held that a measure would only fall within the exemption contemplated by Article 1(5) where the legislative process pursued had enabled the objectives of the directive to be achieved. In particular, the Court highlighted that the legislative process pursued must facilitate the supplying of information and that the information available to Parliament when the details of the project are adopted must be equivalent to that which would be before the competent national authority in the ordinary course of the development content procedure. It is for the national court to determine whether the requirements of the directive have been satisfied.

These recent decisions in *Bozen* and *Linster* provide further evidence of the Court of Justice's robust attitude to the requirements of the directive, and to its apparent determination to set limits – including by encouraging the process of national judicial review thereof – to the scope of discretion left by the directive. It is interesting to note that the Court has also taken a vigorous, purposive approach in interpreting a related directive, Directive 90/313/EEC[28] on freedom of access to information on the environment held by public authorities (*Mecklenburg*,[29] *Commission v. Germany*).[30] These decisions serve to emphasise the importance the Court seems to attach to meaningful participation by concerned individuals and environmental groups in development consent procedures.

More recent amendments to the EIA directive aim to address many of the issues which were highlighted in the Court's case law to date (Directive 97/11/EC).[31] It remains to be seen whether these amendments will resolve or ameliorate some of the practical difficulties in the interpretation and application of the directive. Detailed proposals have also been put forward to revise the directive on freedom of access to information on the environment with a view to strengthening its provisions.[32]

The ECJ's Approach to National Court Review of Administrative Discretion in the Context of the Implementation of EC Law

Although not in the field of environmental law, the decision of the ECJ in *Upjohn*[33] is significant in providing some guidance as to the ECJ's approach to national judicial review of administrative action in an area of complex decision-making that is governed by Community law. The respondent licensing authority, acting under Directive 65/65/EEC relating to proprietary medicinal products, revoked marketing licences for a drug marketed by Upjohn. Upjohn challenged that decision in judicial review proceedings. The Court of Appeal made a reference to the ECJ asking for guidance as to the way in which the national court should proceed in examining Upjohn's challenge to the licensing decision. The ECJ ruled that although the directive required Member States to provide that decisions revoking marketing authorisations should be open to challenge by way of legal proceedings, it was clear that it:

---

28 [1990] OJ L158/56.

29 Case C-321/96 *Mecklenburg v. Kreis Pinneberg-Der Landrat* [1998] ECR I-3809.

30 Case C-217/97 *Commission v. Germany* [1999] ECR I-5087.

31 Above Fn. 1.

32 *Report from the Commission to the Council and the Parliament on the experience gained in the application of Council Directive 90/313/EEC of 7 June, 1990, on freedom of access to information on the environment* COM (2000) 400 final (29.06.2000) and *Proposal for a Directive of the European Parliament and of the Council on public access to environmental information* COM (2000) 402 final 2000/0169(COD) (29.06.2000)

33 Case C-120/97 *Upjohn Ltd. v. The Licensing Authority established by the Medicines Act 1968* [1998] ECR I-223.

> [did] not lay down detailed rules for the exercise of the right of recourse; it leaves to the Member States the task of organising their own systems of judicial review of decisions refusing, suspending or revoking marketing authorisations for proprietary medicinal products. (paragraph 29)

The Court of Appeal had asked whether it was the duty of the national court when ruling on the compatibility of the licensing authority's decision with EC law:

> to decide whether or not the ... decision was the *correct* decision as opposed to a decision which the licensing authority could *reasonably* have reached on the material before it? (emphasis added)

The ECJ recited its ruling in *Peterbroeck*[34] and stressed that it was for the domestic legal system to set down procedural rules governing actions for safeguarding rights which individuals derive from Community law (which include judicial review proceedings) subject to the twin principles of equivalence and effectiveness. The Court went on to rule in paragraph 33:

> As regards decisions revoking marketing authorisations taken by the competent national authorities following complex assessments in the medico-pharmacological field, it does not appear that the only appropriate means of preventing the exercise of rights conferred by Community law from being rendered virtually impossible or excessively difficult would be a procedure for judicial review of national decisions revoking marketing authorisations, empowering the competent national courts and tribunals to substitute their assessment of the facts and, in particular, of the scientific evidence relied on in support of the revocation decision for the assessment made by the national authorities competent to revoke such authorisations.

The ECJ went on consider its own role in judicial review proceedings when called on to review the decision of a Community authority which is required to make complex assessments in the course of the performance of its duties. According to the Court's settled case law:

> [Such authorities] enjoy a wide measure of discretion, the exercise of which is subject to a *limited* judicial review in the course of which the Community judicature may not substitute its assessment of the facts for the assessment made by the authority concerned ... [and must therefore] restrict itself to examining the accuracy of the findings of fact and law made by the authority concerned and to verifying, in particular, that the action taken by that authority is not vitiated by manifest error or a misuse of powers and that it did not clearly exceed the bounds of its discretion. (emphasis added) (paragraph 34)

Accordingly, the Court ruled that:

> Community law does not require the Member States to establish a procedure for judicial review of national decisions revoking marketing authorisations ... in the exercise of

---

34 See Fn. 7, above.

> complex assessments, which involves a more extensive review than that carried out by the Court itself. (paragraph 35)

This is an interesting "parallelist" form of argument similar to that employed by the Court in *Brasserie du Pêcheur*[35] to align the standard of liability of public authorities in EC law under Article 288 EC (ex Article 215) with that of liability of Member State authorities.

In *Upjohn* the Court concluded by emphasising the importance of the principle of effectiveness in the following terms:

> ...any national procedure for judicial review of decisions of national authorities revoking marketing authorisations must enable the court or tribunal seised of an application for annulment of such a decision *effectively to apply the relevant principles and rules of Community law when reviewing its legality*. (emphasis added) (paragraph 36)

The decision in *Upjohn* illustrates a two-fold reasoning by the ECJ in appearing not to require a stronger, more intense standard of review on the part of the national courts when dealing with the application of EC law than that which they normally apply under national administrative law. First, the Court endorses the *Peterbroeck* principle of national procedural autonomy, subject only to the twin principles of equivalence and effectiveness. It then moves on to invoke what could be described as the reverse of the "equivalence" argument, to the effect that national courts do not have to develop or apply a stronger, more intensive form of review of administrative discretion than that which the ECJ itself applies when reviewing discretionary decisions of the EC authorities in complex policy areas. This approach is not dissimilar to that adopted in *Edis* where the Court ruled that once the principles of equivalence and effectiveness are satisfied, Member States do not have to extend their most favourable procedural rules to claims based on Community law. In *Upjohn*, the ECJ is also emphasising that national courts do not have to create stronger forms of remedy than those which the EC judiciary employs.

This "parallelism" point is interesting when considered in light of the arguments advanced by both the Court of First Instance[36] and the ECJ in refusing to broaden the rules on *locus standi* in the context of environmental challenges brought against Community institutions pursuant to Article 230 EC (ex Article 173). In *Greenpeace*[37] the ECJ relied *inter alia* on the fact that there was standing to bring judicial review proceedings before the national courts in Spain in relation to an alleged breach of the EIA directive, not as an argument for recognising a similarly "broad" *locus standi* against Community institutions, but instead as a partial justification for not granting any wider *locus standi* than the narrow "direct and individual concern" formula. Furthermore, although the Court did not actually

35 Case C-46/93 *Brasserie du Pêcheur SA v. Germany* [1996] ECR I-1029.

36 Case T-585/93 *Stichting Greenpeace Council v. Commission* [1995] ECR II-2205.

37 Case C-321/95 P *Stichting Greenpeace Council v. Commission* [1997] ECR I-1651.

investigate or consider the standard of review, or any other procedural rules that applied to environmental litigants before the Spanish courts, the ECJ nonetheless asserted that:

> in the circumstances of the present case [the applicant's rights under directive 85/337/EEC] are fully protected by the national courts which may, if need be, refer a question to this Court for a preliminary ruling under Article 177 of the Treaty. (paragraph 33)

It appears from *Greenpeace* that the Court is prepared to assume adequate protection of rights deriving from the EIA directive by the national courts without entering into a detailed examination of the nature or intensity of review being applied by the national courts in such cases.

As noted above, in *Kraaijeveld* the Court articulated a tighter interpretation of the substantive requirements of Article 4(2) of the directive than that proposed by the national authority in question. One of the key points arising in *Kraaijeveld* was whether the national court hearing an action for annulment of a decision approving a zoning plan was required to raise of its own motion the question of whether an EIA should have been carried out pursuant to the directive. The ECJ cited *Van Schindel*, where it had ruled that if the national courts must, of their own motion, raise points of law based on binding domestic rules which were not raised by the parties, then the same obligation would also exist in relation to Community law.[38] However, in *Kraaijeveld* the Court went on to rule that this obligation also applied where national law conferred a *discretion* on national courts to apply binding rules of law of their own motion.[39]

This latter point appears to give rise to a certain ambiguity. Is it the case that a discretion on the part of a national court to raise points of law of its own motion becomes a firm obligation when Community law is at issue? The effect of the Court's ruling in *Kraaijeveld* seems to be that, in the context of the EIA directive, a national court enjoying a discretion to raise points of national law of its own motion, *must* examine whether the legislative or administrative authorities have exceeded their discretion under Article 2(1) and Article 4(2) of the directive. This approach imposes a strong obligation on national courts to ensure that the rights which individuals derive from Community law are protected.

In paragraph 61 of its ruling in *Kraaijeveld* the Court held that:

> if [the legislative or administrative authorities of a Member State have exceeded their discretion under the directive] and *consequently the national provisions must be set aside in that respect*, it is for the authorities of the Member State, according to their respective powers, to take all the general or particular measures necessary to ensure that projects are examined in order to determine whether they are likely to have significant effects on the environment and, if so, to ensure that they are subject to an assessment. (emphasis added)

---

38 At paragraph 57.

39 At paragraph 58.

Again, there is a certain element of ambiguity here about whether it follows automatically as a matter of EC law that the national measures which have been found to exceed the discretion must be set aside or whether the appropriateness of annulment is something for the national court to decide. The *Kraaijeveld* ruling certainly suggests the former course of action is required under Community law. It is also unclear what exactly the Court means by the expression "national provisions" which must be set aside. Does this refer to the national legislative provisions that are incompatible with the provisions of the directive or the individual decision taken by the national administrative authority in respect of the project or both? It is suggested in this chapter that the preferred interpretation of the ruling is that national courts are in fact required to set aside any national legislative or administrative measures which are incompatible with the directive.

The ambiguity is however again evident in the terms of the ECJ's ruling in *Bozen*. Here the Court ruled that:

> It is for the national court to review whether, on the basis of the individual examination carried out by the competent authorities which resulted in the exclusion of the specific project at issue in the main proceedings from the assessment procedure established by the Directive, *those authorities correctly assessed, in accordance with the Directive, the significance of the effects of that project on the environment*. (emphasis added) (paragraph 48)

Later in its judgment the Court (following *Kraaijeveld*) confirmed that:

> where the discretion conferred by [Articles 2(1) and Articles 4(2) the EIA Directive] has been exceeded by the legislative or administrative authorities of a Member State, individuals may rely on those provisions before a court of that Member State against national authorities and thus obtain from the latter the setting aside of the national rules or measures incompatible with those provisions. In such a case, it is for the authorities of the Member State to take, according to their relevant powers, all the general or particular measures necessary to ensure that projects are examined in order to determine whether they are likely to have significant effects on the environment and, if so, to ensure that they are subject to an impact assessment. (paragraph 71)

Kraaijeveld and *Bozen* therefore confirm that even though Member States have a discretion under Articles 2(1) and 4(2) this does not prevent judicial review of the question whether the national authorities (both legislative and administrative) have exceeded this discretion. While the Court does not adopt the traditional language of direct effect, there is now no doubt that individuals may invoke the directive in the national courts and petition the national court to set aside any national rules or measures that are incompatible with the provisions of the directive. This approach was again confirmed in the Court's recent ruling in *Linster*.[40]

---

40 At paragraphs 31-39.

Another decision which is noteworthy in this context is *Standley*.[41] While not concerned with the EIA directive, the decision sheds some light on how the Court views the role of the national courts when called upon to examine environmental directives which leave considerable discretion to national authorities. *Standley* concerned a challenge to decisions designating certain waters as waters that could be affected by nitrate pollution and designating certain areas of land that drained into those waters as nitrate vulnerable zones. These decisions were taken pursuant to national measures designed to implement Directive 91/676/EEC on the protection of waters from pollution caused by agricultural sources. In the course of its judgment the Court noted that:

> When national courts review the legality of measures identifying waters affected by pollution in accordance with Article 3(1) of the Directive... they must take account of the wide discretion enjoyed by the Member States which is inherent in the complexity of the assessments required of them in that context. (paragraph 37)
>
> However, Community law cannot provide precise criteria for establishing in each case whether the discharge of nitrogen compounds of agricultural origin makes a significant contribution to the pollution. (paragraph 38)
>
> The Directive may thus be applied by the Member States in different ways. Nevertheless, such a consequence is not incompatible with the nature of the Directive, since it does not seek to harmonise the relevant national laws but to create the instruments needed in order to ensure that waters in the Community are protected against pollution caused by nitrates from agricultural sources. (paragraph 39)

Having noted the discretion that the directive leaves to national authorities, the Court went on to consider the claim that the Directive breached the principle of proportionality. The applicants in the main proceedings before the national court had argued that the action programme adopted by the United Kingdom authorities to implement the directive imposed excessive obligations on farmers to ensure that the threshold of nitrates in waters was not exceeded. The Court disagreed that the impact of the directive was disproportionate. In the Court's view:

> ... the Directive contains flexible provisions enabling the Member States to observe the principle of proportionality in the application of the measures which they adopt. It is for the national courts to ensure that the principle [of proportionality] is observed. (paragraph 50)

Therefore, according to the ECJ, it falls to the national courts to review measures adopted to implement the directive to ensure that such measures comply with the principle of proportionality. This is one particular requirement or constraint which the ECJ has specified for national courts in exercising their

41 Case C-293/97 *R. v. Secretary of State for the Environment ex parte Standley* [1999] ECR I-2603.

judicial review function in relation to the manner in which EC environmental law measures which confer an element of discretion have been implemented.

Conclusion

There seems to be a certain tension between the apparently deferential approach of the ECJ to national judicial procedures examined in the first part of this contribution[42] (which is also reflected in the approach taken by the Court in *Upjohn*) and the recent rulings of the Court in the context of the EIA directive discussed in the later sections.[43] This may be indicative of the fact that the Court's jurisprudence on national procedures is not generally applicable, but may vary depending on the particular policy sector in issue, and in this case the ECJ may have evolved more stringent rules to limit national autonomy in the environmental policy sector.[44] The recent EIA jurisprudence indicates unequivocally that the Court requires that the discretion left to national authorities should be firmly controlled by national judicial review to ensure that the rights which individuals derive from the directive and the substantive obligations which are imposed therein are protected. Clearly, significant questions remain about the precise extent and meaning of the discretion which is left to national authorities – and indeed also to national courts in reviewing the exercise of that discretion – but it seems that the discretion will in any case be exceeded where the *substantive core* of one of the obligations in the Directive has not been met. In such a case, the ECJ's jurisprudence seems unequivocal in its insistence that the offending national provisions be set aside, and that in such circumstances the effectiveness of environmental obligations must trump concerns for national procedural autonomy.

---

42 See the section headed "The ECJ's Approach to Procedures Before National Courts Concerning the Enforcement of Community Law".

43 Namely, the sections headed "The ECJ's Approach to the Discretion Left to Member States Under the Environmental Impact Assessment (EIA) Directive" and "The ECJ's Approach to National Court Review of Administrative Discretion in the Context of the Implementation of EC Law".

44 Claire Kilpatrick has recently advocated a more sectoral examination of the development of EC remedies, rather than assuming a commonality of approach across the entire field of European policy areas. She suggests that such an approach "might provide a new and challenging research agenda for re-assessing the past and considering the future of remedies in the Luxembourg Court's jurisprudence". See "Introduction" in C. Kilpatrick, T. Novitz and P. Skidmore (eds) *The Future of Remedies in Europe* (Oxford: Hart Publishing, 2000).